The Routledge Pocket Guide to Legal Latin

The Routledge Pocket Guide to Legal Latin is an invaluable legal reference tool, providing a quick and informative guide to Latin words and phrases commonly used in legal settings.

This useful guide offers readers an extensive collection of over 4700 Latin words and phrases, 500 Latin abbreviations, and hundreds of informative legal maxims, principles, and interesting quotations drawn from the field of law, including terms and legal concepts related to commercial, international, political, personal, and societal as well as property and inheritance laws for which use of the Latin language has remained indispensable. Also included is a helpful pronunciation guide and a miscellaneous section featuring Latin prepositions, particles, common prefixes, Roman numerals, and more. Included at the end of this reference work is an extensive English-Latin index to assist readers in swiftly locating legal words and phrases.

Offering quick, accessible definitions and helpful explanations of Latin words and phrases, *The Routledge Pocket Guide to Legal Latin* is the ideal reference work for professionals across the legal field, including lawyers, judges, and paralegals as well as law students and all interested readers.

Jon R. Stone is a best-selling author and Professor of Theory and Research Methods at California State University, Long Beach. He is the author of *Latin for the Illiterati*, *More Latin for the Illiterati*, *The Routledge Dictionary of Latin Quotations*, and *The Routledge Book of World Proverbs*, among many others.

The Routledge Latin Pocket Guides
(in Three Separate Volumes):

Volume 1: *The Routledge Pocket Guide to Medical Latin*
Volume 2: *The Routledge Pocket Guide to Legal Latin*
Volume 3: *The Routledge Pocket Guide to Religious Latin*

Also by Jon R. Stone

Dictionnaire Rose des Locutions Latines (2007)
Latin for the Illiterati, 2nd ed. (2009)
More Latin for the Illiterati (1999)
The Routledge Book of World Proverbs (2006)
The Routledge Dictionary of Latin Quotations (2005)

and

The Craft of Religious Studies (1998)
The Essential Max Müller: On Language, Mythology, and Religion (2002)
Expecting Armageddon: Essential Readings in Failed Prophecy (2000)
A Guide to the End of the World (1993)
On the Boundaries of American Evangelicalism (1997)
Prime-Time Religion: An Encyclopedia of Religious Broadcasting (1997)
Readings in Faith & Race in America (2021)

The Routledge Pocket Guide to Legal Latin

Jon R. Stone

LONDON AND NEW YORK

Designed cover image: Brian Jackson/Alamy Stock Photo

First published 2025
by Routledge
4 Park Square, Milton Park, Abingdon, Oxon OX14 4RN

and by Routledge
605 Third Avenue, New York, NY 10158

Routledge is an imprint of the Taylor & Francis Group, an informa business

© 2025 Jon R. Stone

The right of Jon R. Stone to be identified as author of this work has been asserted in accordance with sections 77 and 78 of the Copyright, Designs and Patents Act 1988.

All rights reserved. No part of this book may be reprinted or reproduced or utilised in any form or by any electronic, mechanical, or other means, now known or hereafter invented, including photocopying and recording, or in any information storage or retrieval system, without permission in writing from the publishers.

Trademark notice: Product or corporate names may be trademarks or registered trademarks, and are used only for identification and explanation without intent to infringe.

British Library Cataloguing-in-Publication Data
A catalogue record for this book is available from the British Library

Library of Congress Cataloging-in-Publication Data
Names: Stone, Jon R., 1959- author.
Title: The Routledge pocket guide to legal Latin / Jon R. Stone.
Description: Abingdon , Oxon [UK] ; New York, NY : Routledge, 2025. | Includes bibliographical references and index.
Identifiers: LCCN 2024053748 (print) | LCCN 2024053749 (ebook) | ISBN 9781032186108 (hardback) | ISBN 9781032186092 (paperback) | ISBN 9781003255369 (ebook)
Subjects: LCSH: Law--Dictionaries--Latin. | Latin language--Law Latin--Dictionaries--English.
Classification: LCC K52.L37 S76 2025 (print) | LCC K52.L37 (ebook) | DDC 422/.471--dc23/eng/20241114
LC record available at https://lccn.loc.gov/2024053748
LC ebook record available at https://lccn.loc.gov/2024053749

ISBN: 978-1-032-18610-8 (hbk)
ISBN: 978-1-032-18609-2 (pbk)
ISBN: 978-1-003-25536-9 (ebk)

DOI: 10.4324/9781003255369

Typeset in Times New Roman
by KnowledgeWorks Global Ltd.

For my sister-in-law
Dr. Mary Morgan Stone
with love and admiration

Nunc autem manent fides, spes, caritas, tria haec:
major autem horum est caritas

Contents

Preface	viii
References and Sources	xiv
Pronunciation Guide	xvii
Latin Legal Words and Phrases	1
Selected Latin Maxims and Legal Principles	168
A Sampling of Latin Quotations Related to Law and Life	204
Latin Abbreviations	211
Miscellanea (Miscellaneous)	227
Some Common Prepositions and Particles 227	
Some Common Prefixes 228	
The Latin Calendar 229	
Roman Numerals 230	
English-Latin Index	233

Preface

At the dawn of the modern era in England, Sir Francis Bacon, solicitor general to Queen Elizabeth I and later Lord Chancellor under King James I, advocated for the inductive method as the foundation of a new approach to scientific knowledge. Rather than continue to build on the past, as the Scholastics had done, Bacon sought to begin anew by formulating universal laws or principles derived from careful observation and experimentation so as to work out a rational chain of cause and effect. In his *New Organon* (1620), Bacon hoped to advance 'the true and lawful marriage between the empirical and the rational faculty'—that is to say, human experience coupled with, if not entirely, wedded to reason (quoted in Scruton 1995:22). But what, he asked, prevented men and women from gaining such knowledge of these universal laws of nature? To answer this, Bacon pointed to what he called the 'idols of the mind,' those aspects of human cognition that kept an individual, even the well-bred, from rising above the mentality of the unenlightened herd. By name, these are the idols of the tribe (*idola tribus*), the cave (*idola specus*), the marketplace (*idola fori*), and the theater (*idola theatri*), representing the personal, social, cultural, and economic spheres that tend to shape and condition unreflective human experience. These idols worked to undermine human reasoning, and thus inductive thought, by blinding people through their preconceived notions and erroneous assumptions about the natural and human worlds.

Although not regarded as one of the fathers of modern science, Sir Francis did bequeath to later generations elements of a scientific method that could be applied across a number of fields of human knowledge. As one direct challenge to established assumptions about the natural world, and the civil order, was a belief that 'science should treat of the real and not of the nominal essences of things' (Scruton 1995:23). And so, said Bacon, just as there are laws governing the natural world (*jus naturale*) discoverable through inductive means, there are also laws governing human civil life (*jus civile*). These Bacon described in an early work, *De Regulis Juris*— and then refined in *The Maximes of the Lawes*—as a science of law derived from rational principles—that is, axioms or maxims or rules (*regulae*) 'gathered and extracted out of the harmony and congruity of cases' (see McCabe 1964:111). These natural laws, or principles, expanded beyond Bacon's original handful of maxims—what we today might identify as among the foundational assumptions behind the art or science of jurisprudence—are not themselves the law but principles that inform the crafting of reasoned law that stretch back to ancient Rome.

The earliest expression of Roman law, known as the *Law of the Twelve Tables* (*Lex Duodecim Tabularum*), was a system built on a set of moral codes framed as rules that governed public and private conduct. These rules were centered on the father of the family (*pater familias*) and his paternal power (*patria potestas*) and radiated outward into Roman society and came to regulate what was permitted (*fas*) and what was forbidden (*nefas*), itself becoming a complex and elaborate process for judging and punishing breaches of private and public conduct. Although the *Twelve Tables* is not extant except in a fragmentary form of clauses, much of their focus concerned issues of property and inheritance. Beside, if not behind, these *Twelve Tables*, there existed moral duties and expectations (*mos* or *mores*) as well as recognized customs (*consuetudines*) that collectively informed the concept of *ius* or *jus*, often translated as right or rights (see Johnston 1999: 2–3, Mousoutakis 2015:32–6, and Marin and Botină 2020:16). To this point, George Mousoutakis (2015) notes that the concept of equity (*aequitas*) 'is reflected in the definition of *ius*, or law in a broad sense' and guided judicial pronouncements. And further, 'the test of the *bonum et aequum* [the good and equitable] in this era was still the *ius gentium* [law of nations], the norms governing civilized society as construed by the Romans. But the Roman *ius gentium* was now declared binding because it was also natural law (*ius naturale*), based on natural reason' (74–75). These two, *jus gentium* and *jus naturale*, were said to form a type of *jus tripertitum*, a three-part or threefold law, with *jus civile* (civil law) as the third (Osborn 1927:151). Among the aspects of law derived from nature is found a definition of a supreme legal precept in the Institutes of the Emperor Justinian, modified from Cicero—namely, to live honestly (or honorably), not to injure another, and to render to each person his due (as recorded by Ulpian, this part of the precept is given as *honeste vivere, alterum non laedere, suum cuique tribuere*; see Pennington 2008:577–8).

Returning then to Sir Francis Bacon, the main purpose behind his small book, *The Maximes of the Lawes* (1696), dedicated to Queen Elizabeth I and as confessed in *The Preface*, was the need for students of the law 'to be a helpe and ornament thereunto'; their profession

performed in some degree by the honest and liberall practice of a profession ... and preserve themselves free from the abuses wherewith the profession is noted to bee infected: but much more is this performed if a man bee able to visite and strengthen the roots and foundation of the science it selfe; thereby not onely gracing it in reputation and dignity, but also amplifying it in perfection & substance. (1636:1)

The main means of accomplishing this, Bacon thought, would be through rules drawn from Latin maxims and aphorisms, 'because this delivering of knowledge in distinct and dis-joyned Aphorismes doth leave the wit of man more free to turne and tosse, and make use of that which is delivered to more severell purposes and applications' (1636:4–5). And, continuing,

for wee see that all the ancient wisdom and science was wont to be delivered in that forme, as may be seen by the parables of *Solomon*, and by the Aphorismes of *Hippocrates*, and the morall verses of *Theognes* and *Phocilides*, but chiefly the president [*sic*] of the Civill law, which hath taken the same course with their rules, did confirme me in my opinion. (1636:5)

The book itself, in which Sir Francis noted some concurrence with as well as 'the diversities between' English law and 'the civill Roman rules of law' (1636:4), is a series of legal commentaries on 25 maxims meant to show how legal practitioners might glean practical application, or rules (*regula* or *regulae*), from one pithy Latin maxim after another that would turn and toss in the reader's mind, being, as Bacon later wrote, 'like the magnetic needle, [that] points at the law, but does not settle it' (quoted in Postema 2012:414). In fact, the very first maxim on which Bacon comments became itself a premier maxim of tort law—namely that, in law, it is the proximate, not the remote, cause that is to be considered (*In jure non remota causa sed proxima spectatur*). Another maxim, discussed under *Regula 12*, is that the safety of the people is the supreme law (*Salus populi est suprema lex*). And still another, *Regula 23*, is that a latent ambiguity in the language may be removed by evidence (*Ambiguitas verborum latens verificatione suppletur*). It is from this small sample of 25 maxims and aphorisms that Bacon vowed hereafter to treat 300 in all, ultimately to be scattered throughout a number of his later writings (1636:8).

Nearly 400 years since the time of Bacon, the Latin language continues to shape the practice and study of law throughout the Western world, with its influence reaching into the Baltic and Balkan regions of Europe and beyond. As Merike Ristikivi (2005) at the University of Tartu in Estonia attests, the position of Latin in the legal literature of Estonia and Finland allows for translinguistic communication which then serves to foster mutual understanding among peoples 'irrespective of the linguistic and cultural differences of the communicators.' Because Latin is a 'neutral and common ground,' therefore a 'basic knowledge of Latin is often essential' for a legal professional's engagement in the world (200–1). For, as Marin and Botină (2020) of Ovidus University of Constanta, Romania, also point out, 'Roman law did not remain only a document of history, like other legislations of antiquity, but it exceeded, in terms of form, the limits of the society that created it.' Indeed, 'Roman law plays in history the role of a true "legal alphabet," the Roman legal concepts giving concrete expression to the most varied and subtle rules of law' (17).

As one way to provide basic knowledge of the Latin language and its use among legal professionals, *The Routledge Pocket Guide to Legal Latin* offers readers—all under one cover—a useful and informative collection of Latin words and phrases drawn generally from the field of law, including legal terms and concepts related to commercial, international, political, personal, and societal as well as property and inheritance laws for which use of the Latin language has remained indispensable. In total, roughly 4700 entries make up the main body of this text, with an additional 500 abbreviations that are both specific to law and to general use. And, in the spirit of Sir Francis Bacon, there is also a section of several hundred Latin maxims and related legal principles and another section of 100 or more Latin quotations related to the law and to life. There is also a section of miscellaneous reference entries of common Latin prepositions, particles, and common prefixes, as well as the list of the months and days of the Roman calendar and a chart of Roman numerals. Also included at the end of this pocket guide is an extensive, though by no means comprehensive, English-Latin index to assist the reader in locating legal words and phrases more quickly.

One of the greatest difficulties in writing a reference work of this kind is achieving perfection in typography and translation. But errors creep in, not all of which can be avoided. In fact, the sources themselves offer numerous opportunities for error. As noted elsewhere in my other Latin reference works, there are variations in spelling, word order, and word choices in Latin texts and translations that are, at times, difficult to reconcile. In some cases, one finds that the use of Latin words and phrases in law and the legal professions has changed over the course of a century or more, the meaning and application of words and phrases having been altered to fit new circumstances. And even though the meanings have changed, the very words themselves have remained unaltered, making difficult for the translator or lexicographer the negotiation between what words mean and how words are used (see Eco 2003:1–6). Given these changes, I have been guided largely by the comparative use of multiple reference and linguistic sources, both older—to some, antiquated—as well as more recent. So, in all of my translations and retranslations, including those herein, I once more beg the reader's kind indulgence.

For this, and for all of my other Latin projects, I express my never-ending gratitude to the editors and production staff at Routledge UK. I truly appreciate their unwavering support over the past 30 years of fruitful professional collaboration. So many sleepless nights! My special appreciation is here offered to Amy Davis-Pointer, Marcia Adams, Lizzi Rich, Sophie Dixon-Dash, Mariam Farooq, Joyce Li, and two unnamed reviewers for their guidance and helpful suggestions on how to improve this present volume.

But it is to my family and close circle of friends that I offer my deepest and most heartfelt gratitude, with special thanks to two of my esteemed lawyer friends, William P. Medlen and R. Bruce Evans. But family comes first. And so, as a small expression of my love and admiration for my sister-in-law, Dr. Mary Morgan Stone, my twin brother David's wife, I dedicate to her this small book. Her life truly exemplifies one of kindness, generosity, and selfless devotion to family and friends. She has touched the lives of everyone around her.

Honeste Vivere, Neminem Laedere, Suum Cuique Tribuere

Jon R. Stone, Ph.D.
California State University, Long Beach
October 2024

References and Sources

Anon. *Latin for Lawyers* (2nd ed.). London: Sweet and Maxwell, 1937.

Bacon, Sir Francis. *A Collection of Some Principal Rules and Maximes of the Common Lawes of England with Their Latitude and Extent, etc*. London: J. More, esq., 1636.

Ballentine, James A. *A Law Dictionary of Words, Terms, Abbreviations and Phrases, etc*. San Francisco: Bancroft-Whitney Company, 1916.

Bennett, Charles E. *New Latin Grammar* (2nd ed., revised; reprinted). Boston: Allyn and Bacon, 1963.

Blackwell, Amy Hackney. *The Essential Law Dictionary*. Naperville, IL: Sphinx Publishing, 2008.

Bouvier, John. *Bouvier's Law Dictionary and Concise Encyclopedia* (3 vols.; 3rd revision by Francis Rawle being the 8th ed.). Kansas City, MO: Vernon Law Book Company; St. Paul, MN: West Publishing Company, 1914.

Bouvier, John. *A Law Dictionary Adapted to the Constitution and Laws of the United States of America, etc*. (2 vols.; 14th ed., revised and greatly enlarged). Philadelphia: J.B. Lippencott, 1874.

Broom, Herbert. *A Selection of Legal Maxims, Classified and Illustrated* (7th American from the 5th London ed.). Philadelphia: T. & J.W. Johnson and Company, 1874.

Burrill, Alexander. *A Law Dictionary and Glossary, etc*. (2 vols.). New York: Baker, Voorhis & Company, 1867–70.

Cochran, William C. *The Students' Law Lexicon: A Dictionary of Legal Words and Phrases with Appendices, etc*. (2nd ed., revised). Cincinnati: The Robert Clarke Company, 1892.

Eco, Umberto. *Mouse or Rat?: Translation as Negotiation*. London: Weidenfeld & Nicolson, 2003.

Garner, Bryan A. (ed. in chief). *Black's Law Dictionary* (9th ed.) St. Paul, MN: Thomson Reuters, 2009.

Glare, P.G.W. (ed.). *Oxford Latin Dictionary* (2nd ed., reprinted with corrections). Oxford: Oxford University Press, 2016.

Greenough, J.B., et al. (eds.). *Allen & Greenough's New Latin Grammar* (reprint of 1903 ed.). New Rochelle, NY: Aristide D. Caratzas, 1983.

Guterman, Norbert (ed.). *The Anchor Book of Latin Quotations*. New York: Anchor Books, 1990.

Johnston, David. *Roman Law in Context*. Cambridge: Cambridge University Press, 1999.

King, William Francis Henry. *Classical and Foreign Quotations, etc.* (2nd ed.). London: Whitaker & Sons, 1889.

Lely, J.M. *Wharton's Law-Lexicon: Forming an Epitome of the Law of England, etc.* (7th ed.). Boston: Soule and Bugbee, 1883.

Lewis, Charlton T., and Charles Short. *A New Latin Dictionary* (revised, enlarged, and rewritten). New York: Harper & Brothers; Oxford: Clarendon Press, 1884.

Marin, Marilena, and Mădălina Botină. "Legal Rules in Ancient Rome between Law, Morality and Religion." *Scientia Moralitas: International Journal of Multidisciplinary Research* 5, 2 (2020): 16–23.

Martin, Charles Trice (comp.). *The Record Interpreter: A Collection of Abbreviations, Latin Words and Names, Used in English Historical Manuscripts and Records* (2nd ed.). London: Stevens and Sons, 1910.

Martin, Elizabeth, and Jonathan Law (eds.). *A Dictionary of Law* (6th ed.). New York: Oxford University Press, 2006.

McCabe, Bernard. "Francis Bacon and the Natural Law Tradition." *Natural Law Forum* Paper 85 (1964): 111–21.

Moreland, Floyd L., and Rita M. Fleischer. *Latin: An Intensive Course*. Berkeley: University of California Press, 1977.

Morwood, James. *A Latin Grammar*. Oxford: Oxford University Press, 1999.

Mousoutakis, George. *Roman Law and the Origins of the Civil Law Tradition*. New York: Springer, 2015.

Osborn, P.G. *A Concise Law Dictionary for Students and Practitioners, etc.* London: Sweet & Maxwell, 1927.

Pennington, Kenneth. "Lex Naturalis and Jus Naturale." *The Jurist* 68 (2008): 569–91.

Postema, Gerald J. "Philosophy of the Common Law." In *The Oxford Handbook of Jurisprudence and Philosophy of Law*, edited by Jules L. Coleman, Kenneth Einar Himma, and Scott J. Shapiro. Oxford: Oxford University Press, 2004; ebook 2012 (unpaginated).

Riley, H.T. (ed.). *A Dictionary of Latin and Greek Quotations, etc.* London: George Bell and Sons, 1891.

Ristikivi, Merike. "Latin: The Common Legal Language of Europe?" *Juridica International* 10 (2005): 199–202.

Scruton, Roger. *A Short History of Modern Philosophy* (2nd ed.). London: Routledge, 1995.

Simpson, D.P. *Cassell's Latin-English/English-Latin Dictionary* (5th ed.). New York: Macmillan, 1977.

Stimson, Frederic Jesup. *A Concise Law Dictionary of Words, Phrases, and Maxims, etc.* (revised edition by Harvey Cortlandt Voorhees). Boston: Little, Brown, and Company, 1911.

Stone, Jon R. *Latin for the Illiterati* (2nd ed.). New York: Routledge, 2009.

Stone, Jon R. *More Latin for the Illiterati*. New York: Routledge, 1999.

Stone, Jon R. *The Routledge Dictionary of Latin Quotations*. New York: Routledge, 2005.

Tayler, Thomas. *The Law Glossary, etc.* Albany, NY: W & A Gould, 1833.

Tellegen-Couperus, Olga (ed.). *Law and Religion in the Roman Republic* (*Mnemosyne* Supplements, vol. 336). Leiden: Brill, 2012.

Trayner, John. *Latin Maxims and Phrases* (2nd ed.). Edinburgh: William Green; London: Stevens & Haynes, 1876.

Webster's II: New Riverside University Dictionary. Boston: Houghton Mifflin, 1984.

Webster's New World Dictionary (3rd college ed.). New York: Prentice Hall, 1988.

Wheelock, Frederic M., and Richard A. LaFleur. *Wheelock's Latin* (6th ed., revised). New York: HarperCollins, 2005.

Wild, Susan Ellis (ed.). *Webster's New World Law Dictionary*. Hoboken, NJ: Wiley, 2006.

Pronunciation Guide

In pronouncing Latin, it is helpful to know that most Latin sounds have corresponding standard American English sounds, but with the rules for long and short vowel sounds being more consistently applied. Indeed, long and short vowel sounds refer simply to the duration of the sound—that is, how long the vowel should be voiced within its given syllable. For convenience, the basic Latin vowel sounds are pronounced accordingly: **a** = ah, **e** = eh, **i** = ee, **o** = oh, **u** = oo.

As examples, the long *a* in *father* is the same sound as the long *a* in the Latin word *pater*. The short *a* in the English words *par* and *far* are very similar in sound to that of the Latin words *pax* and *fax*. The short *e* in *pet* is similar in sound to the Latin *et*, as is the short *i* in *twig* the same as the *i* in the Latin word *signum*. The long *o* in *Ohio* sounds very much like the *o* in the Latin word *dolor*. Similarly, the short *o* in *pot* is pronounced similarly to the short *o* in *populus*. Likewise, the Latin *u* in *runa* and *pudicus*, one long and the other short, sound the same as the long and short *u* vowels in *rude* and *put*.

Readers should also keep in mind that in Latin, unlike English, all the syllables in a word are pronounced, including the final *e* and *es*, such as in the words *arte* and *artes*, *duce* and *duces*, *fide* and *fides*, *opinione*, and *legiones*.

With respect to Latin consonants, one should nearly always pronounce them as those in standard American English (e.g., **b** = b, **d** = d, **f** = f, **l** = l, **m** = m, **n** = n, **p** = p, **r** = r, **s** = s, **t** = t, etc.), with the exception of **c**, **g**, **h**, and **v**, which are always pronounced like **k** (as in kirk), **g** (as in give, gave, and go), **h** (as in hard), and **v** as v or w (as in vine and vise or we and was), respectively. The letters **i** and **j**, when placed before another vowel, such as *iam/jam* and *ius/jus*, are pronounced like the consonant **y** (as in you, yam, and yeti), not the consonant **j**. The convention of substituting the letter **j** for **i**, when used as a consonant, appeared after the Classical period. For the sake of simplicity, both **i** and **j** are used here.

Last, with respect to vowel diphthongs, most Classical Latin linguists prefer to pronounce them as follows: **ae** as if it were a long *i* (as in pine); **oe** as *oi* (as in boy); **au** as *ou* or *ow* (as in bough or now); **ei** as a long *a* (as in weight); **eu** as *eu* (as in feud); and **ui** as *wee* (as in the French *oui*).

For further discussion, guidelines, and helpful examples, please consult LaFleur's *Wheelock's Latin* (6th ed.), *Allen & Greenough's New Latin Grammar*, Bennett's *New Latin Grammar*, and Morwood's *A Latin Grammar*.

CORPVS IVRIS CIVILIS,
IN IV. PARTES DISTINCTVM.

Eruditissimis DIONYSII GOTHOFREDI I.C. Clarissimi notis illustratum.

In hac postrema LVGDVNENSI Editione Pandectæ purissimæ sunt: Textus cum optimis Codicibus collatus, & infinitis prope mendis purgatus: Legionque allegationes in notis adductæ incuriâ Typographorum anteà corruptæ, nunc suis locis fideliter repositæ, diligenti studio & curâ N. ANTONII, Iurium Professoris.

Quæ in hoc opere contineantur quarta pagina indicabit.

LVGDVNI,
Sumptibus LAVRENTII ANISSON.

M. DC. LXII.
CVM PRIVILEGIO REGIS.

Latin Legal Words and Phrases

A

a bene placito: at one's pleasure; at will (see also, **ad libitum**)
a capite ad calcem: from head to heel (i.e., from top to bottom)
a coelo usque ad centrum: from the heavens to the center of the earth
a consiliis: of counsel
a contrario sensu: on the other hand
a dato or **a datu:** from the date
a dextra: on the right
a die: from that day or date
a fortiori: with greater force; by greater force of reason; more conclusively
a gratia: with favor; as a favor; out of kindness
a jure suo cadunt: they lose their right
a latere: from the side (i.e., collateral)
a maximis ad minima: from the greatest to the least
a mensa et thoro [from table and bed]: from bed and board (i.e., a limited divorce)
a minima: for being too small (i.e., to refer a case to a lower court)
a minori ad majus: from the lesser to the greater
a multo fortiori: from much the stronger; by far the stronger
a nativitate: from birth
a non domino: by or from the non-owner (i.e., granted by someone not holding the title)
a pari: equally; in like manner
a posse ad esse: from possibility to realization
a posteriori [from after]: reasoning from specific instances to general conclusions (i.e., inductive or empirical knowledge)
a primo: from the first
a principio: from the beginning
a priori [from before]: reasoning from premise to logical conclusions (i.e., deductive or presumptive knowledge)

a pueris or **a puero** [from boyhood]: from childhood; from youth

a quo: from which (i.e., the beginning point, as opposed to **ad quem**)

a retro: from back; from behind (i.e., in arrears)

a rubro ad nigrum [from the red to the black]: from title to text (i.e., the entire statute has legal force)

a sinistra: on the left

a sociis: by its associates

a solis ortu usque ad occasum: from sunrise to sunset

a sursum usque deorsum: from top to bottom

a teneris annis [from tender years]: from childhood or youth

a tergo [in the rear]: behind; from behind

a verbis ad verbera: from words to blows

a vinculo: from the bond or tie

a vinculo matrimonii [from the bond of matrimony]: a divorce (i.e., a complete dissolution of the marriage)

ab absurdo: from the absurd

ab actis: a register; a notary

ab agendo: unable to act or transact business

ab ante: in advance; beforehand

ab antecedente: beforehand

ab antiquo: from of old; from antiquity; from ancient time(s)

ab epistolis or **ab epistulis** [of letters]: secretarial matters (e.g., correspondence)

ab extra [from without]: from the outside

ab inconvenienti: from the inconvenience involved (i.e., in reference to a law that should not be passed because of certain hardships or inconveniences it would create)

ab incunabulis [from the cradle]: from childhood

ab inde: from that time forward

ab initio (ab init.): from the beginning; from the start

ab initio mundi: from the beginning of the world

ab intestato: from a person dying intestate (i.e., without a will)

ab intra [from within]: from the inside

ab invito: unwillingly; against one's will

ab irato [from anger]: in a fit of anger (i.e., not to be taken too seriously)

ab olim [of old]: formerly; in times past

ab omni parte: from every side

ab orco usque ad coelum [from Hades to Heaven]: from the ground to the sky

ab origine [from the origin]: from the beginning

ab ovo [from the egg]: from the beginning

ab parvulis: from childhood

ab uno ad omnes: from one to all

ab utraque parte: of both parties (i.e., common property)

abandum: abandoned; forfeited; also, confiscated

abatamentum: abatement; a making less

abatus per vent: thrown down by the wind

abdite latet: he or she lies hid

aberratio ictus [mistake in the blow]: unintended harm, such as harm to a bystander

abest (pl. **absunt**): he or she is absent

abhinc or **ab hinc:** hereafter; from here on

abinde: from thence; thenceforth

aborticidum: killing the fetus *in utero*

abortivus: abortive

abortus: aborted; prematurely born

abscissio infiniti [the cutting off the infinite]: in logic, the process by which the true conclusion is reached by a systematic comparison and rejection of hypotheses

abscondita: hidden places

absens: absent

absente reo (**abs. re.**): the defendant being absent (see also, **reo absente**)

absit invidia: let there be no ill will (i.e., no offense intended)

absolutum et directum dominium: entire and direct ownership (i.e., full private ownership)

absolutus: absolute

absque: without

absque consideratione curiae: without the consideration of the court

absque hoc [without this]: without this fact
absque impetitione vasti: without impeachment of waste (i.e., the tenant not being liable for non-malicious waste)
absque injuria: without injury
absque misericordia: without mercy
absque paucis casibus: except for a few cases
absque probabili causa: without probable cause
absque tali causa: without such cause
absque ulla conditione: without any condition
absque ulla nota: without any mark or marking
absque vasti: without waste
absum: I am absent
ac etiam or **acetiam:** and also
accedas ad curiam [you may approach the court]: a common law writ to remove a case to a higher court
accepta: receipts; credits
accidere: to happen; to befall
accitus: a summons
accola [a person living nearby]: a neighbor; a tenant laborer or tenant farmer
accomenda: a maritime contract (i.e., a contract in which a person entrusts his or her property for transport that is then to be sold for the benefit of both parties)
accommodatus: suitable; appropriate
accumulatio jura juribus: by adding rights to rights (i.e., a right being conferred does not displace any existing rights)
accusatio: an accusation
accusatus: accused; indicted
acervatim [in heaps]: summarily
acta diurna: daily records
acta publica: matters of public concern
actio: action; a legal action
actio ad exhibendum: an action to compel a defendant to bring forth or display an item in his or her possession
actio arbitraria: an action at the discretion of the judge

Latin Legal Words and Phrases 5

actio bonae fidei: an action undertaken in good faith (i.e., in an equitable manner)

actio calumniae: an action for malicious prosecution

actio commodati contraria: an action by a borrower against the lender

actio commodati directa: an action initiated by a lender against the borrower

actio communi dividundo: an action for the division of commonly held property

actio damni injuria: an action for damages

actio de dolo malo: an action of fraud

actio de in rem verso: an action for unjust enrichment

actio empti: an action of the buyer to compel delivery of a purchased item or good

actio familiae erciscundae: an action to divide an inheritance among the heirs

actio finium regundorum: an action reestablishing the boundaries between adjoining lands

actio furti: an action of theft

actio in personam: an action against a person

actio in rem: an action against a thing (i.e., property)

actio judicati: an action to compel the execution of a judgment

actio mandati: an action concerning breach of contract (i.e., an action brought to receive compensation, reimbursement for expenses, or to recover losses suffered in the performance of one's contracted duties; the other party may also seek compensation for breach of contract)

actio non accrevit infra sex annos: the action did not accrue within six years (i.e., the action was not brought within the statute of limitations)

actio pro socio: an action of partnership (i.e., an action to compel one's business associates to carry out the agreed terms of the partnership)

actio redhibitoria [action to rescind]**:** an action to return a damaged or defective purchase and to receive a refund of the purchase price

actio utilis: an equitable action (i.e., just and fair to all parties involved)

actio venditi: an action of the seller to receive payment

actionem non habere (actio. non): a denial of a plaintiff's charge

actiones bonae fidei: actions of good faith (i.e., in an equitable manner)

actiones in personam: personal actions

actiones innominatae: writs for which there were no precedents (as opposed to **actiones nominatae**)

actiones nominatae: writs for which there were precedents (as opposed to **actiones innominatae**)

actiones penales: penal actions

actiones populares: public actions

actiones rei persecutoriae: actions for the recovery of something belonging to the one bringing the action

actiones stricti juris: actions of strict law

actor: a plaintiff

actor dominae: the manager of an estate

actor ecclesiae: the manager of church property (e.g., a sexton)

actum agere: to do what has already been done

actum et tractatum: done and transacted

actus (pl. acta) [act]: an action or an actuality

actus animi [an act of the mind]**:** an intention

actus Dei: act of God

actus legitimus: a legal act

actus reus: a criminal act

ad: at; to; for; according to

ad absurdum [to what is absurd]**:** an argument that demonstrates the absurdity of an opponent's proposition

ad abundantiorem cautelam: for more abundant caution

ad acta (a.a.) [to the archives or files]**:** shelved (i.e., to close the case or the matter)

ad aliud examen: to another tribunal

ad alium diem: at or to another day

ad amussim [according to a rule]**:** accurately or exactly

ad annum: a year from now

ad arbitrium: at will

ad audiendum et (de)terminandum: to hear and determine

ad auxilium vocatus: one called upon to help (i.e., an advocate)

ad avizandum: to consider further (i.e., to decide the case at a later date)

ad baculum [to the rod]: an argument or appeal that resorts to force rather than reason

ad barram evocatus: called to the bar

ad bona: for or of the goods (used in reference to the guardian of the estate of a minor) (see also, **curator ad bona**)

ad campi partem: for a share of the field or land

ad captandum: an argument or appeal that is presented for the sake of pleasing the audience

ad captandum lucrum: for the purpose of making money

ad captum vulgi [to the common understanding]: easily understood

ad cautelam: as a precaution

ad certum diem: at a certain day

ad civilem effectum: as to the civil effect

ad colligenda bona: for collecting the goods

ad colligendum: for collecting

ad commune nocumentum: to the common nuisance

ad communem legem: at common law

ad comparendum et ad standum juri: to appear and to stand to the law

ad computum reddendum: to render an account

ad consimiles casus: to similar cases

ad convincendam conscientiam judicis: sufficient to satisfy the conscience of the judge

ad crumenam [to the purse]: an argument or appeal to one's personal interests

ad culpam: until misconduct

ad curiam: at court

ad curiam vocare: to summon to court

ad custagia: at the costs

ad custum: at the cost
ad damnum: to the loss or damage (i.e., a clause stating monetary loss in a complaint) (see also, **ad quod damnum**)
ad damnum ipsorum: to their loss
ad defendendum: to defend
ad die datus: given from a certain day (i.e., a rental period)
ad diem [at a day]: on a specific day; at the appointed day
ad effectum: to the effect
ad effectum sequentem: to the effect following
ad effectum videndi: to have the effect of being seen (i.e., that remains to be seen)
ad eundem gradum (ad eund.): to the same degree or standing
ad excambium: for exchange; for compensation
ad exhibendum: for open display
ad exiguum tempus: for a short time
ad exitum: at issue; at the end (of the pleading)
ad extremum [to the extreme]: to the last; to the end
ad faciendam juratam illam: to make up that jury
ad faciendum: to do or to make (i.e., a task to do or complete)
ad factum praestandum: for the performance of a certain act
ad fidem: in allegiance; under allegiance; owing allegiance
ad filum aquae: to the thread or center of the stream
ad filum viae: to the middle of the way (i.e., a road)
ad finem (ad fin.) [to or at the end]: finally
ad fontes: at or to the source
ad goalam deliberandam: to deliver to jail
ad gravamen: to the grievance or the injury
ad gustum: according to taste
ad hanc vocem (a.h.v.): to or at this word
ad hoc [to or for this]: for this purpose (i.e., an action taken for a specific purpose, case, or situation)
ad hominem [to or at the person]: an argument that appeals to personal prejudice or emotions rather than to reason
ad hominem tu quoque: to at the person, you as well (i.e., responding to an *ad hominem* attack by accusing the accuser of the same offense)

Latin Legal Words and Phrases 9

ad horam compositam: at the agreed hour

ad hunc diem (a.h.d.): to or at this day

ad hunc locum (a.h.l.): to or at this place

ad idem [to the same point]: the essential agreement (e.g., the terms being understood and accepted by both parties in a contract)

ad ignorantiam [to ignorance]: an argument or appeal to those ignorant of the needed facts

ad illic: in that place

ad inde: to that; to them; thereto

ad inde requisitus: from thence or thereunto required

ad inferos: to the depths; to the center of the earth

ad infinitum (ad inf. or **ad infin.)** [to infinity]: endless; limitless; forever

ad informandum judicem: for the judge's information

ad informationem judicis: for the judge's information

ad initium (ad init.): at the beginning

ad inopiam: toward poverty or insolvency (see also, **vergens ad inopiam**)

ad inquirendum: for inquiry (i.e., an inquiry to obtain additional information or a clarification in a pending case)

ad instantiam: at the instance

ad instantiam partis: at the instance of a party

ad instar after the fashion of; like

ad interim (ad int. or **ad inter.):** in the meantime; temporarily

ad internecionem: to the point of extermination

ad invidiam [to envy]: an argument that appeals to prejudice or envy

ad judicium [to judgment]: an argument that appeals to common sense

ad jungendum auxilium: to join in aid

ad jura regis: to or for the rights of the king

ad largum: at large; at liberty; to have escaped (see also, **ire ad largum**)

ad levandam conscientiam: for the purpose of easing the conscience

ad libitum (ad lib.) [at pleasure]: at will; to improvise (see also, **a bene placito**)

ad limina [to the threshold]: to the highest authority

ad litem: to or for the suit; to the matter under litigation (e.g., in reference to a court-appointed guardian or representative)

ad literam or **ad litteram** [to the letter]: literally

ad locum (ad loc.): to or at the place

ad longum: at length

ad lunam: by moonlight

ad majorem cautelam: for greater caution or security

ad manum: at hand (i.e., ready for use)

ad melius inquirendum: a writ directing a coroner to hold a second inquest

ad misericordiam [to pity]: an argument that appeals to pity

ad modum: in or after the manner of; like

ad multus annos: for many years

ad nauseam [to nausea]: to the point of disgust

ad nocumentum: to the hurt or injury; to the detriment; also, to the nuisance or annoyance

ad omnes casus: for all causes (i.e., contingences)

ad omnia placita: to all the pleas

ad opus [to the work]: for the use; for the benefit

ad ostium ecclesiae [at the church door]: at the marriage

ad pares casus: to similar cases (see also, **ad similes casus**)

ad perpetuam rei memoriam: for a perpetual remembrance (record) of the matter

ad perpetuam remanentiam: to remain forever

ad perpetuitatem: in perpetuity; forever

ad pios usus: for pious purposes

ad plenum: fully; copiously; to the brim

ad populum [to the people]: an argument that appeals to people's passions or prejudices

ad postremum: lastly; for the last time

ad pristinum statum: to the pristine or former condition

ad probationem: to probe (i.e., to gather evidence to use as proof)

ad punctum temporis: at the point in time

ad quaerimoniam: on complaint of

ad quem [to which]: the ending point (as opposed to **a quo**; see also, **post quem**)

ad quod damnum: according to the loss or damage (i.e., a clause stating monetary loss in a complaint) (see also, **ad damnum**)

ad rationem ponere [to give a reason]: to cite a person to appear to give reason (e.g., for an expense)

ad recognoscendum: to recognize

ad rectum [to right]: to meet an accusation

ad referendum [for reference]: for further consideration; subject to approval (by a superior)

ad rem: to the matter; relevant to the point at issue

ad respondendum: to answer

ad rimandam veritatem: for the purpose of investigating the truth

ad satisfaciendum: to satisfy (see also, **capias ad satisfaciendum**)

ad sectam (**ads.** or **adsm.**; also **ats.**): at the suit of

ad similes casus: to like or similar cases (see also, **ad pares casus**)

ad solemnitatem: to solemnity (i.e., to perform all that the law requires)

ad summam [on the whole]: in general; in sum; in short

ad tempus [at the time]: in due time; according to the circumstances

ad terminum annorum: for a term of years

ad terminum qui praeteriti: a writ allowing entry of the owner at the expiration of a lease

ad tertiam vicem (**ad ter. vic.**): for the third time

ad tunc: then and there

ad tunc et ibidem: at the very time and in the same place (i.e., then and there)

ad ultimum: at the last moment; at last; finally

ad unum [to one]: without exception

ad unum omnes [all to one]: everyone without exception (i.e., unanimously)

ad usum (**ad us.**): according to custom or use

ad valentiam: to the value

ad valorem (**ad val.**): according to the value; also, proportional to the value (as in a tax)

ad ventrem inspiciendum: to inspect the womb (i.e., to determine if the condemned woman is pregnant before carrying out the execution) (see also, **de ventre inspiciendo**)

ad verbum: to the letter; word for word (i.e., *verbatim*)

ad verecundiam [to modesty]: an argument that appeals to modesty; also, an argument that appeals to the authority of the speaker (i.e., compared to someone of lower social status or of modest learning)

ad vicem: in place of; instead of

ad vindictam publicam: for defense of the public interest

ad vitam: for life

ad vitam aeternam [for eternal life]: for all time

ad vitam aut culpam [for life or until fault]: held for life (i.e., until death or delinquency removes one from office)

ad vitandum perjurium: for avoiding perjury

ad vivum [to the life]: from life; lifelike

adde huc or **adde eo:** add to this; add to that; also, consider this as well

addendum (pl. **addenda**): something to be added (i.e., an addition to the end of a book or manuscript); also, a supplement

addictio [adjudication]: the awarding of the property of the debtor to the creditor in the form of a conveyance

addictio in diem: assignment for a fixed period or postponement to a date (i.e., a clause in a contract that allows the contract to be terminated if the seller receives a better offer within a given period) (see also, **in diem addictio**)

additum (pl. **addita**): something added

additur: it is added (e.g., an addition to a judgment for damages to avoid further appeal) (see also, **remittitur**)

ademptio: revocation of a legacy
adeo: so; as
adfinis (pl. **adfines**): a relative of one's spouse
adfinitas: the familial connections of a husband and a wife (i.e., their relatives broadly speaking)
adhibere: to use or exercise
adhibere diligentiam: to use or exercise care
adhuc: while; as yet
adhuc sub judice lis est: the case is still before the court
adiratus (pl. **adirata**): lost; strayed
aditio hereditatis: an heir's acceptance of an inheritance
aditus: a public road or access
adjournatur: it is adjourned
adjudicata: decided; settled
adjumentum: assistance; help
adjuvans: helping; assisting
admanuensis: one who takes an oath or swears on a Bible
adolescens: youth
adscripti glebae: joined to the land
adsum: I am present
adsumptio: in logic, the minor premise of a syllogism
adulterium: a fine for committing adultery
adultus (pl. **adulti**): an adult
advena: a sojourner; a non-citizen
adventitius: adventitious (i.e., unusual)
adventurae maris: adventures of the sea (i.e., things lost at sea)
adventus: an arrival
adversa fortuna: ill fortune
adversaria [written observations]**:** a diary; a journal
adversarius: a legal adversary, such as in a lawsuit
adversus or **adversum (adv.):** against; opposed to (see also, **versus**)
adversus bonos mores (adv. bon. mor.): contrary to or against good morals (see also, **contra bonos mores**)
advisare: to advise; to consult; to consider

advocatus diaboli: a devil's advocate
aedes: a dwelling
aedificare: to build a house
aegis [a shield]: sponsorship; protection
aegrotat (pl. **aegrotant**) [he or she is ill]: a medical excuse
aequalis (aeq.): equal
aequalitas: equality
aequitas: equity
aequo animo [with an equal mind]: calmly; with composure
aequum est: it is just
aequum et bonum: just and good (i.e., reasonable)
aequus: equal; equitable
aes alienum [money belonging to another]: debt or debts
aetas: age
aetatis (aet. or **aetat.):** of the age; of one's lifetime
aetatis suae (A.S.): of his or her age; of his or her lifetime
affectio: affection; feeling; disposition
affectio conjugalis: conjugal affection
affectio justitiae: affection for justice
affectio maritalis: marital affection
affectio societatis [disposition for sociality or partnership]: an intent to form a mutually beneficial partnership
affectus: disposition of mind; intent
affectus sine effectu [intent without effect]: an intention that is not acted upon or carried out
affidatus: a loyal tenant
affidavit [he has stated on oath]: a sworn written statement of fact
affinis: having affinity with
affinitas affinitatis [affinity of affinity]: related by affinity of marriage but not by law or by blood (e.g., the brother of a husband is related by affinity of marriage to the sister of his brother's wife)
affixus: affixed; fastened
agendum est: the matter to be treated is...
ager: land; a field; also, an acre

ager limitatus (pl. **agri limitati**): lands or property limited by natural boundaries or by the lines of government survey

ager publicus: public land

aggregatio mentium: a meeting of the minds

aggressus: an attack

agnomen: a nickname

agrestis: wild; rustic; pertaining to the field or countryside; also, uncultivated or rude

agricola: a farmer

aio et nego: I say yes and I say no

alba et atra: white and black

album: a record book (e.g., a compilation of laws)

alia: other things

alia de causa: for another reason

alia enormia: other enormities; other serious wrongs (see also, **et alia enormia**)

alia manu (a.m. or **al. man.**): by another hand

alias: otherwise; also, on other occasions

alias dictus [otherwise called]: an alias

alibi: elsewhere; at another place

alienatio: alienation; conveyance (i.e., the transfer of ownership)

alieni generis: of another kind

alieni juris: subject to the authority of another, as in a legal dependent (as opposed to **sui juris**)

alieno solo: on another's land

alimenta: provisions; food stuffs (i.e., things necessary to support life)

alio intuitu: with another intent; from another view (i.e., in view of another case or condition)

alio pacto: in another way

alioquin: otherwise

aliqua ex parte: in some respect

aliqualis probatio: a proof of some sort (i.e., the best available evidence under the circumstances)

aliqualiter: in any way

aliquando: at times; sometimes
aliquis: someone; anyone; something
aliquo: somewhere
aliquot: some; a few; a fraction of the whole
aliter: otherwise
aliunde [otherwise]: from elsewhere; from another source
alius: other; another
alius alias: one now, another later
alius aliter: in different ways
allegata et probata: things alleged and things proved
allegatio falsi: a false allegation; a false statement
alluvium: the movable surface of the earth, such as soil and other deposits
alta proditio: high treason
alta via: a highway (see also, **via alta**)
alter: other; the other; another
alter ego [one's other self]: a second self; a best friend; a bosom buddy
alter idem [another of the same kind]: a second self
alternis annis: every other year
alternis diebus: every other day
alternis vicibus: alternately, by turns
alternus: alternate; one after the other
alterum non laedere: to injure no one
alterum tantum [as much again]: twice as much
alteruter: one or the other
altius non tollendi: of not raising higher (i.e., a reference to codes regulating the height of tenement buildings) (as opposed to **altius tollendi**)
altius tollendi: of raising higher (i.e., a reference to the unregulated height of buildings) (as opposed to **altius non tollendi**)
alto et basso: high and low
altum mare: the high seas
alumnus (f. **alumna**; pl. **alumni**): a foster child; also, a college graduate
alvei mutatio: a change in the course of a stream

alveus: a riverbed (i.e., a bed or channel through which a river or stream normally flows)

amanuensis: a personal secretary

ambidexter [a person skillful with both hands]: (inf.) an attorney who receives pay from both sides; also, a bribed juror

ambigendi locus: room for doubt

ambiguitas latens: a latent ambiguity

ambiguitas patens: a patent or clear ambiguity

ambiguus: ambiguous; going two ways; uncertain

ambitiosus: ambitious

ambo [two together]: both

ambulatoria voluntas: an ambulatory intention; a revocable will or intention

amens: insane

amentia: insanity; idiocy

amiciter: in a friendly way

amicus curiae [a friend of the court]: a disinterested adviser

amita: a paternal aunt (i.e., father's sister) (cf., **matertera**)

amor: love

anatocismus: compound interest

androgynus: an androgyne

anecius: the firstborn child; the eldest or senior-most member (see also, **primogenitus**)

Anglice: in English

anguis in herba [a snake in the grass]: an unsuspected danger

animal rationale: a reasoning person

animi causa: for the sake of pleasure (as opposed to **negotii causa**)

animo: with intent or design

animo cancellandi: with the intent of canceling

animo capiendi: with the intent of taking

animo custodiendi: with the intent of keeping

animo defamandi: with the intent of defaming

animo differendi: with the intent of obtaining delay

animo donandi: with the intent of making a donation

animo et corpore: by the mind and by the body (i.e., with intent and act)
animo et facto: with intent and fact
animo felonico: with felonious intent
animo furandi: with the intent of stealing
animo lucrandi: with the intent of profiting
animo manendi: with the intent of remaining
animo morandi: with the intent of delaying
animo obligandi: with the intent of entering into an obligation
animo recipiendi: with the intent of receiving
animo remanendi: with the intent of remaining abroad
animo republicandi: with the intent of republishing
animo revertendi: with the intent of returning
animo revocandi: with the intent of revoking
animo signandi: with the intent of signing
animo testandi: with the intent of making a will
animus: will; intent; also, the mind
animus belligerendi: the intent to wage war
animus cancellandi: the intent of canceling
animus capiendi: the intent of taking
animus contrahendi: the intent of entering into a contractual agreement
animus defamandi: the intent of defaming
animus delinquendi: the intent of abandoning
animus derelinquendi: the intent of leaving or disowning
animus domini: the intent of owning (i.e., to establish legal residency)
animus donandi: the intent of giving
animus et factum: intent and act (i.e., intent fulfilled by a corresponding action)
animus et factus: will and deed
animus felonicus: the intent of committing a felony
animus furandi: the intent of stealing
animus injuriandi: the intent of injuring (properly, **cum animo injuriandi**)
animus laedendi: the intent of injuring

Latin Legal Words and Phrases 19

animus lucrandi: the intent of gaining (i.e., to make a profit)
animus malus: evil intent
animus manendi: the intent of remaining
animus necandi: the intent of killing
animus nocendi: the intent of harming
animus occidendi: the intent of killing
animus possidendi: the intent of possessing
animus quo: the intent with which (i.e., the motive behind an action)
animus recipiendi: the intent of receiving
animus recuperandi: the intent of recovering
animus republicandi: the intent of republishing
animus residendi: the intent of residing or establishing a residence
animus restituendi: the intent of restoring
animus revertendi: the intent of returning
animus revocandi: the intent of revoking
animus solvendi: the intent of paying a debt
animus testandi: the intent of making a will
annales (ann.): records; chronicles
anni continui: successive years (i.e., continuing without interruption)
anni et tempora [years and times]: annals; yearbooks
anni nubiles: the legal marriageable age for girls
anni utiles: the years during which a right may be exercised
anniculus: a one-year-old child
anno aetatis suae (A.A.S.): in the year of his or her age
anno Domini (A.D.): in the year of our Lord
anno interjecto or **anno interiecto:** after the interval of a year
anno Regni or **anno regni (A.R.):** in the year of the reign
anno vertente: in the course of the year
annona: a yearly crop
annos vixit (a.v.): he or she lived (so many years)
annua pecunia: an annuity
annus (pl. **anni**): year
annus bisextus: leap year

annus continuus: a continuous year (i.e., without interruption)

annus deliberandi: the year for deliberating (i.e., a reference to succession or inheritance)

annus et dies: a year and a day

annus luctus or **annum luctus:** a year of mourning (i.e., the period between the husband's death and when his widow was allowed to remarry)

annuus: annually; yearly

annuus reditus or **annuus redditus:** an annuity; a yearly rent

annuus utilis: a year of useful advantage (i.e., the exercise of one's legal rights)

ante (a.): before; ahead of

ante bellum: before the war

ante diem (a.d.): before the day

ante exhibitionem billae: before the showing of the bill (i.e., before the suit is filed)

ante factum [done before]: a previous act or fact

ante gestum: a previous act

ante juramentum or **antejuramentum:** an oath formerly taken before the suit

ante litem motam: before litigation has begun; before a legal dispute arose

ante lucem: before daybreak

ante meridianus: before midday

ante meridiem (A.M. or **a.m.):** before noon

ante mortem: before death

ante natus or **antenatus** (pl. **antenati**): a person born before a certain time or important event, especially one that affects a legal right or privilege (e.g., before the parents are married)

ante omnia [before all things]: first of all; in the first place

ante partum or **antepartum** [before birth]: before childbirth

ante redditas rationes: before accounts are rendered

antea: formerly; heretofore; beforehand

antehac [before this time]: formerly

anterior: at the front; the front part

anti: against; opposed to

antiqua custuma: ancient customs

antiqua et nova: old and new (rights)

antiqua statuta: ancient statutes

apertum breve (pl. **aperta brevia**): an open, unsealed writ

apertum factum: an overt act

apertus: opened; uncovered

apex [summit]: the top-most point or part (i.e., a reference to the top of a mineral vein nearest the surface of the earth)

apex juris [summit of the law]: an extreme point or subtly of the law carried to either extreme

apices litigandi: the finer points or subtleties of litigation

apinae: trifles

apo: from; away from

apparatus (app.): equipment; also, a set of materials summarizing textual evidence

appendicula: a little addition

appenditia: appurtenances

appendix [appendage]: an addition

aptus: suitable

apud [according to]: in the writings of

apud acta: among the acts (i.e., among the recorded proceedings)

aqua (aq.): water

aqua cedit solo: water passes with the soil (i.e., the water goes with the land)

aquae ductus or **aquaeductus:** the right to pipe or convey water over or through the property of another (e.g., drainage)

aquae haustus or **aquaehaustus:** a right to water cattle or livestock at any stream or pond

aquaticus: related to water; aquatic

arator: a farmer of arable land

aratrum terrae: plow land (i.e., the amount of land that can be plowed with a single plow) (cf., **bovata terrae**)

arbiter: arbitrator

arbitrio suo: under one's own authority or control

arbitrium: an award

arbor civilis [civil tree]: a family tree

arbor consanguinitatis [blood relationship tree]: a genealogical tree

arbor infelix [infelicitous or unhappy tree]: the gallows

arcana imperii: state secrets

arcanus: secret

arena [sand]: ground; arena

argentarius (pl. **argentarii**): moneylender (i.e., a banker)

argentum (Ag. or **ag.):** silver

argentum Dei [God's money]: earnest money (i.e., money deposited to bind a contract or financial agreement)

arguendo (arg.) [in arguing]: in the course of arguing; by way of argument

argumentum: an argument; a proof

argumentum a contrario: an argument from the opposite position or viewpoint

argumentum a majori ad minus: an argument from greater to the lesser (i.e., the right to the greater also assumes a right to the lesser)

argumentum ab auctoritate: an argument from authority

argumentum ab inconvenienti: an argument from inconvenience (i.e., one that appeals to the hardship it might present)

argumentum ad absurdum: an argument to prove the absurdity of an opponent's argument

argumentum ad antiquitatem [argument to or from antiquity]: an argument that appeals to tradition

argumentum ad baculum [argument to or from the rod]: an argument that appeals to force or the threat of force (see also, **argumentum baculinum**)

argumentum ad captandum: an argument made by arousing popular passions

argumentum ad consequentiam [argument to the consequence]: an argument that appeals to the consequences of an action

argumentum ad crumenam [argument to the purse]: an argument that appeals to a person's self-interest (i.e., an appeal to wealth or privilege; as opposed to **argumentum ad lazarum**)

argumentum ad hominem [argument to or at the person]: an evasive argument that attacks an opponent's character rather than the point under dispute

argumentum ad ignorantiam: an argument based on an opponent's ignorance of the facts or on his or her inability to prove the opposite

argumentum ad invidiam: an argument that appeals to prejudice or base passions

argumentum ad judicium: an argument that appeals to good judgment or common sense

argumentum ad lazarum [argument to poverty]: an argument that appeals to one's belief in the inherent goodness of the poor (as opposed to **argumentum ad crumenam**)

argumentum ad misericordiam: an argument that appeals to pity

argumentum ad populum: an argument that appeals to people's passions and prejudices rather than to their intellect

argumentum ad rem: an argument that bears on the actual point or issue at hand

argumentum ad verecundiam: an argument from authority that appeals to a person's sense of reverence (e.g., a reliance on the prestige of a great or respected person rather than on the independent consideration of the question itself) (cf., **ipse dixit**)

argumentum baculinum: an argument that appeals to force or to the threat of force (see also, **argumentum ad baculum**)

argumentum ex concesso: an argument that is based on points already held by one's opponent

arma: arms; weapons

arma in armatos: to take up arms against arms

armata vis: armed force

armatus: armed; also, provided with

ars: art; method; practice; skill

articulo mortis: at the moment of death
artificialis: artificial
arvus: arable land; a ploughed or cultivated field
assensio mentium [a meeting of the minds]: mutual consent
assidue: constantly
assisa armorum: a statute ordering the keeping of arms
assisus: lands farmed or rented out for income
assumpsit [he or she undertook]: a suit to recover damages for breach of a contract or actionable promise, whether expressed or implied
asylum (pl. **asyla**): a sanctuary; a place of refuge
atra et alba: black and white
auctor: author
auctor ignotus: an unknown author
auctor in rem suam: one who acts on his or her own behalf
auctoritas: authority
audacia: boldness; daring
audi alteram partem: hear the other side (i.e., the right of the defendant to answer a charge or to speak in his or her own defense)
audita querela [the complaint having been heard]: a common-law writ giving the defendant opportunity to appeal
auditus: hearing; also, hearsay
aula: a hall or palace
aula regis or **aula regia:** a royal court
aura vitalis: the life principle
aurea mediocritas: the golden mean (i.e., moderation in all things)
aurum (**Au.** or **au.**): gold (see also, **chrysos**)
aut eo circiter: or thereabout
auter: another
auto da fe [act of faith]: the public burning of heretics
auxilium: an aid
auxilium curiae: a request by one party for another party to appear in court

auxilium regis: the king's aid (i.e., taxes levied for public services)
averium (pl. **averia**): a beast of burden; also, goods or property
aversio periculi: averting peril or danger
averum: property; holding
avia: a grandmother
avunculus: a maternal uncle (i.e., mother's brother) (cf., **patruus**)
avus: a grandfather

B

ballium or **balium:** bail
bancus [bench]: court or tribunal; also, the judges of a court seated together, as in a quorum
Bancus Communium Placitorum (or simply, **Bancus**): Court of Common Pleas
Bancus Reginae: the Queen's Bench
Bancus Regis: the King's Bench
bannitus: a banished or outlawed person
bannum: an edict or court-ordered prohibition aimed at keeping the peace (i.e., a ban)
basis (pl. **bases**): base; bottom
belli: at war
belli denuntiatio: a declaration of war
bellicus or **bellicosus:** warlike
bellum: war
bellum atrocissimum: a war of atrocities
bellum inter duos [war between two]: a duel
bene: well; good
bene decessit [he or she died well]: he or she died naturally
bene exeat [let him or her go forth well]: a certificate of good character
bene facta or **benefacta:** good deeds
bene placitum or **beneplacitum:** good pleasure
beneficium: a privilege or favor; also, a benefice

beneficium abstinendi: the right of an heir to decline an inheritance

beneficium ordinis [the benefit of order]: the right of the surety to require the creditor to exhaust the resources of the debtor first before the surety assumed liability for the debt (see also, **ordinis beneficium**)

benignus: kind; generous (as opposed to **malignus**)

bibliotheca: a library

biduum: a period or space of two days

biennium: a period of two years

bihorium: a period of two hours

billa: a bill; a statement; a proposed statute

billa cassetur or **quod billa cassetur** [that the bill be quashed]: let the bill or case be set aside (i.e., discontinued) (see also, **cassetur billa**)

billa excambii: a bill of exchange

billa vera: true bill (i.e., a bill of indictment containing sufficient evidence to warrant a trial)

bipartito: in two parts

bipartitus: divided in two

birretum [biretta]: a traditional cap or other headpiece worn by judges

bis: twice

bis petitum: twice demanded

bogus: false; spurious

bona: property; goods

bona confiscata: confiscated goods

bona et catalla: goods and chattels

bona fide [in good faith]: honestly; sincerely; genuinely (as opposed to **mala fide**)

bona fides [good faith]: honest intention; also, a person with genuine credentials

bona fiscalia: public property

bona forisfacta: forfeited goods (i.e., seized by the state due to a violation of the law)

bona gestura: good behavior

bona gratia: goodwill; voluntarily
bona immobilia: immovable goods
bona memoria: with good memory
bona mobilia: movable goods
bona notabilia: notable or noteworthy things (i.e., property of the deceased that requires probate)
bona paraphernalia or **paraphernalia:** separate goods, specifically the separate property of the wife beyond her dowry
bona peritura: perishable goods
bona vacantia: unclaimed goods
bona waviata: goods cast off or dropped by a thief in flight
bonis non amovendis: that the goods not be removed
bono et malo: for good and bad
bonorum omnium heres: the sole heir
bonum nomen: a good payer (i.e., a good security risk)
bonum publicum (b.p. or **bon. pub.):** the common good
bonum vacans: unowned property that belongs to whomever makes the first claim to it
bonus: good
bovata terrae: as much land as one ox can plow (cf., **aratrum terrae**)
breve (pl. **brevia**)**:** a writ
breve de recto: a writ of right
breve originale: an original writ
brevi manu [with a short hand]**:** briefly; summarily (see also, **manu brevi**)
brevia anticipantia: writs of prevention
brevia de cursu: writs of course (see also, **de cursu**)
brevia judicialia: judicial writs
brevis: brief; short
brevitatis causa: for the sake of brevity
breviter: briefly; shortly
brutum fulmen (pl. **bruta fulmina**) [a harmless thunderbolt]**:** an empty threat
brutus: dull-minded; irrational; without reason

C

cadaver: a corpse

cadit quaestio: the question falls to the ground (i.e., the dispute or discussion has come to an end)

caecus: blind

caeteris tacentibus: the others being silent (i.e., the other judges expressing no formal opinion)

calefagium: a right to take fuel yearly

calendarium: calendar; account book

calumnia: malicious prosecution

calumniae jus jurandum or **calumniae jusjurandum:** an oath against calumny

cambium: change or exchange (e.g., money or land) (see also, **excambium**)

camera: a chamber (viz., a judge's chambers)

camera regis (obscure pl. **regiae camerae**) [chamber of the king]: a harbor; a place of royal commercial privilege

Camera Stellata [Star Chamber]: a tribunal or inquisitorial council (fig., a severe and arbitrary court)

campertum: a field of grain (e.g., a cornfield)

canfara: trial by hot iron

capacitas: capacity

capax doli: capable of committing crime

capias [take]: that you may seize (i.e., a writ issued for the arrest of a person who has been accused of committing a crime)

capias ad audiendum judicium: a writ to bring a defendant to court to hear sentence when found guilty of a misdemeanor

capias ad computandum: a writ to compel a defendant to give an account to an auditor

capias ad respondendum (ca. ad re. or **ca. re.** or **ca. res.):** a writ of arrest intended to keep the defendant safely in custody until trial

capias ad satisfaciendum (ca. ad sa. or **ca. sa.):** a writ of arrest to hold the defendant and present him or her in court to satisfy a plaintiff's complaint (see also, **ad satisfaciendum**)

capias pro fine or **capiatur pro fine:** a writ against a defendant who fails to pay a court-ordered fine

capias respondendum (ca. re. or **ca. res.):** a writ of arrest intended to keep the defendant safely in custody until trial

capita [heads]: persons individually considered (see also, **per capita**)

capitatim: by the head

capitis deminutio: a change in or reduction of legal status; the loss of civil rights (see also, **deminutio capitis**)

Capitula de Judaeis: historically, a register of mortgages made to the Jews

captus: seized

caput (pl. **capita**): head

caput anni: the beginning or first day of the year

caput lupinum [wolf's head]: an outlaw; fugitive from the law

caput mortuum [dead head]: dead; obsolete (i.e., a matter of no legal validity that is void to all persons and for all purposes)

carcer: prison

cardo controversiae: the hinge of the controversy (i.e., the main point under dispute)

carnifex: an executioner; a hangman

carta [paper]: charter; deed (see also, **charta**)

cassetur billa [that the bill be quashed]: let the bill or case be set aside (i.e., discontinued) (see also, **billa cassetur**)

casus [a falling or fall]: an occasion; an event; an occurrence; also, a case

casus amissionis: the circumstances of the loss

casus belli: an act of war

casus conscientiae: a case of conscience

casus foederis [a case of the treaty]: a case within the stipulations of a treaty

casus fortuitus (cas. fortuit.) [a case of fortune]: a chance happening; an accident; a loss happening despite a person's best preparation and effort

casus omissus: a case omitted or not provided for

casus omissus et oblivionis: a case omitted and forgotten

causa: cause; reason; also, a case
causa causans: the immediate cause; the cause of an action
causa cognita: the cause or fact being known (i.e., the facts being ascertained after investigation)
causa data et non secuta: consideration given and not followed
causa debendi: the cause of debt
causa hospitandi: for the sake of hospitality
causa impotentiae: by reason of impotence
causa mali [an evil cause]: a cause of mischief
causa mortis: by reason of death; also, in anticipation of death
causa patet: a plain or manifest cause (i.e., the reason is clear)
causa privata: a private or civil case
causa proxima: the direct or immediate cause
causa publica: a public or criminal case
causa qua supra: for the reason stated above
causa remota: the indirect or remote cause
causa secunda: secondary cause
causa sine qua non: an indispensable condition without which the injury would not have taken place (see also, **sine qua non**)
causa tenuis et inops: a weak and tenuous case
causa turpis: for a base or evil cause
causator: a party to a legal action (i.e., a litigant)
causu proviso: in the case provided
caute: carefully; cautiously
cautio: security; bond; bail
cautio fidejussoria: a bond or security paid by a third party
cautio juratoria: a bond or security given by oath
cautio pignoratitia: a bond or security given by deposit of goods
cautio pro expensis: a bond or security for costs or expenses
cautum: caution; concern
cautus: careful; cautious; wary
cave canem [beware the dog]: beware of dog
cave felem [beware the cat]: beware of cat
caveat [let the person beware]: a warning or caution

caveat actor: let the doer beware
caveat conductus: let the one who has been hired beware
caveat emptor: let the buyer beware
caveat venditor: let the seller beware
caveat viator: let the traveler beware
censor morum: a censor of morals
centrum: center; middle point
centum (C. or **cent.):** one hundred; a hundred
cepi: I have taken
cepi corpus (c.c.) [I have taken a body]: the official reply by the sheriff after fulfilling a *capias* writ
cepit: he or she has taken
cepit in alio loco: he or she took in another place (i.e., in a location not named by the plantiff)
cera impressa [wax impression]: a wax seal
certiorari [to be certified]: a writ calling up the records of a lower court
certis nominibus: on good security
certo [certainly]: yes
cessio bonorum: a surrender of goods (i.e., assignment of a debtor's property to creditors)
cetera desunt or **caetera desunt** (**c.d.** or **cet. d.**): the rest is lacking
ceteris paribus or **caeteris paribus** (**cet. par.**): other things being equal
ceteris rebus: as regards the rest
ceterus: the other part
charta (**chart.**) [paper]: charter; deed (see also, **carta**)
charta chyrographata (or **chirographata**): a charter or deed of indenture in which each party held their half of the document that was divided in the middle by the word 'chyrograph' or by the full alphabet (properly, **charta chyrographata vel communis**)
charta communis: a charter or deed of indenture
chartae libertatum: charters granting certain liberties, as in the Magna Carta

chirographum or **chyrographum** [handwritten]: an autograph copy; a handwritten document of debt

chrysos: gold (see also, **aurum**)

cibatus: food; nourishment

cibus (cib.): food; a meal

cicatrix manet: the scar remains

circa (c. or **ca.):** about; near; around

circiter (c. or **circ.):** about

circuitus verborum [a circuit of words]: circumlocution

circulatim: in circles; in groups

circulus vitiosus [a vicious circle]: circular reasoning

circum (c. or **circ.):** around; about

circus: a circular enclosure

cito: swiftly; quickly

citatio ad reassumendam causam: a citation issued, at the death of the plaintiff or defendant in a pending suit, for or against the heir of either

citra causae cognitionem: without investigating the cause

civiliter: civilly (as opposed to **criminaliter**)

civiliter mortuus [civilly dead]: an outlaw

civis: a citizen

civis bonus: a good citizen; a patriot

civitas: a city

civitatis amissio: loss of citizenship

clam: secretly; covertly

clare constat: it clearly appears

clauditas: lameness

clausula derogativa: a clause in a will invalidating subsequent wills (e.g., to guard against involuntary amendments)

clausum: shut; closed; an enclosed space (i.e., a body of water or a piece of land)

clausura: closed; an enclosure

clausus: closed; covered; also, a clause

clementia: clemency

clericale privilegium: the privilege of clerics (see also, **privilegium clericale**)

Latin Legal Words and Phrases   33

clericus: a clerk; a clergy member

codex [book]**:** a code; a collection of laws

Codex Juris Civilis or **Codex Iuris Civilis:** Code of Civil Law

cognati [connected by blood]**:** relations on the mother's side

cognatus: related by birth

cognomen: a surname; a family name

cognovit or **cognovit actionem** [he has acknowledged the action]**:** the defendant's acknowledgment of the plaintiff's claim

cohaeres or **coheres:** a joint heir

coitus or **coetus:** sexual union; intercourse

collegialiter: in a corporate capacity

collegium (pl. **collegia**)**:** a college; a corporate body; a guild

collistrigium: the pillory

colloquium [conversation]**:** colloquium; convocation

colluvies vitiorum (coll. vit.) [a collection of filthy vices]**:** a den of iniquity

colore officii: by color of office

combustio: burning (i.e., the ancient practice of burning persons as punishment for apostasy or treason)

combustio domorum: the burning of houses

combustio pecuniae: the practice of testing the purity of milled or coined money by melting it down upon receipt

comes: a count or earl; also, a companion or associate

comes stabuli: a constable or sheriff

comitas inter gentes [comity among nations]**:** civility among peaceful nations

comitatus: a county or shire

commeatus: free passage; a leave of absence (i.e., a furlough); also, travel supplies

commendatus: one commended to another for protection

commercia belli: an armistice between warring nations; also, contracts made between persons of warring countries

comminatorium: a clause admonishing the sheriff to be faithful in carrying out his or her duties

commodatum: a loan (i.e., a contract of deposit for a temporary loan of movable property)

commodum: advantage; opportunity; also, leisure

commodus: proper; appropriate; suitable; satisfactory

commorientes: persons who perish at the same time and place as a result of the same calamity

commune bonum: the common good

commune forum: the common forum (i.e., a court of common session)

commune placitum: a common plea

commune vinculum: a common bond

communi consensu: by common consent

communia placita: common pleas (i.e., civil actions between individuals) (see also, **placita communia**)

communibus annis: on a yearly average

communio bonorum: a community of goods

communis: common

communis annis [in ordinary years]: on the annual average

communis error: common error (i.e., an opinion or practice that is commonly held but not adequately founded in the law)

communis opinio: common opinion

communis scriptura: a writing common to both parties (e.g., a chirograph)

communis stirpes: common stock; a common ancestor

comparatio literarum: a comparison of handwritings

compendium: an abridgment

compensatio criminum or **compensatio criminis:** a compensating crime (i.e., the doctrine of recrimination in which the defendant may contest the charge of the plaintiff on the grounds of equal guilt, as in a divorce)

complementum justi: full justice

componere lites: to settle disputes

compos mentis [sound of mind]: in one's right mind

compos sui: master of himself (i.e., having use of one's limbs or the power of bodily motion)

compromisarius: an arbitrator

conatus: an attempt, such as to commit a crime

concedo [I admit]**:** I grant (i.e., a concession made in an argument)

concessi: I have granted

concessio: a grant; a lease

concessit or **concessum:** granted; allowed

concessit solvere: he or she agreed to pay

concilium: a council

concordatus: a pact or agreement, historically between civil and religious authorities

concordia [harmony]**:** an agreement

concubinatus: concubinage

condictio [a summons]**:** an action to recover, such as a debt (broadly understood)

conditio sine qua non: an indispensible condition (also, **sine qua non**)

condominium (pl. **condominia**)**:** common domain (i.e., a domain belonging to all parties)

confer (cf.): compare

confiscare: to confiscate

confitens reus: an accused person who admits his or her guilt

confusio: blending; mixing; merging

confusio bonorum: confusion of goods (i.e., the mixing of private property of different owners)

confusio jurium: confusion of rights (i.e., the merging of the rights of debtor and creditor in the same person)

conjudex (pl. **conjudices**)**:** an associate judge

conjugium: marriage

conjuncta: things joined together (as opposed to **disjuncta**)

conjunctim: jointly

conjunctim et divisim: jointly and severally

conjunx or **conjux** (**con.** or **conj.**)**:** wife; spouse; a marriage partner

connubium or **conubium:** marriage; intermarriage

consanguineus: related by blood

consanguineus frater [blood brother]: a brother who has the same father (i.e., a half brother)
consanguineus uterinus: a half sibling by the same mother
consanguinitas: relationship by blood
conscientia: conscience
conscientia mala: a bad conscience
conscientia recta: a good conscience
consensus: agreement; consent
consensus ad idem: consent or agreement as to the same (i.e., common consent)
consensus audacium [agreement of the rash]: a conspiracy
consensus gentium: consent of the nations
consensus omnium: universal consent
consequentia: a consequence
conservatio: preservation
conservus (f. **conserva**): a fellow servant or slave
consessor: an assessor
consessus: an assembly
considerabitur pro querente: judgment shall be given to the plaintiff
consideratio curiae: the judgment of the court (given after deliberation and study)
consideratum est per curiam: it is the judgment of the court
consideratur: it is the judgment
consiliarius: a counselor
consilium: counsel (i.e., the day appointed to hear the counsel of both parties)
consobrini: first cousins, in general terms
consociatio: an association
consolidus: bound together
consortium: a company or partnership; also, the conjugal companionship of husband and wife
consortium vitae: cohabitation
constabularius: a constable
constat [it appears]: it is clear or evident
constat de persona: it is clear as to the person meant

consuetudo (pl. **consuetudines**): custom; usage
consuetudo amatoria: courtship
consuetudo anglicana: English custom (i.e., English common law)
consuetudo curiae: the custom or practice of the court
consuetudo majorum: ancestral custom (see also, **mos majorum**)
consuetudo mercatorum: the custom or practice of merchants (see also, **lex mercatoria**)
consuetudo universa: universal custom
contemporanea expositio: a contemporaneous interpretation
contemptibiliter: contemptuously
conterminus: bordering on; adjacent
contestatio litis: contestation of the suit (i.e., the legal process by which a suit is brought before a judge, viz., the complaint and response by plaintiff and defendant)
continens: joined together
continentia: a continuance
continuando: continuing (e.g., a continuing breach of the law, such as trespassing)
contra (**con.** or **cont.**) [opposite]: against; on the opposite side (i.e., on the contrary)
contra bonos mores (**cont. bon. mor.**): contrary to good morals (see also, **adversus bonos mores**)
contra formam collationis: contrary to the form of the contribution or gift
contra formam statuti: against the form of the statute; against the letter of the law
contra jus belli: against or contrary to the law of war
contra jus commune: against or contrary to common law
contra jus fasque: against all law, human and divine
contra jus gentium: against the law of nations
contra legem: against the law
contra legem facere: to do what is prohibited by the law
contra legem terrae: against the law of the land
contra naturam: against nature
contra omnes gentes: against all the people
contra pacem: against the peace

contra placitum: a counterplea
contra proferentem: against the one who makes the offer (i.e., ambiguous wording [in a contract] should not favor the party that offered the wording)
contra rem publica: to the disadvantage of the state
contra scriptum testimonium: against written testimony
contractus: a contract
contradictio in adjecto: a contradiction in terms
contratenere: to withhold
contravenire: to contravene; to violate
controversia: a legal dispute
controversus: disputed
contumax: an outlaw (i.e., an accused person who refuses to appear and answer to a charge)
contumelia: physical violence; a verbal insult
contumeliosus: abusive; insulting
conveniens: convenient; suitable
convenit: it is agreed
conventio in unum: the agreement between two parties on the sense of the contract proposed
conventus: an assembly
conventus juridicus: judicial assembly (i.e., a Roman provincial court that heard civil cases)
convicium: censure; reproof; also, outcry
convivium: a feast or banquet
copia: plenty
copia vera: a true copy
copiosus: plentiful; wealthy
copulatio: union; connection
cor: heart
coram [before]**:** in the presence of; face-to-face
coram judice: before a judge
coram nobis [before us]**:** in the court of King's Bench (**Bancus Regis**)
coram non judice [before a judge without jurisdiction]**:** before one not the proper judge

coram paribus [before equals]: before one's peers
coram populo [in public]: in the sight of spectators
coram vobis [before you]: a writ to correct an error of fact
corona [crown]: the Crown
coronator: a coroner
corpore et animo: by physical act and mental intent
corpus (pl. **corpora**): body or corpse; also, a body or collection of writings
corpus comitatus [the body of the county]: the inhabitants of a county
corpus corporatum: a corporation
corpus delicti [the body of the crime]: the body of evidence (i.e., the substance or fundamental facts of a crime)
corpus humanum: the human body
corpus juris [body of law]: a collection of laws of a country or jurisdiction
Corpus Juris Canonici or **corpus juris canonici:** the body of canon law
Corpus Juris Civilis or **corpus juris civilis:** the body of civil or Roman law
corpus pro corpore: body for body
correi credendi: joint creditors
corrigendum (pl. **corrigenda**): to be corrected (i.e., the corrections to be made in a manuscript before its publication)
corruptus: corrupted; spoiled
cotidie or **cotidianus** (**cotid.**): daily
cras: tomorrow
crassa ignorantia: gross ignorance
crassa negligentia or **crassa neglegentia:** gross negligence
crastino: tomorrow; the next day
crastinus (**crast.**): of tomorrow; on the morrow
credere in Deum: to entrust oneself to God
creditum: a loan
crepusculum (**crepus.**): twilight; in the evening
cretio: the period of deliberation allowed for an heir to decide whether to take an inheritance

crimen (pl. **crimina**): crime; guilt

crimen falsi: the crime of falsification (e.g., perjury and forgery) (see also, **falsi crimen**)

crimen furti: the crime of theft

crimen incendii: an incendiary crime (i.e., arson)

crimen laesae majestatis: the crime or charge of high treason

crimen majestatis: crime against the Crown (i.e., treason)

crimen raptus: the crime of rape

crimen repentundarum: the crime of bribery

crimen roberiae: the crime of robbery

criminaliter: criminally (as opposed to **civiliter**)

criminosus: criminal

cubiculum: a bedroom

cui: which; to or for whom

cui ante divortium: to whom before the divorce (i.e., a writ brought by a divorced woman to recover lands of hers that had been held back by her husband) (see also, **cui in vita**)

cui bono?: for whose benefit?

cui bono fuisset? or **cui fuisset bono?:** for whose benefit or advantage?

cui in vita: to whom in life (i.e., a writ brought by a divorced woman to recover lands of hers that had been held back by her husband) (see also, **cui ante divortium**)

cui malo?: whom will it harm?

cui prodest?: who benefits?

cujus or **cuius** (**cuj.**): of which or whose

cujus libet (**cuj. lib.**): of whatever pleases

culpa: fault; negligence; guilt

culpa in eligendo: fault in choosing or selecting (i.e., negligence through a poorly made decision or choice)

culpa in faciendo: fault by negligent doing, causing harm to another's person or property

culpa in vigilando: a fault in vigilance (i.e., guilt by failure to supervise properly or exercise due diligence)

culpa lata [wide or extensive fault]: gross negligence (as opposed to **culpa levis**)

Latin Legal Words and Phrases 41

culpa levis [slight fault]: excusable negligence (as opposed to **culpa lata**)
culpa levissima [the slightest fault]: slight fault or neglect (see also, **levissima culpa**)
culpabilis (**cul.**): culpable; guilty
cum (c̄): with
cum animo injuriandi: the intent of injuring (see also, **animus injuriandi**)
cum causa: with cause
cum domibus et aedificiis: with houses and buildings
cum effectu: with effect
cum grano salis: with a grain of salt (i.e., with reservation)
cum multis aliis (**c.m.a.**): with many others
cum nota [with a mark]: with reservation
cum omni causa: with every advantage
cum onere: with the burden [of proof]
cum onere debitorum defuncti: under burden of the debts of the deceased
cum pertinentiis: with the appurtenances (i.e., with additional rights)
cum suo onere: with its burden
cum telo: armed
cum testamento annexo: with the will or testament annexed
cum uxoribus et liberis: with wife and child
cumulatus or **cumulativus:** cumulative; accruing
cura: care; custody
curator (f. **curatrix**): a curator
curator ad bona: curator of the goods (i.e., the guardian of the estate of a minor) (see also, **ad bona**)
curator ad hoc: a specially appointed curator (i.e., a guardian)
curator ad litem: guardian for the lawsuit (i.e., a court-appointed representative of a minor)
curator bonis: a curator of property, especially for a minor or for a disabled person
curator bonorum: a court-appointed administrator for the estate of an insolvent person

curatus: cared for

curia (cur.): a court of justice

curia advisari vult (cur. adv. vult or c.a.v.): the court wishes to be advised or to consider the matter

curia christianitatis: an ecclesiastical court

curia claudenda: historically, a court order compelling a plaintiff's neighbor to erect a wall or fence between their adjoining lands

curia comitatus: the county court

Curia Magna: the Great Court (i.e., the English Parliament)

Curia Regis: the King's Court

curriculum: a course of study

curriculum vitae (c.v.): a résumé (also **vitae curriculum** or **vita**)

currit quatuor pedibus: it runs on four feet (i.e., these cases are similar)

cursus: course; practice

curtus: shortened

custa (sing. **custum**) or **custantia:** costs (see also, **custus**)

custagium (pl. **custagia**): cost

custodes pacis: guardians of the peace

custodia: custody; guardianship

custodia legis: in the custody of the law (see also, **in custodia legis**)

custodia libera: house arrest

custodiae causa: for the purpose of preserving

custos (pl. **custodes**): a guard; warden; keeper; custodian

custos ferarum: a game warden

custos maris [warden of the sea]: an admiral

custos morum: a custodian of morals

custos rotulorum (C.R.) [custodian of rolls]: principal justice of the peace in an English county

custos sigilli: keeper of the seal

custos terrae: keeper of the land

custus or **custum** [cost]: charges; expense (see also, **custa**)

D

damnatus [damned]: declared guilty; condemned; sentenced

damnosa haereditas [a damaging inheritance]: an inheritance that entails loss

damnum (pl. **damna**) [damage]: physical harm; material loss

damnum absque injuria [loss without injury]: loss due to lawful competition

damnum et injuria: loss and injury

damnum et interesse: loss plus interest

damnum fatale [fatal damage]: acts of God (i.e., unavoidable loss)

damnum infectum: threatened loss

damnum sine injuria: damage without injury (i.e., without wrongful act) (cf., **injuria sine damno**)

dare cervices [give the neck]: submit to the executioner

data et accepta [things given and received]: expenditures and receipts

datio [giving]: the right of alienation

datio in solutum: giving in payment (i.e., a transfer of goods in lieu of payment)

datio tutoris: appointment of a guardian

datum (pl. **data**): the thing or information that is given; also, the date of an instrument

datus: the date of giving

de: of; concerning; from

de aetate probanda: for proving age (i.e., a writ to determine the rightful age of an heir)

de alto et basso [of high and low]: the absolute submission of all differences to arbitration

de ambitu [of going around]: of devious methods to secure a position or some favor (e.g., bribery)

de audiendo et terminando: to hear and determine

de auditu: by or from hearsay

de banco: of the bench

de bene esse [of well being]: provisionally; as conditionally allowed (i.e., for the time being)

de bonis asportatis: of goods carried away (e.g., trespassing in the process of theft)
de bonis non administratis (or simply, **de bonis non**): of the goods not yet administered
de bonis non amovendis: a writ for not removing goods
de bonis propriis [out of one's own goods]: out of one's own pocket
de bono et malo [for good and bad]: for better or for worse
de bono gestu: for good behavior
de causa in causam: from one cause to another
de claro die: by the light of day
de consilio: of counsel
de corpore: of the body
de cursu: of course (see also, **brevia de cursu**)
de die: while still day
de die claro [by clear day]: by daylight
de die in diem (de d. in d.): from day to day; also, continuously
de dolo malo: concerning fraud
de domo reparanda: to repair a house (i.e., a suit brought against a neighbor asking that neighbor to repair his or her house before it falls and damages one's house or property) (also, **domo reparanda**)
de facto: in fact; in deed; in reality or actuality (as opposed to **de jure**)
de fideli administratione: of faithful administration
de finibus levatis: of or concerning fines levied
de futuro [regarding the future]: at a future time
de gestu et fama: of behavior and reputation
de gratia [of grace]: by favor
de homine replegiando: a writ to bail a person out of prison
de incremento: of increase; in addition
de industria: intentionally; purposely
de ingressu: of entry
de injuria: of wrong
de integro: anew; a second time
de jactura evitanda: for avoiding a loss

de jure [by right]: rightful or rightfully; according to law (as opposed **de facto**)

de jure communi: at or by common law

de latere: from the side; collaterally

de lege ferenda [from law to be passed]: what the law ought to be (as opposed to **de lege lata**)

de lege lata [from law passed]: what the law actually is (as opposed to **de lege ferenda**)

de lege naturae: by the laws of nature

de lucro captando: for obtaining an advantage or material gain

de lunatico inquirendo: a writ to inquire into the sanity of a person

de malo lecti: of illness in bed (i.e., an excuse for not appearing in court)

de manucaptiare or **de manucaptione** [of mainprise]: bail or surety

de manutenendo: of maintenance

de materia in exitu: of the matter in or at issue

de medietatis linguae [of half-tongue]: a reference to a jury comprised of non-English-speaking persons (perhaps including non-native speakers) (see also, **medietatis linguae**)

de melioribus damnis [of the better damages]: in reference to a plaintiff's freedom to elect which award to receive when successfully suing several defendants

de mercatoribus: of merchants

de minimis [of the least]: minimal; trifling

de momenta in momentum: from moment to moment

de more: habitually

de nocte: while still night

de novo: anew; afresh; a second time

de novodamus: we give anew

de odio et atia: of hatred and ill will

de pace infracta: of breach of the peace

de placito debit: of a plea of debt

de plano [from ground level]: (fig.) in a summary manner

de praesenti or **de presenti** [regarding the present]: at present; at the present time

de praxi: according to practice
de quodam ignoto: from a certain person unknown
de recenti: of recent; recently
de tabulis exhibendis: of exhibiting the written documents (e.g., a will)
de tenero ungui: from childhood
de una parte: of one part (as opposed to **inter partes**)
de vasto: of waste
de ventre inspiciendo or **ventre inspiciendo:** examining the womb (historically, a writ commanding a sheriff to examine a woman, in the presence of 12 male jurors and 12 women, to determine if she truly is with child and, if so, when the child is likely to be born) (see also, **ad ventrem inspiciendum**)
de verbo in verbum or **de verbo:** word for word; literally
de vicineto [of a vicinage]: from a neighborhood (i.e., in reference to filling a jury pool)
debet: he or she owes
debet et detinet: he owes and detains (i.e., an action of the creditor against the debtor)
debilitas: weakness
debita fundi: debts attached to the soil or secured on land
debito tempore: in due time
debitor: debtor
debitum (pl. **debita**): a debt
debitum recuperatum: a debt recovered
debitum subesse: that the debt is due
decem tales [ten of such]: a summons to fill vacancies on a jury
decessit sine prole (d.s.p.s.): died without issue
decessit sine prole supersite (d.s.p.s.): died without surviving issue
decimus: the tenth
decollatio: beheading
decollatus: beheaded
decrementum maris: the receding of the sea from the land
decretum (d.): a decree; an ordinance
dedi: I have given

dedi et concessi: I have given and granted
dedimus potestatem or **dedimus** [we have given power]: a commission to take depositions
dediticii or **dedititii** [those who have surrendered]: in Roman law, low-born or foreign criminals who were marked permanently on the face or body with fire or a firebrand
deductis debitis: the debts being deducted
defalcatio: deduction; abatement; also, a non-fraudulent default
defalta: default; failure to appear
defectus: weakness; defect
defectus discretionis judicii: lack of judicial discretion
defectus sanguinis: failure of issue
deformis: deformed
deformitas: deformity
defunctus: dead; the deceased
defunctus sine prole: dead without issue
Dei judicium [judgment of God]: trial by ordeal
delatio: denunciation; informing against; a charge or accusation of crime
delator: an informer; a spy
delectamentum: amusement
delectus: choosing; choice
delegatio: assignment of a debt
delenda: things to be deleted
deliberabundus: deliberating; carefully considering
deliberatio: deliberation; consideration
delictum (pl. **delicta**) [a fault or crime]: an offense or misdemeanor; a tort
delineavit (**del.**): he or she drew it
delirium tremens (**D.T.**) [trembling delirium]: mental delusions caused by alcohol poisoning
demens [out of one's mind]: insane (i.e., one who has lost his or her mind through illness or some other cause)
dementia: insanity
dementia praecox: a form of early insanity
deminutio or **diminutio:** reduction; deprivation; loss

deminutio capitis: a change in or reduction of legal status; the loss of civil rights (see also, **capitis deminutio**)

demortuus: the late (i.e., deceased)

demum: at length

denique: at last; finally

denuntiatio: a public notice or summons

derisus: mockery

desperandum: to be hopeless

despitus: a despicable person

desunt cetera or **desunt caetera** (**d.c.** or **d. cet.**): the rest is wanting (e.g., the missing part of a quotation)

devastavit [he has wasted]: mismanagement by the executor of an estate

dexter (**dext.**): right

dextra or **dextera:** the right hand

dextras dare [to give right hands]: to shake hands as a pledge of good faith

diarium: daily food

dicis causa: for the sake of form

dicitur [it is said]: they say

dictores: arbitrators

dictum (pl. **dicta**) [it is said]: a word or speech; a truism; a witty saying; also, a command or award

dictum de dicto [report on hearsay]: a secondhand story

dictum factum: said and done

diebus alternis (**dieb. alt.**): every other day

diem ex die (**d. ex d.**): from day to day

dies: day; daytime

dies a quo: the day from which

dies ad quem: the day to which; the last day (i.e., an expiration date)

dies communes in banco: regular days for appearance in court

dies datus [a day given]: a day appointed for hearing a lawsuit

dies datus partibus [a day given to the parties]: a continuance; an adjournment

dies Dominicus [the Lord's day]: Sunday

dies fasti (sing. **dies fastus**) [permitted days]: days on which business could be transacted or on which justice could be administered (as opposed to **dies nefasti**)

dies festus: a festival or holiday

dies gratiae: a day of grace

dies nefasti (sing. **dies nefastus**) [forbidden days]: days on which no business could be transacted or on which no justice could be administered (as opposed to **dies fasti**)

dies juridicus: a day on which the court sits

dies natalis: birthday

dies non juridicus or **dies non:** a day on which the court does not sit

dies utiles: days available

dieta: a day's journey; a day's work; a day's expenses

dijudicatio: a decision or judgment between two parties

dilatio: delaying; a postponement or delay

dilecto et fideli (di. et fi.): to his or her beloved and faithful

diligiatus [not under legal protection]: an outlaw

diluculum (diluc.): the break of day; in the morning

diminutio or **deminutio:** reduction; deprivation; loss

dioicus: unisexual

disjecta membra: scattered parts or remains (i.e., fragments)

disjuncta: things disjoined or separated (as opposed to **conjuncta**)

disputatio fori: argument in court

diu: for a long time

diurnus: lasting for a day; daylong

diutius: longer

diverso intuitu: from a different point of view; with a different purpose; by a different course

dives (favored by the gods): rich; a rich person

dividatur (div.): let it be divided

divide (div.): divide

dividenda [to be divided]: an indenture; one part of an indenture

divinatio: divination (i.e., an ancient Roman process for selecting a prosecutor in a case)

divulgatio legis: publication of a law

dixi: I have spoken

do ut des: I give that you may give

do ut facias: I give that you may do

dodrans: three-quarters; three-fourths

doli capex [capable of deceit]: capable of distinguishing right from wrong

doli incapex [incapable of deceit]: incapable of distinguishing right from wrong

dolores corporis: bodily ills

dolosus: deceitful; cunning

dolus: fraud; deceit

dolus bonus: permissible deceit

dolus malus: unlawful deceit (i.e., fraud)

domesticus: domestic

domi [in the house]: at home

domicilium: home; domicile; dwelling place

domicilium citandi et executandi [home for summoning and executing]: an address for receiving legal summons and notices

dominium: control of property (i.e., ownership)

dominium directum: ownership as distinguished from enjoyment

dominium directum et utile: ownership and enjoyment of a property

dominium utile: a beneficial ownership (i.e., use or enjoyment of one's property)

dominus [lord]: owner; proprietor

domo carens: homeless

domo profugus: (fig.) a refugee

domo reparanda: to repair a house (i.e., a suit brought against a neighbor asking that neighbor to repair his or her house before it falls and damages one's house or property) (also, **de domo reparanda**)

domus: house

donatio: a gift; donation (see also, **donum**)

Latin Legal Words and Phrases 51

donatio causa mortis: a gift by one who is dying (i.e., an inheritance)

donatio inter vivos: a gift between living persons

donec (don.): until

donec aliter provideatur: until something else is provided

dono dedit (d.d.): given as a gift

donum: a gift (see also, **donatio**)

dormitorius: a place for sleeping

dos: a dower or dowry

dubii juris [of doubtful law or right]: an unsettled legal point (see also, **juris dubii**)

dubitante: doubting (i.e., having doubts about a legal issue though not willing officially to disagree)

dubitatur (dub.): it is doubted

dubitavit (dub.): it has been doubted

dubius: doubtful

duces tecum [bring with you]: a subpoena to appear in court with the specified records or documents (see also, **subpoena duces tecum**)

duellum [a duel]: trial by combat; also, a judicial contest

dum: while; on the condition that

dum bene se gesserit: while he shall conduct himself; during good behavior

dum casta (or **castus**) **vixerit:** for as long as she (or he) lives chaste (i.e., until the surviving spouse remarries)

dum recens fuit maleficium: while the misdeed (or offense) was recent

dum sola: while alone (i.e., single or unmarried)

dum sola fuerit: while she remains alone (i.e., single or unmarried)

duodecemvirale judicium: trial by a jury of twelve persons

duodecima manus (twelve hands): a jury

duodena [the twelve]: a dozen; a jury of twelve members

duodena manu [twelve hands]: twelve witnesses to purge a criminal of an offense

duplex: double; twofold

duplicatio: the defendant's second answer to the plaintiff
duplicatum jus: a double right (i.e., a *droit droit*)
duplum (dup.): twice as much; double the price (see also, **simplum**)
durante: during; continuing
durante absentia: during absence
durante bene placito [during (our) good pleasure]: appointments made and unmade at the pleasure of the king or a royal magistrate
durante furore: during madness or insanity (i.e., while the madness endures)
durante itinere: during a journey; during travel
durante minore absentia: during the absence of the minor
durante minore aetate: during minority
durante viduitate: during widowhood
durante virginitate: during virginity
durante vita: during life
duritia: duress

E

e or **ex:** from; out of
e contra: on the contrary
e converso: conversely; on the contrary; on the other hand
e re nata: under the present circumstance(s); as the matter stands (see also, **pro re nata**)
e republica or **e re publica:** in the public interest; for the benefit of the state
e verbo [in word]: literally
eadem (ead.): the same
eat inde sine die [that he may go thence without a day]: a full acquittal
ebriolus: mildly intoxicated
ebrius: drunk; intoxicated
ecce homo: behold the man
ecce signum [behold the sign]: here is the proof

Latin Legal Words and Phrases 53

edictum (pl. **edicta**): an edict; a decree; a mandate or demand
editicius: proposed; set forth; announced
editicius judices: proposed judges (i.e., judges chosen by a plaintiff; but in some contexts, the meaning is of jurors chosen by the plaintiff but subject to challenge by the defendant)
editio tribuum: a proposal by a plaintiff for the choice of a jury
editus: issued
efficaciter: effectively
efficiens: being efficient; effective
efforcialiter: forcibly
effractor: one who commits burglary
ego: I
ego ipse: I myself
einetia: the share of the eldest-born son
einetius: the firstborn son
ejectum: that which is thrown up by the sea
ejus generis: of the same kind; of the same nature
ejus modi [of this kind]: in that manner
ejusdem (**ejusd.**): the like; of the same
ejusdem generis: of the same kind or class
ejusdem negotii: part of the same transaction
elapsus: elapsed
electio est creditoris: the creditor has the choice
electio est debtoris: the debtor has the choice
electus: elected; chosen
elegit: he or she has chosen
elongata: carried away to a distance (i.e., not to be found here)
elongatus: having been conveyed to another jurisdiction
elogium: an epitaph on a tombstone; a codicil to a will
emenda: amends (i.e., a reparation for loss or trespass)
emendatio: improvement; amendment
emeritus (f. **emerita**) [veteran]: a title of honor denoting long and distinguished service
emporium: a place of wholesale trade; a market
emptio (pl. **emptiones**) [purchase]: the act of buying
emptio bonorum: the purchase of goods

emptio et venditio: buying and selling
emptor (pl. **emptores**): a buyer
emunctae naris [of wiped nose]: a shrewd or discerning person; a young person of mature judgment
ens: being; existence
ens legis: a being created by law
eo animo: with that intention
eo instante: at that moment
eo ipso [by that itself]: by that fact
eo loci: at that very place
eo nomine [by that name]: under that name (in an account)
epigramma: an inscription
epistola or **epistula:** a letter; written communication
epistola excusatoria or **epistula excusatoria:** a letter of excuse
epistolium or **epistulium:** a brief letter; a note
erectus: upright
ergo: therefore
erratum (pl. **errata**): an error; a mistake
errore lapsus: a lapse or mistake through error
esse in possessione: to be in possession
essentia: essence
et: and
et adjournatur: and it is adjourned
et alia (et al.): and other things
et alia enormia: and other enormities; and other serious wrongs (see also, **alia enormia**)
et aliae or **et alii (et al.):** and others
et alibi (et al.): and elsewhere
et alii or **et aliae (et al.):** and others
et cetera (etc.): and the rest; and so on; and so forth
et conjunx (et conj.): and spouse (either husband or wife)
et habuit: and he or she had it
et hoc paratus est verificare: and this one is prepared to verify
et non: and not
et non allocatur: and it is not allocated
et sequens (et seq.): and the following

et sequente (et seq.): and in what follows
et sequentes (et seq. or **et seqq.):** and what follows
et sequentes paginae (et seq. pag.): and the following pages
et sequentia (et seqq.): and what follows
et sequitur (et seq.): and the one following
et sic: and thus; and so
et sic fecit: and he or she did so
et sic pendet: and thus it hangs (i.e., the point or matter is left undetermined)
et sic ulterius: and so on; and so forth
et similia: and the like
et uxor (et ux.): and wife
et vir: and husband
etiam causa non cognita: even where the cause is not known (i.e., without investigation)
etiam in articulo mortis: even at the point of death
eundo, morando, et redeundo [going, remaining, and returning]: a protection from arrest while attending to official business
eundo et redeundo: going and returning
evanidus: vanishing; passing away
evasio: an escape from prison or custody
eventum or **eventus:** event; issue; consequence
eversio: ruin
evestigatus [traced out]: tracked down; discovered
evidens: clear; evident
ex or **e:** out of; from
ex abrupto [abruptly]: without preparation
ex abundanti: more than sufficient; superfluous
ex abundanti cautela or **ex abundante cautem:** out of abundant caution
ex adverso [from the opposite side]: in opposition
ex aequitate: out of or according to equity
ex aequo: equally; with equal merit
ex aequo et bono: according to what is equitable and good (i.e., justly and equitably)

ex altera parte: of the other part
ex animo [from the heart]: sincerely
ex ante: from before
ex arbitrio judicis: at or upon the discretion of the judge
ex assensu curiae: with the consent of the court
ex assensu patris: with the father's consent
ex auditu: from or by hearsay
ex bona fide [in good faith]: on one's honor; sincerely
ex capite: on the ground of; by reason of
ex capite doli: on the ground of deceit; by reason of deceit
ex capite fraudis: on the ground of fraud; by reason of fraud
ex capite metus: on the ground of fear; by reason of fear
ex cathedra [from the chair]: with authority (e.g., a papal pronouncement)
ex certa scientia: for certain knowledge
ex colore: under color of (i.e., by pretense); under protection of
ex comitate: out of comity or courtesy
ex commodato: from a loan
ex comparatione scriptorum [by comparison of writings]: by comparing handwritings
ex concessione: by grant
ex concessis: from the premises granted
ex concesso [out of concession]: from what has been granted
ex consuetudine mea: according to my custom
ex consulto or **ex consultu:** from consultation or deliberation
ex continenti: immediately (i.e., without an interval of time)
ex contractu: from a contract
ex contrario: on the contrary; on the other side
ex culpa levissima: from the slightest fault
ex curia: out of court
ex debito justitiae: as a matter of legal right
ex delicto: from offense (i.e., by reason of an actionable wrong or a criminal deed)
ex demissione (ex dem.): on the demise
ex dicto majoris partis: by the voice of the majority
ex directo: directly

ex diverso: conversely; on the other hand
ex dolo malo [from evil intent]: out of fraud or deceit
ex dono: as a gift (i.e., a donation)
ex eadem causa: from the same cause
ex empto: from purchase
ex equitate: equitably
ex errore (**ex err.**): in error
ex eventu: after the event
ex facie [on the face]: apparently; evidently
ex facili: easily
ex facto: according to fact (i.e., in consequence of an act or a thing done)
ex fictione juris: by fiction of law
ex figura verborum: by the form of the words used
ex gratia [out of grace]: by grace; as a matter of favor (i.e., in absence of a legal right)
ex hypothesi: by hypothesis
ex incommodo: on account of inconvenience
ex incontinenti: without delay; summarily
ex industria: with a deliberate design or purpose
ex instituto: according to traditional usage
ex integro [from the whole]: anew; afresh
ex jure naturae: according to the law of nature (viz., legal and moral principles derived from universal concepts of human nature and divine justice) (see also, **jure naturae**)
ex justa causa: from a just or lawful cause
ex justitia: according to justice; justly
ex latere: from the side; collaterally
ex lege [arising from the law]: as a matter of law; by virtue of law
ex legibus: according to the laws
ex libris: from the library of (i.e., a bookplate or inscription denoting a book's owner)
ex longinquo: from a distance
ex longo: for long; for a long time
ex maleficio: from malfeasance; from misconduct

ex mandato: according to the mandate
ex memoria [from memory]: by heart
ex mero motu [of a mere impulse]: of one's own accord
ex mora [from delay]: in consequence of delay
ex mora debitoris: on account of the delay of the debtor
ex more [according to custom]: by custom; habitually
ex natura: according to nature
ex natura rei: according to the nature of the thing
ex naturali jure: according to natural law
ex necessitate: of necessity
ex necessitate legis: from the necessity of law
ex necessitate rei: from the necessity of the thing
ex officio (e.o.): by virtue of one's office
ex pari: in the same manner
ex parte [from one party]: in part; in the interests of one side only
ex parte materna: on the mother's side
ex parte paterna: on the father's side
ex paucis: from a few words; from a few things
ex pietate: from natural affection and duty
ex post facto: after the fact (i.e., after the deed is done) (see also, **post facto**)
ex praecogitata malicia: with malice aforethought
ex professo: by profession (i.e., expressly); also, as an expert
ex propriis: from one's own resources
ex proprio motu: of its own motion; of its own accord
ex proprio vigore: by its own force
ex pueris: from childhood
ex quasi contractu: as if from a contract (i.e., as though it were from a contract)
ex quo [from which time]: since
ex quo tempore: since that time
ex quocunque capite: for whatever reason
ex re et ex tempore: according to time and circumstance
ex relatione (ex rel.): from relation; by information
ex statuto: by statute

Latin Legal Words and Phrases 59

ex stricto jure: according to strict law
ex summa necessitate: from the greatest necessity
ex tacito: tacitly
ex tempore: on or at the moment; temporarily; on the spur of the moment; without premeditation
ex testamento [from a testament]: under a will
ex tota materia: from the whole matter
ex toto: on the whole
ex usu [of use]: useful; advantageous; expedient
ex utraque parte: on either side
ex vi aut metu: on account of force or fear
ex vi termini: by force of the term, limit, or restriction
ex visceribus: from the vital part (i.e., the very essence of a thing)
ex visceribus verborum: from the essence of the words (i.e., nothing beyond the words themselves)
ex visu scriptionis: from having seen the writing (i.e., eyewitness to a written document)
ex voto: according to one's vow
excambium: an exchange (see also, **cambium**)
exceptio: an exception; an objection
exceptio doli: an exception for or plea of fraud
exceptio rei judicatae: an exception or objection to a matter already adjudged
exceptis excipiendis: with due or necessary exceptions or objections being made
excerpta: excerpts; extracts
excudit (exc.) [he fashioned it]: he or she printed or engraved it
excursus: a digression
excusatio: an excuse
excusatus: excused
exeat: permission to leave or to go out
executor (f. **executrix**): an executor
exempli causa: for instance
exempli gratia (e.g.) [for the sake of example]: for example
exemplum (pl. **exempla**): an example; a sample or copy

exequatur: permission granted to a foreign consul to enter into office

exercitor maris: owner of a sea vessel

exercitor navis: a person who charters or temporarily owns a ship

exlegalitas: an outlaw (as a class); also, those outside the protection of the law

exlegatus: an outlaw (see also, **exlex**)

exitus: issue (i.e., a child or children)

exodium: the introductory section of a speech or written document (e.g., the introductory part of a will)

exoneretur: let him or her be discharged or relieved (i.e., the discharge of bail or a surety when the conditions of the bond have been fulfilled)

exhaeres or **exheres:** disinherited

exhibeatur (exhib.): let it be exhibited or given

exilium or **exsilium:** exile; banishment

exitus [offspring]: an export duty; rents or profits from landholdings

exlex: outside the law; an outlaw (see also, **exlegatus**)

exoticus: foreign; exotic

expedit mihi: it is in my interest or to my advantage

expeditio: dispatch

expeditio brevis: the service of a writ

expensae litis: the costs of litigation

expers: free from; exempted; also, deprived

experto credite: believe the one with experience (i.e., trust the expert)

expertus: an experienced person; an expert

expressio falsi: a false statement

expressis verbis: in express terms; explicitly

extendi facias: that you cause to be extended or appraised (at its value)

externus: external

extra: out of; outside; beside; beyond

extra consuetudinem: beyond or beside the usual custom

extra curtem domini: beyond the jurisdiction of one's superior

extra familiam: outside the family
extra foedum: out of the fee
extra judicium: out of court
extra jus: beyond the law
extra legem: beyond the protection of the law
extra muros: beyond the walls; outside the corporate limits
extra ordinem: out of the ordinary manner (i.e., a judgment pronounced at the discretion of the judge)
extra praesentiam mariti: out of her husband's presence
extra quatuor maria: beyond the seas
extra regnum: outside the kingdom
extra territorium judicis: beyond the jurisdiction of the judge (i.e., exercising judgment beyond one's jurisdiction)
extra viam: off the path or the roadway (i.e., trespassing); also, out of the usual way
extra vires: beyond the powers of (see also, **ultra vires**)

F

fac simile or **facsimile** [make it like]: an exact copy
facere sacramentum: to swear an oath
facias: that you may do; that you may cause
facile: easily
facilis: easy
facit: he or she does
factio testamenti: the making of a will
factitius: artificial; manufactured
factotum [a 'do everything']: a jack-of-all-trades
factum: fact; an act or a deed
factum est: it is done
factum probantia: a fact given in evidence to prove other facts at issue
factum probatum: a fact to be proved or proven
facultas: ability; opportunity; also possession (i.e., mental capacity)
faex populi: the dregs of society

fallax: deceptive; fallacious

falsi crimen: the crime of falsification (e.g., perjury and forgery) (see also, **crimen falsi**)

falsonarius: a forger

fama [fame]: character; reputation; also, rumor

famulatus: slavery; servitude; service

famulus: a slave or attendant

fas: divine law

fas est [it is allowed]: it is lawful; it is permitted

fatum: fate

fatuum judicium: a foolish judgment or verdict

fauces terrae: ocean headlands or promontories

favor legitimationis: in favor of legitimacy (i.e., an assumption of a child's biological legitimacy at birth)

favor matrimonii: in favor of [the validity of] marriage (i.e., certain judgments or incentives protective of or favorable to marriage)

favor negotii: in favor of business (i.e., the non-interference in the affairs of business by a court without a compelling reason to do so)

favor testamenti: in the favor of the testament (i.e., a will is assumed to be legally valid)

favorem vitae: favor of life

fecerunt (ff.) [they made it]: appended to the artists' names on a painting

fecit (fec.) [he or she made it]: appended to an artist's name on a painting

felix: happy

felo-de-se (pl. **felones-de-se**): suicide; also, an illegal act that results in the death of the felon

felonia: felony

femina (f. or **fem.):** female; a woman

femininum (f. or **fem.):** feminine

fenestra [a window]: a loophole

ferae bestiae: wild beasts

ferae naturae [of a wild nature]: untamed; undomesticated

ferea via [iron road]: a railroad

feria: weekday; holiday

feriae: public and religious holidays (i.e., those days on which judicial business was suspended)

fertilis: fertile; fruitful

fertilitas: fertility

ferus [a wild animal]: wild; uncivilized

fervente die: in the heat of the day

fessa aetas: old age

fessi rerum: distress; misery; misfortune; also, weary of matters; tired of life (see also, **res fessae**)

festinum remedium: a speedy remedy

fetus or **foetus:** offspring

feudum antiquum: land acquired through succession (as opposed to **feudum novum**)

feudum novum: land acquired through conquest (as opposed to **feudum antiquum**)

fiat (f. or **ft.):** let it be so; let it be done; also, a decree

fiat ut petitur: let it be done as asked

ficta confessio [fictitious confession]: the admission of guilt by non-denial (i.e., not to refute is to confess)

ficta traditio [fictitious delivery]: a pretend delivery (i.e., because the buyer is already in possession of that which was purchased, the seller thus deems it to have been delivered)

fide mea: on my word of honor

fides: faith; trust

fides publica: a promise of protection or of safe-conduct

fiducia: trust; assurance; property held by another in trust (to be restored at a later date)

fieri facias (fi. fa.) [cause it to be done]: a writ commanding the sheriff to execute a judgment)

fieri feci (fi. fe.) [I have caused it to be done]: the sheriff's official reply to a writ of *fieri facias*)

filia: daughter

filia mulieratus: a legitimate daughter

filius: son

filius familias or **filiusfamilias:** a son still under the power of his father

filius mulieratus: a legitimate son; also, the first legitimate son born to a woman who has had a child by her husband before their marriage

filius nullius [a son of nobody]**:** an illegitimate son

filius populi [a son of the people]**:** a bastard

filum [a thread]**:** a boundary

filum aquae [a thread of water]**:** the middle of a river or thread of a stream

filum forestae: the border of the forest

filum viae: the middle line of the way or road

finalis concordia: a decisive or final argument

finem facere: to impose a fine; to pay a fine

finis (fin.): the end

finium regundorum actio: an action for regulating boundaries

fixus: fixed

flagrans: burning; raging

flagrans bellum: a raging war

flagrans crimen: a fresh or recent crime

flagrante crimine: in the act or immediately after the act of committing the crime

flagrante delicto: in the very act of the crime

floruit (fl. or flor.): flourished

flotsam: cargo or other floating wreckage from a vessel usually lost at sea, sometimes later to wash up on shore (see also, **jetsam** and **ligan**)

foedata: polluted; violated

foedus: league; treaty; compact

foenus nauticum: marine interest (i.e., interest gained through a shipping venture)

folia (ff.): pages

folium (f. or fol.): a leaf of a book or a manuscript page

forinsecus [on the outside]**:** outward; external; also, foreign or a foreignor

foris: outdoors; abroad

forisbanitus or **forbannitus:** banished

forisfactum: forfeited

forisfactura plena: the complete forfeiture of a person's property

forisfactus: a criminal (i.e., a person who has forfeited his or her life through commission of a capital offense)

forisjudicatio: a judgment resulting in the forfeiture of property

forisjudicatus: deprived of property by judgment of the court

forisjurare: to forswear; to abandon

forma: form; shape

forma verborum: the form of the words

formalis: formal; having a set form

formaliter: formally

formatus: formed

fornix: a brothel

fors: chance; luck

fortior: stronger

fortis: strong; brave

forum [an open place]: a court of justice

forum actus: the place where the act was done

forum competens: a competent court

forum conscientiae [court of conscience]: a tribunal or court of equity

forum contentiosum [forum of contention]: a court of justice where litigation takes place

forum contractus: a court in the place where the contract is made

forum conveniens: a convenient court (i.e., the most suitable or appropriate court for the case)

forum domesticum: a domestic court

forum domicilii: the court of a person's domicile, usually of the defendant

forum ecclesiasticum: an ecclesiastical court

forum non competens: an inappropriate court (i.e., one lacking jurisdiction)

forum non conveniens or **forum inconveniens** [an inconvenient court]: an inconvenient location for judicial proceedings (i.e., the right to have a case tried in a more convenient court)

forum originis: the court in or the jurisdiction of the place of a person's birth or citizenship

forum regium: a royal court; the king's court

forum rei gestae: the court where an act or transaction took place

forum rei sitae: a court in the place where the thing or matter is situated

forum seculare: a secular court

fossa: ditch (i.e., a ditch full of water wherein women felons were executed by drowning)

fractus: broken

fragilis: fragile; brittle

frater (pl. **fratres**): a brother

frater consanguineus: a brother born of the same father, though the mother may differ (i.e., a half-brother)

frater nutricius: a bastard brother

frater uterinus: a brother born from the same mother, but not the same father (i.e., a half-brother)

fratres: brothers and sisters

fratres conjurati: brothers (or companions) sworn to the same purpose

fraus: fraud

frequenter (freq.): frequently

frontis: front

fructus: fruit; increase

fructus civiles: all profit or increase regarded as taxable (e.g., rent and interest)

fructus industriales: profit or increase gained through cultivation, such as crops

fructus legis: fruits of the law (i.e., court proceeds gained through judgments and executions)

fructus naturales: the fruit or products of nature produced by the power of nature alone

fructus pendentes: hanging fruit not yet gathered

fruges: crops or edible produce
frustrum terra: a piece, tract, or fragment of land
fugam fecit: he or she fled
fulmen brutum [a harmless thunderbolt]: an empty threat
fulmine ictus: struck by lightning
fumus: smoke
fumus boni juris [smoke of a good right]: to have sufficient basis to bring legal action
functus officio [having performed the office]: no longer useful; no longer functioning in its previous capacity
fundo annexa: things annexed or attached to the soil
fundus: land or ground
fungibiles res or **res fungibiles:** fungible things (i.e., commercially interchangeable)
fur: thief
fur manifestus: manifest thief (i.e., a thief caught in the act of stealing)
furca [pitchfork]: a gallows
furca et flagellum [gallows and whip]: service for life or limb
furca et fossa [gallows and pit]: legal authority to punish felons, the men by hanging and the women by drowning
furcifer [yoke bearer]: a villain; scoundrel; rogue; (fig.) a jailbird
furiosus: a lunatic
furor: madness
furor brevis: a brief madness (i.e., in the heat of passion)
furtim: by stealth
furtum: robbery; theft
furtum grave: aggravated theft
furtum manifestum [open theft]: caught in the act of stealing
furtum rei [theft of a thing]: ordinary theft

G

gardia: custody; guardianship
gardianus: guardian; protector; also, a warden
geminus (pl. **gemini**): a twin; a double

gemmarius: a jeweler
gener: a son-in-law
genus or **generis:** genus; kind; manner
genus humanum or **humanum genus:** humankind
georgicus: agricultural
gerere pro patrono: to act on behalf of the master (i.e., to represent one's master or patron in legal matters)
geraticus: old age
germanitas: brotherhood; sisterhood
germanus: of the same parents
gestio: behavior; conduct; also, management of a thing (i.e., a transaction)
gestu et fama: conduct and reputation
gestum (pl. **gesta**): deed; act; also, business
gestus: posture; carriage (of the body)
gilda: a guild
glossa: a gloss (i.e., an explanation or interpretation)
glossae marginales: explanatory marginal notes
gradatim (grad.) [step by step]: gradually or by degrees
gradus: a step; degree
gradus parentelae: a genealogy; a pedigree; a family tree
graffarius: notary
graffium or **grafium:** a ledger book; register; registry of deeds
gratis: free of cost; a favor; also, without reward
gratis dictum: a mere assertion; a voluntary statement
gratuitus: gratuitous; voluntary; without force
gratus (grat.): grateful; thankful; agreeable
gravis: grave; serious; weighty (i.e., a matter of importance)
gravitas: seriousness; weightiness; also, severity
gregarius: of the flock or herd; sociable
grege facto: in close order
grex: flock; herd; a band of people
gubernator (f. **gubernatrix**): a governor; the pilot of a ship
gustus: taste

H

habeas corpus (hab. corp.) [that you have the body] or properly, **habeas corpus ad subjiciendum** [that you have the body to submit to]: a writ requiring that officials bring a detained individual before a court to decide the legality of that individual's detention or imprisonment

habeas corpus ad prosequendum: a writ of *habeas corpus* to move a prisoner to the proper jurisdiction

habeas corpus ad respondendum: a writ of *habeas corpus* to remove a person from the custody of one court to that of another

habeas corpus ad satisfaciendum: a writ of *habeas corpus* to remove a prisoner to be charged in another court

habeas corpus ad testificandum: a writ of *habeas corpus* to bring a witness to court (usually one already in custody at the time)

habeas corpus cum causa: a writ of *habeas corpus* requiring that officials produce the defendant and provide the reason for the arrest or detention

habemus confitentem reum: we have an accused person who pleads guilty

habendum et tenendum (or simply, **habendum**): to have and to hold (i.e., the part of a deed defining ownership)

habentes homines [the men who have]: the rich; the well-heeled

habere facias possessionem [that you cause to have possession]: an action taken to recover property by eviction of a tenant

habere facias seisinam [that you cause to be seized]: an action taken to recover property by evicting a tenant

habere facias visum [that you cause to be viewed]: an action taken to view property occupied by a tenant

habilis: suitable

habitatio: dwelling; habitation

habitus: habit; dress; also, appearance

hac die: on this day

hac lege [with this law]: with this proviso

hac mercede placet: I accept the terms (of the offer)

haec est conventio [this is the custom]**:** this is a term of the agreement

haec est finalis concordia: this is the final agreement

haec verba: these words (see also, **in haec verba**)

haeredes nati et facti or **heredes nati et facti:** heirs born and made

haeredes proximi or **heredes proximi:** the children or direct descendants of a deceased person

haeredes remotiores or **heredes remotiores:** the kinsfolk of a deceased person, other than children or descendants

haereditarius or **hereditarius:** inherited; hereditary

haereditas or **hereditas:** an inheritance (as opposed to **quaestus**)

haereditas jacens or **hereditas jacens:** an estate in abeyance (i.e., the interval between the owner's death and possession of the estate by the heirs)

haeredium or **heredium:** patrimony

haeres or **heres** (**haer.** or **her.**; pl. **haeredes** or **heredes**): an heir

haeres ex asse or **heres ex asse:** a sole heir

haeres ex besse or **heres ex besse:** heir to two-thirds of the property

haeres ex dodrante or **heres ex dodrante:** heir to three-quarters of the estate

haeres factus or **heres factus:** an heir appointed by the will of the decedent

haeres natus or **heres natus:** an heir by descent

haeres rectus: or **heres rectus:** a right heir

hebdomada (**hebdom.**)**:** a week; any seven-day period

heri: yesterday

hesternus: of yesterday

hibernus [of winter]**:** for the winter

hic, haec or **hoc:** this; in this place

hic casus non dignus est quem consideremus: this case is not worth considering

Latin Legal Words and Phrases 71

hic et nunc: here and now
hic finis fandi: here ends the discussion
hic iacet (H.I.) or **hic jacet:** here lies
hic iacet sepultus (H.I.S.): here lies buried
hic sepultus (H.S.): here [lies] buried
hic sepultus est (H.S.E.): here lies buried
hinc atque illinc: on this side and on that
hippodromos: a horse track
his testibus or **hiis testibus:** these being witnesses
hoc anno (h.a.): in this year
hoc indictum volo [I wish this unsaid]: I withdraw the statement
hoc loco (h.l.): in this place
hoc mense (h.m.): in this month
hoc nomine (h.n.): in this name
hoc ordine (h.o.): in this order
hoc quaere (h.q.): look for this
hoc sensu (h.s.): in this sense
hoc tempore (h.t.): at this time
hoc titulo (h.t.): under this title
hoc voce (h.v.): under this word or phrase
hodie: today
homicidium [homicide]: murder; manslaughter
homicidium in rixa: homicide committed during a quarrel
hominis iussu or **hominis jussu:** with the sanction of a person
homo (pl. **homines**): human being; man
homo exercitalis: a soldier
homo feodalis: a vassal or tenant
homo forensis: an advocate
homo francus: a free person
homo ingenuus: a free and lawful person; a yeoman
homo liber: a free person
homo ligius: a subject or vassal
homo maleficus: an evildoer (see also, **maleficus**)
homo regius: a king's vassal
homo reus: an accused or guilty person

homo sapiens [wise man]: the human species of the genus Homo

homo trium literarum [a man of three letters]: a thief (i.e., **fur**, a thief)

honeste vivere: to live respectably

honorarium: an honorary gift or gratuity (i.e., monetary compensation received by a person for additional services or outside employment)

honoris causa [for the sake of honor]: as a mark of honor (e.g., an honorary degree)

honoris gratia: honorary

hora (H. or **hor.):** hour

horae judiciae: the hours in which a court sits to decide judicial matters

hortatus: advised

hospes or **hospita** [stranger]: guest; host

hospitator communis: an innkeeper

hostelagium or **hostalagium:** the ancient right of lords to receive lodging and entertainment in the homes of their tenants

hostes humani generis [enemies of the human race]: pirates

hostia: a victim

hostis (pl. **hostes**): an enemy

hujusmodi: of this kind

humanum genus or **genus humanum:** humankind

humanus: human; pertaining to human beings

humi: on the ground

hunc in modum: in this way or manner

hybridus or **hibridus:** hybrid

hypomnema: a note or memorandum; also, a public record

I

ibi: there and then; also, in that place; in that matter

ibidem (ib. or **ibid.):** in the same place (e.g., in a book)

id demum: that and that alone

id est (i.e.): that is; that is to say
id ipsum: that very thing
idem (id.): the same; the same as above
idem quod (i.q.): the same as
idem sonans: sounding the same (e.g., a homonym)
identidem: repeatedly
ideo consideratum est: therefore it is considered
idonea cautio: sufficient security
idonea paries: a wall sufficient or able to bear the weight
idoneus: suitable; fitting; appropriate; adequate; sufficient
idoneus homo: a fit and capable person; also, one who is financially responsible or solvent
ignis judicium: trial by fire
ignitegium [cover fire]**:** curfew; the curfew bell (see also, **pyritegium**)
ignoramus [we are ignorant]**:** the reply of a grand jury when it finds the evidence insufficient to try the defendant
ignorantia elenchi [ignorant reasoning]**:** the fallacy of refutation by indirection (i.e., by arguing an irrelevant point)
ignorantia facti: ignorance of fact
ignotus (ign.): unknown
illegibilis (illeg.): illegible
illicite: unlawfully
illicitus or **inlicitus:** illegal; illicit; forbidden
illico (illic.): immediately
illiterati: the unlettered
illustratio: illustration; example
immunis: exempt
imparatus: unprepared
impedimentum: a hindrance
imperium [the right to command]**:** the right to use the force of the state to enforce its laws
imperium in imperio: a government within a government
impermissus: forbidden; unlawful; illicit
imperpetuum: forever
impervius: impassable

impescatus: impeached
impetus: attack; assault; also, impulse
impietas: impiety; disloyalty
impignorata: pledged; mortgaged
implicatus: implicated; entangled; entwined
imprimis: first; first of all; in the first place
improbitas: depravity
improbus: inferior; morally bad; perverse
impromptus: not ready; unprepared
imprudencia temeraria: reckless negligence
impugnatio: an attack
impunitas: impunity (i.e., exemption from punishment)
impurus: impure
in absentia (i.a.): in absence
in acquirenda possessione: in the course of taking possession
in actu: in action; in practice
in adversum: against an unwilling party
in aequali jure: in equal right
in aequali manu [in equal hand]**:** held equally by both parties
in aequo: on equal terms
in alieno solo: in another's land
in alio loco: in another place
in ambiguo: in doubt
in ante: before
in apicibus juris: among the subtleties of the law (i.e., the extremes)
in aqua scribis [you are writing in water]**:** it is without effect
in arbitrio alieno: according to the judgment of another
in arbitrium judicis: at the pleasure of the judge (i.e., at the judge's discretion)
in arcta et salva custodia: in close and safe custody
in armis [in arms]**:** under arms
in articulo: at that moment; immediately
in articulo mortis: at the point or moment of death
in auditu [within the hearing]**:** within earshot
in autea: in the future

in banco: in full court

in banco regis: in the king's bench

in bello: in time of war

in bonis: in or among the goods or property; in actual possession

in bonis defuncti: among the goods of the deceased

in bonis esse: to be among the goods (i.e., to be someone's property)

in camera [in chamber]**:** in or at chambers (i.e., in private, not in open court); also, a meeting that is held in secret

in campo: in the field

in capita [to or by the heads]**:** to take equal shares of an inheritance

in capite [in chief]**:** lands bestowed upon a feudal lord by the Crown

in carcerem: in prison

in cauda venenum [in the tail is poison]**:** beware of danger

in causa: in the cause

in circuitu: in a circuit; in the surrounding

in clientelam recipere: to receive under protection

in colloquio: in a discourse

in commendam: in trust (i.e., as commended)

in communi: in common

in consideratione legis: in consideration of law

in consimili casu: in a like or similar case

in conspectu ejus: in his view

in continenti: immediately; without any interval

in contumaciam: in contempt of; in disobedience to

in corpore: in a body

in crastino: on the morrow

in cujus rei testimonium: in witness or testimony whereof

in curia: in open court

in cursu rebellionis: in the course of rebellion

in custodia legis: in the custody of the law (see also, **custodia legis**)

in custodiam: in custody; in prison

in damno vitando: in attempting to avoid injury or damage

in delicto: in fault (i.e., guilty)
in deposito: on deposit (i.e., as a pledge)
in diem: for a day; for each day (see also, **per diem**)
in diem addictio: assignment for a fixed period or postponement to a date (i.e., a clause in a contract that allows the contract to be terminated if the seller receives a better offer within a given period) (see also, **addictio in diem**)
in dies (in d.) or **indies (ind.):** from day to day; daily
in dorso: on the back
in dorso recordi: on the back of the record
in dubio (pl. **in dubiis**)**:** in doubt; undetermined; in a doubtful case
in dubio mitius: greater leniency in a doubtful case
in duplo: in double
in duriorem sortem: to the harder lot (i.e., to the more burdensome debt)
in eadem causa: in the same state or condition
in emulationem vicini: in hatred or envy of a neighbor
in equilibrio: in equilibrium; in even balance
in esse: in being; in existence (as opposed to **in posse**)
in essentialibus: in the essential parts
in eventu: in the event
in excambio: in exchange
in exilium or **in exsilium:** in exile
in exitu: in issue
in extenso: at full length (i.e., unabridged)
in extremis: in the extreme; at the point of death
in facie curiae: in the presence of or before the court
in faciendo: in doing; for the performance
in facto: in fact
in facto dicit: in fact it says
in favorem libertatis: in favor of liberty
in favorem vitae: in favor of life
in felicitate viri: for the husband's happiness
in feodo: in fee
in fieri [in being made]**:** in course of completion

Latin Legal Words and Phrases 77

in fine: in the end; in conclusion; toward the conclusion
in flagrante delicto [while the crime is blazing]: in the very act of the crime
in forma pauperis [in the manner of a pauper]: not liable to costs (i.e., to be relieved of court costs due to inability to pay)
in forma praedicta: in the form aforesaid
in foro [in a forum]: in court
in foro conscientiae: in the court or tribunal of conscience (viz., moral obligation)
in foro contentioso: in a court of litigation
in foro domestico: in a domestic court (as opposed to a foreign court)
in fraudem creditorum: with intent to defraud creditors
in fraudem legis: in fraud of the law (i.e., with intent to break, evade, or skirt the law)
in fructu: among the fruits
in furto vel latrocinio: in theft or larceny
in futuro: at a future time (as opposed to **in praesenti**)
in genere [in kind]: generally speaking
in gremio legis [in the bosom of the law]: under the protection of the law; also, in abeyance
in hac parte: on this part or side; in or on this behalf
in haec verba: in these words; in the same words (i.e., *verbatim*)
in hoc statu: in this position; in the present state
in horas: hourly
in hunc modum: in this manner; after this manner
in hypothesi: in a supposed or hypothetical case
in iisdem causis: in the same cases
in iisdem terminis: in the same terms
in incertum: for an indefinite period
in infinitum [to infinity]: endless; without limit; forever
in initialibus: in the preliminaries
in initio: in or at the beginning
in initio litis: at the outset of the suit
in integrum: in or to the original condition

in invidiam [in ill will]: to excite prejudice
in invitum [against the unwilling]: compulsory
in ipsis faucibus [in the very throat]: in the entranceway
in ipso termino: at the very end; on the last day
in itinere: on the way; during the journey
in judicio: in a judicial proceeding
in jure [in law]: according to the law; by right
in jure alterius: in another's right; on another's behalf
in jure proprio: in one's own right; on one's own behalf
in jus vocare: to summon to court
in lecto: in bed
in lecto mortali: on the deathbed
in limine (in lim.) [on the threshold]: in or at the beginning; preliminary
in limine judicii: at the beginning or outset of the suit
in limine litis: at the beginning or outset of the legal process (i.e., litigation)
in linea recta: in the direct line (i.e., the line of succession)
in litem: to or for the suit
in loco: in place of; in lieu of; instead
in loco citato (i.l.c. or **in loc. cit.):** in the place cited (see also, **loco citato**)
in loco haeredis: in place of the heir
in loco parentis: in the place of a parent
in majorem cautelam: for greater caution; for greater security
in mala fide: in bad faith
in malam partem: in a bad sense
in maleficio: in wickedness; with malicious intent
in manibus [in the hands]: on hand
in manu [in hand]: in possession
in materia: in the matter; in the cause
in medias res: in or into the midst of things
in medio: in the middle; intermediate
in meditatione fugae: in contemplation of flight
in memoriam [in memory]: in memory of
in mero jure: of mere right

in misericordia: by way of mercy

in mitiori sensu: in a gentler or milder sense (see also, **mitior sensus** or **mitiori sensu**)

in mitius: gentler; in the milder

in modum adminiculi: as corroborating evidence

in modum poene: by way of penalty or fine

in modum probationis: by way of proof

in mora [in delay]: in default

in mortua manu [in a dead hand]: property held by a religious or charitable society

in mundo: in the world; (fig.) in a clean or extended copy

in naturalibus [in a state of nature]: in the nude

in nomine: in the name of

in nomine Dei: in the name of God

in nomine Domini: in the name of the Lord

in nomine solum: in name only

in notis: in the notes

in nubibus [in the clouds]: nebulous; in abeyance; also, protected by the law

in nuce: in a nutshell

in nullius bonis: in the goods of no one

in nullo est erratum [in nothing is there error]: no error has been committed

in obliquo: obliquely; indirectly (as opposed to **in recto**)

in octavis: in eight (days)

in oculis civium [in the eyes of citizens]: in public view

in odium: in hatred or detestation

in odium spoliatoris: in hatred of a despoiler (i.e., one who destroys evidence)

in omnes partes: in all directions; in every respect

in omnibus [in all things]: in all respects; on all points

in ovo [in the egg]: undeveloped

in pari causa: in a like or similar case; in similar conditions (see also, **pari causa**)

in pari delicto [in equal fault]: equally at fault; guilty to the same extent (see also, **pari delicto**)

in pari jure: in equal right

in pari materia [in the same matter]: in an analogous case (i.e., as a matter of legal precedent) (see also, **pari materia**)

in pari passu [at an equal pace]: on equal footing; proportionally; equally; without partiality (see also, **pari passu**)

in pari ratione: for the equal reason; by a like mode of reasoning (see also, **pari ratione**)

in partes: between parts; between parties

in partes aequales: into equal parts (see also, **partes aequales**)

in patiendo: in permitting; in tolerating

in pectore [in the breast]: in secret; in reserve

in pectore judicis: in the heart of the judge

in pejorem partem: in the worst part; on the worst side

in pendente or **in pendenti:** in suspension; in abeyance

in perpetuum: in perpetuity; forever

in perpetuam rei memoriam: for the perpetual memory of the thing

in perpetuum rei testimonium [in perpetual testimony of the matter]: for the purpose of settling the matter forever

in persona: in person

in personam: to or against the person (i.e., a suit against a particular person as distinguished from *in rem*, a particular thing)

in pios usus: for religious purposes

in plena vita: in full life

in pleno: in full; in full court

in pleno comitatu: in full county court

in pleno lumine [in the light of day]: in public; common knowledge

in poenam: as a penalty

in posse [in possibility]: potentially (as opposed to **in esse**)

in posterum [for the next day]: for the future; also, in the hereafter

in potentia: in possibility; potentially

in potestate parentis: in the power of a parent

in praemissis: in the premises

Latin Legal Words and Phrases 81

in praesens: for the present; for the moment
in praesenti: at the present time; immediately effective (as opposed to **in futuro**)
in primis: in the first place
in principio: in or at the beginning
in privato: in private
in promptu [in readiness]: impromptu; at a moment's notice
in propria causa: in one's own cause (e.g., lawsuit)
in propria persona: in one's own person (see also, **propria persona**)
in proximo gradu: in the nearest degree
in publica custodia: in the public custody (i.e., a reference to public records)
in publico: in public
in quantum: insofar as
in quantum lucratus est: insofar as he or she has prospered
in quovis: in whatever
in re: in the matter of; regarding; concerning (see also, **re**)
in re aliena: in the affairs of another
in re communi: in a partnership
in re propria: in one's own affairs
in re trepida: (fig.) at a critical juncture
in rebus: in things, cases, or matters
in recto: directly (as opposed to **in obliquo**)
in rei exemplum: by way of example
in rem [in a thing]: to the point; to or against the property (i.e., against a particular thing as distinguished from *in personam*, a particular person)
in rem suam: in one's own affairs
in rerum natura: in the nature of things
in retentis: in retention (i.e., being held back or secretly kept safe until wanted or needed)
in rigore juris: in strictness of law
in rixa: in a quarrel or fight
in separali: in several; in severalty

in simul or **insimul:** jointly; together; at the same time (see also, **simul**)

in situ [in its place]: in proper position

in solido: as a whole; entirely

in solidum: for the whole; for the entire sum (i.e., jointly liable for the full amount)

in solo: in the soil; on the ground

in solutum: in payment

in spe: in hope or expectation

in specie: in kind; in the same form; also, payment made in coin as opposed to paper money

in statu quo: in the state in which it was before

in stirpes: according to lineage

in stricto jure: in strict right

in subsidium [as a subsidy]: in aid; in support

in substantialibus: of a substantial nature; substantially

in summa: on the whole

in superficie: superficially

in suspenso: in suspense

in tam amplo modo: in as ample a manner

in tantum: in so much; so far; to that extent

in tempus: for a time; temporarily

in tenebris [in the dark]: in the night

in terminis terminantibus: in express or determinate terms

in terrorem: in terror or warning; in fear; also, by way of threat

in terrorem populi: to the terror of the people

in testimonium: in witness; in evidence whereof

in totidem verbis: in so many words

in toto: in total; on the whole; completely; altogether

in transitu (in trans.): in transit; on the way

in tuto: in safety

in ultima voluntate: in the last will

in universum: on the whole; universal or universally

in usu: in use; at the moment of usage

in utero (in ut.): in the womb

in utraque re: in both cases

in utroque jure: under both laws (i.e., civil and canon)
in vacuo: in a vacuum
in vadio: in pledge
in valorem: according to the value
in verbis: in words
in vicem: alternately; by turns
in vinculis: in chains; in prison
in viridi observantia: in fresh observance (i.e., in full force and operation)
in virtute: by virtue of; by reason of
in vita: in life
in vita testatoris: in the testator's lifetime
in vitro (in vit.) [in a glass]: in a test tube or petri dish
incerti temporis: of uncertain time or date
incerto patre: from an uncertain father
incertus (incert.): uncertain; doubtful
incidenter: incidentally
incipitur: it is begun
incisio: a clause (see also, **clausus**)
incognita causa: without examination
incognito: unknown; unexamined
incolumis: safe; unharmed
incomitatus: unaccompanied
incommodo tuo: to your inconvenience; to your disadvantage
incommodus: inconvenient; troublesome
inconcessus: not allowed; forbidden
incrementum (pl. incrementa): increase; an addition
indebitatus: indebted
indebitatus nunquam: never indebted
indebiti solutio: the payment of something not due
indebitum: not due; not owing
indefensus [undefended]: one sued who has nothing to answer
indemnificatus: indemnified
indicium (pl. indicia): sign; mark; also, evidence or other type of proof
indicta causa: without a hearing

indictus: unsaid; not said
indies (ind.) or **in dies (in d.):** from day to day; daily
indigena: a native-born inhabitant
indivisum or **indivisus:** undivided; held in common
indoctus: untrained; unskilled
industrialis: industrial
ineditus: not published
inemptus: unbought
ineptiae: trifling
inest de jure: it is implied in the right
infans: infant
infantiae proximus: next to infancy (i.e., under seven years of age)
inferior: lower (in position or grade) (as opposed to **superior**)
inferus: below; lower (as opposed to **superus**)
infidelis: unfaithful
infimus or **infumus:** lowest; the lowest part (as opposed to **summus**)
infinitum: without end; unlimited
infra (inf.): below; under; beneath; underneath; within
infra aetatem: within or under age
infra annos nubiles: not of marriageable age
infra annum: within a year
infra annum luctus: within the year of mourning
infra brachia: within her arms
infra civitatem: within the state
infra comitatum vel extra: within the country or without
infra corpus comitatus: within the body of a county
infra dignitatem (inf. dig.): beneath one's dignity
infra dignitatem curiae: beneath the dignity of the court
infra furorem: during madness (i.e., while in a state of insanity)
infra gildam: within a guild
infra hospitium: within an inn or hospice
infra jurisdictionem: within the jurisdiction
infra libertates vel extra: within liberties or without
infra metas: within the limit(s)
infra metas et divisas: within the metes and bounds

infra petita: less than requested

infra praesidia [within the defenses]: under protection (i.e., a place of safe custody); historically, a reference to possession of goods or persons taken during wartime

infra quatuor maria: within the four seas

infra quatuor parietes: within the four walls

infra regnum: within the realm

infra sex annos: within six years

infra summonitium justiciorum: within the summons of the justices

infra tempus semestre: within six months

infra triduum: within three days

ingratus: ungrateful; disagreeable

inhumatus: unburied

inimicus: a public enemy

injuria (pl. **injuriae**) [injury]: an actionable wrong; a tort offense

injuria absque damno: injury without damage

injuria sine damno: injury without damage (cf., **damnum sine injuria**)

injustus: unjust

inlex: lawless

inlicitus or **illicitus:** illegal; illicit; forbidden

innocens: harmless; innocent (as opposed to **nocens**)

innocentia: innocence

innotescimus: we make known

inofficiosum: undutiful

inops: poor; weak; helpless; destitute

inops consilii: without counsel; deprived of counsel

inquirendo [by inquiring]: the authority to inquire into something for the Crown

inquit: he or she says

inquiunt: they say

insanus: of unsound mind; insane

inscriptio (**inscr.**): an inscription; a heading

insequor or **insequitur:** to follow after, either in space or time

insidiae: an ambush; a plot
insidiatio viarum: the crime of ambush or waylaying (i.e., highway robbery)
insilium: pernicious advice or council
inspectio corporis: inspection of the body
inspeximus: we have inspected (see also, **vidimus**)
instanter: instantly; urgently; immediately; at once
instar: like; resembling
instar dentium [resembling teeth]: indented; indenture
instar omnium: equal to all
instinctu naturae: natural instinct
institor: a peddler (pedlar); also a shopkeeper or store clerk
intentio: an accusation; a stated charge, declaration, or claim; also, a count in a series of charges against a defendant
inter: between; among
inter absentes: between or among persons who are absent
inter alia: among other things
inter alios: among other persons
inter amicos: between or among friends
inter apices juris: among the subtleties of the law
inter arma: in time of war
inter caeteros: between or among others
inter canem et lupum [between dog and wolf]: twilight
inter conjuges: between husband and wife
inter eosdem: between the same persons
inter nos [between ourselves]: mutually
inter pares: among equals
inter partes: between or among the parties involved (as opposed to **de una parte**)
inter quatuor parietes: within the four walls (i.e., secretly; in confidence)
inter rusticos: among the unlearned
inter se or **inter sese:** between or among themselves
inter terrorem: by way of threat
inter terrorem populi: to the terror of the people
inter virum et uxorem: between husband and wife

inter vivos: between or among the living (e.g., the transfer of property from parent to child)

interdictum: a prohibition

interdum: now and then; sometimes

interea: in the meantime

interesse termini: interest of term or end (i.e., a tenant's right to enter and possess leased property)

interim: in the meantime; meanwhile (see also, **ad interim**)

intermedius: intermediate

internecinus: deadly; utterly destructive

internecivus: murderous; devastating

internus (int.): inward; internal

interposita persona: an intermediary (i.e., refers to a front man used to disguise an unlawful transaction)

intime: intimately

intra: inside; within

intra anni spatium: within the space of a year

intra fidem: within belief (i.e., credible)

intra fines: inside the boundaries

intra legem: within the law (i.e., legal)

intra luctus tempus: within the time of mourning

intra parietes [within the walls]: among friends; also, a matter settled out of court

intra praesidia: within the defenses

intra quatuor maria: within the four seas (i.e., a reference to England)

intra verba peccare: to offend in words only

intra vires: within the powers (of)

intuitu matrimonii: in the prospect of marriage

intuitu mortis: in the prospect of death

intuitu pecuniae: in view of the money; on account of the money

intuitu personae: in view of the person; on account of the person

intus: inside; within; also, on the inside; from within

intutus: unsafe; unprotected

inultus: unavenged; unpunished
inurbanus: rude; boorish
inure: to habituate; also, to take effect; to vest
invecta et illata: things brought and carried in (e.g., furniture and other belongings)
invenit (inv.): he or she designed it
inveteratus: established
invicem: by turns; alternatively
invictus: invincible
invito debitore: without the consent of the debtor
invito domino: against the will of the owner (i.e., without the owner's consent)
invito superiore: without the consent of the superior
invitus [unwilling]: without consent
ipse [he himself]: he or she alone
ipse dixit: he himself said it (i.e., an unproven assertion) (cf., **argumentum ad verecundiam**)
ipsissima verba: the very words
ipsissimis verbis: in the very words (i.e., the identical words)
ipso facto [by the fact itself]: by that very fact (see also, **de facto**)
ipso jure: by the law itself (see also, **de jure**)
ira motus: excited by anger or passion
ire ad largum: to go at large; to have escaped; to be set free (see also, **ad largum**)
irrevocabile verbum: an irrevocably spoken word
is qui cognoscit: he who acknowledges
ita est: so it is
ita lex scripta est [thus the law is written]: such is the law
ita quod: so that; wherefore; whereby
ita te Deus adjuvet: so help you God
iter [a walkway]: the right of passage
iter criminis: the path of crime
iudex or **judex:** a judge
iudicare or **judicare:** to judge; to give judgment or pronounce sentence

iudicatio or **judicatio:** a legal judgment or opinion; the pronouncing of sentence

iuratus or **juratus:** under oath

iure or **jure:** by right or by law; rightly

iuris consultus or **juris consultus (jurisconsultus):** a lawyer

iuris peritus or **juris peritus (jurisperitus):** skilled or learned in the law; a legal expert (see also, **legis peritus** or **legisperitus**)

iurisdictio or **jurisdictio:** judicial authority

ius or **jus** (pl. **iures** or **jures**): law; a legal right

iusiurandum or **jusjurandum** (pl. **iusiuranda** or **jusjuranda**): an oath

iussu or **jussu:** by order; by command

iustitia or **justitia:** justice; equity

iustus or **justus:** just; equitable

iuxta or **juxta (iux.** or **jux.):** near; next to; close by; according to

J

jacet in ore: it lies in the mouth

jactura: loss by jettison (cf., **jetsam**)

jam: now

januis clausis [with closed doors]: in secret

jetsam: goods or other cargo voluntarily thrown overboard from a sea vessel to lighten its load during storm or other emergency (see also, **flotsam** and **ligan**)

jocus partitus: a divided chance (i.e., the liberty to choose between two options)

jubere: to order or command; to decree

judex or **iudex:** a judge

judex a quo: the judge from whom (i.e., from whom an appeal is made)

judex ad quem: the judge to whom (i.e., to whom an appeal is made)

judex datus: the judge assigned to try a case

judex delegatus: a delegated judge (i.e., one to whom a special case is assigned)

judex incorruptus: an impartial judge

judicare or **iudicare:** to judge; to give judgment or pronounce sentence

judicatio or **iudicatio:** a legal judgment or opinion; the pronouncing of sentence

judicia summaria: summary proceedings

judicis: a panel of jurors

judicium: a trial; a legal decision

judicium aquae [the judgment of water]: trial by water ordeal

judicium capitale: capital punishment

judicium Dei [the judgment of God]: trial by ordeal

judicium parium [judgment of peers]: trial by jury

judicium perversum: a miscarriage of justice

junior: younger

jura: rights; laws

jura ad rem: rights to a thing (as opposed to **jura in re**)

jura et munera: rights and obligations

jura fiscalia fiscal rights

jura fixa: fixed or immovable rights

jura in re: rights in a thing (as opposed to **jura ad rem**)

jura personarum: the rights of persons (i.e., obligations of one person to another)

jura privata: private or civil rights

jura publica: public or political rights

jura regalia: royal rights; the rights or prerogatives of a sovereign (see also, **regalia**)

jura rerum: the rights of things

juramentae corporales: corporal oaths (e.g., to swear on the Bible)

juramento: by oath

juramentum: an oath

juramentum necessarium: a compulsory oath

juramentum voluntarium: a voluntary oath

jurare in verba magistri [to swear the words of the master]: a confession

jurat [sworn]: a written certification that the affidavit has been properly sworn

jurata: a jury of twelve persons
jurator (pl. **juratores**): a juror
juratus or **iuratus:** under oath
jure belli: by the law of war
jure civili: by the civil law
jure coronae: by right of crown
jure divino: by divine right
jure et legibus: by common and statute law
jure gentium: by the law of nations
jure humano [by human law]: by the will of the people
jure mariti: by the right of the husband; by the right of marriage
jure naturae: according to the law of nature (viz., legal and moral principles derived from universal concepts of human nature and divine justice) (see also, **ex jure naturae**)
jure patronatus: by right of patronage
jure propinquitatis: by right of relationship
jure proprio: by proper law or right
jure representationis: by the right of representation
jure sanguinis: by right of blood
jure uxoris: by the right of the wife
juridicus: juridical
juris: of law; of right
juris consultus or **jurisconsultus** (pl. **jurisconsulti**): a legal consultant (i.e., a lawyer)
juris divini: of divine right
Juris Doctor [J.D.]: Doctor of Law
juris dubii [of doubtful law or right]: an unsettled legal point (see also, **dubii juris**)
juris ecclesiae: by the right of the church; by ecclesiastical law
juris peritus or **jurisperitus:** skilled or learned in the law; a legal expert (see also, **legis peritus** or **legisperitus**)
juris praecepta: precepts of the law
juris privati: of private right (see also, **privati juris**)
juris publici: of public right (i.e., according to common or public use) (see also, **publici juris**)

Juris Utriusque Doctor [J.U.D.]: Doctor of Canon and Civil Law

jurisdictio or **iuisdictio:** judicial authority

jurisperitus or **juris peritus:** skilled or learned in the law; an expert in the law

jurisprudentes: students of the law

jurisprudentia: jurisprudence

jus or **ius** (pl. **jures**): law; a legal right

jus abstinendi: the right of abstaining (i.e., renouncing or declining one's inheritance)

jus abutendi: the right of abusing (i.e., the right to use, sell, or dispose of the thing, such as one's property or inheritance, as opposed to **jus utendi**)

jus accrescendi: the right of survivorship

jus ad bellum: the right to wage war (i.e., just war)

jus ad rem: a right to a thing; a personal right

jus ad vim: the just or legal use of force

jus aequum: equitable law

jus aesneciae: the right of primogeniture (i.e., the firstborn child) (see also, **jus primogeniturae**)

jus anglorum: the law of the Anglo-Saxons

jus antiquum: the old law

jus aquaeductus: the right to convey and/or drain water over another's land

jus aquam ducendi: the right to pipe or convey water over another's property

jus belli: the law of war

jus bellum dicendi: the right to declare war

jus canonicum: canon law

jus civile: civil law

jus civitatis: the right of citizenship

jus commune: common law; common right

jus contra bellum: (fig.) law concerning the prevention of war

jus coronae: the right of the crown

jus dare: to give or to make law

jus deliberandi: the right of deliberating

jus dicere: to declare the law

jus disponendi: the right of disposing

jus divinum: divine law

jus duplicatum [a double right]: the right to have and to hold

jus edicendi: the right to issue edicts (i.e., rules)

jus et lex: law and statute

jus et norma loquendi [the law and rule of speech]: ordinary usage

jus ex non scripto: unwritten law (e.g., custom, judicial precedent, etc.) (see also, **jus non scriptum**)

jus fiduciarum: a right held in trust; a moral right

jus fodiendi: the right to dig on another person's land

jus fruendi [the right of enjoying]: the right to use another person's property without altering, damaging, or reducing its value

jus gentium [law of nations]: international law

jus gladii [law of the sword]: the right to punish crime

jus habendi: the right to own and to profit from ownership

jus haereditatis or **jus hereditatis:** the right of inheritance

jus honorarium: the body of Roman law

jus imaginis: the right to display ancestral statues; the right to bear a coat of arms

jus immunitatis: the right of immunity from public service

jus in bello [just conduct in war]: laws that govern or regulate warfare

jus in personam: a personal right (i.e., the right to take legal action) (see also, **jura in personam**)

jus in re [a right in the thing]: a right to property and possession

jus in re aliena: a right in the property of another (i.e., an encumbrance)

jus in re propria: the right in one's own property (i.e., full ownership)

jus in rem: a right in the thing itself

jus incognitum: an unknown law

jus individuum: an individual or indivisible right

jus judicium: a judicial right

jus legitimum: a legal right (i.e., a right that may be enforced by the law)

jus mariti: the right of a husband

jus merum: a bare or mere right (i.e., without possession)

jus naturae or **jus naturale:** the law of nature; natural law; natural right (i.e., legal and moral principles derived from universal concepts of human nature and divine justice) (see also, **lex naturale**)

jus navigandi: the right of navigation

jus necis: the right of death (i.e., an ancient right of the father over household members living under his paternal power) (see also, **jus vitae necisque**)

jus non sacrum: secular law

jus non scriptum: unwritten law (see also, **jus ex non scripto**)

jus novum: new law

jus nullum: absence of justice

jus officii: by right of office

jus pascendi: the right of pasture (i.e., grazing)

jus personarum: the right of persons

jus pignoris: right of pledge

jus portus: the right of port or harbor

jus possessionis: right of possession

jus postliminii: law of postliminium (i.e., restoration or repatriation of goods or persons captured during war)

jus praesens [present right]: a vested right

jus precarium: a precarious right (i.e., as a courtesy or honor)

jus primae noctis: the right of the first night

jus primogeniturae: the right of the firstborn child (see also, **jus aesneciae**)

jus privatum: private law; private right (as opposed to **jus publicum**)

jus proprietatis: the right of property

jus proprietatis et possessionis: the right of property and possession

jus publicum: public law; public right (as opposed to **jus privatum**)

jus quaesitum: the right of demanding (i.e., the right to ask or recover)

jus regium: the right of royalty

jus relictae or **jus relicti:** the right of the widow to her deceased husband's estate (viz., one-third if there be surviving issue; one-half if there be no issue or surviving issue)

jus rerum: the right of things; the law of things

jus sanguinis: the law of consanguinity (i.e., the citizenship of the parents determines the citizenship of the child)

jus scriptum: written law

jus sibi dicere: to take the law into one's own hands

jus soli: the law of the soil (i.e., the place of birth determines the citizenship of the child)

jus strictum or **strictum jus:** strict law (i.e., interpreted according to the strict letter of the law)

jus suffragii: the right of a citizen to vote

jus tertii: the right or interest of a third party

jus tripertitum [a threefold right]**:** the ancient law of wills

jus trium liberorum: the right of three children (i.e., certain historic privileges bestowed upon citizens with three or more children)

jus utendi: the right to use (as opposed to **jus abutendi**)

jus venandi et piscandi: the right of hunting and fishing

jus vetus: old law

jus vitae necisque: the right of life and death (i.e., an ancient right of the father over household members living under his paternal power) (see also, **jus necis**)

jusjurandum or **iusiurandum** (pl. **jusjuranda** or **iusiuranda**)**:** an oath

jussu or **iussu:** by order; by command

justa causa: a just cause

justae nuptiae: legal marriage

justitia or **iustitia:** justice; equity

justitium: a suspension of the court's business or proceedings

justo tempore: at the right time (i.e., in due time)

justus or **iustus:** just; equitable

juvenilis: youthful

juvenis: young; youthful

juventus (f. **juventa**): youth; adolescence; the prime of life

juxta or **iuxta** (**jux.** or **iux.**): near; next to; close by; according to

juxta conventionem: according to the covenant

juxta formam statuti: according to the form of the statute

juxta ratam: according to the rate

juxta tenorem sequentem: according to the following tenor (i.e., the text as written)

L

labor or **laboris:** labor; work

lacrimae simulatae [simulated tears]: crocodile tears

lacuna (**lac.**): gap; deficiency (e.g., missing words in a text or manuscript)

laesa majestas [injured majesty]: high treason

laevo: on the left

laevus (**laev.**): left

ligan: goods or other items cast into the sea tied to buoys so as to be found and retrieved later by their owners (see also, **flotsam** and **jetsam**)

lapsus: lapse; error

lapsus bonis: in straitened circumstances

lapsus calami: a slip of the pen

lapsus linguae: a slip of the tongue

lapsus memoriae: a slip of the memory

lapsus plumae: a slip of the quill (i.e., the pen)

lata culpa [wide or extensive fault]: gross negligence (see also, **culpa lata**)

lata negligentia or **lata neglegentia:** extreme negligence

latinarius: an interpreter of Latin

lato sensu: in a broad sense (as opposed to **stricto sensu**)

latrocinium: larceny

legalis homo: a lawful person (i.e., a person with full legal rights)

legatum: a legacy
legatus [legate]**:** a deputy; a delegate
legem facere: to make law or oath
legem habere: to be capable of giving evidence under oath
legem promulgare: to publish the law
legem rogare: to propose a law
legenda: things to be read
leges Anglia: the laws of England
leges non scriptae: unwritten laws
leges nullae: lawlessness; anarchy
leges scriptae (sing. **lex scripta**)**:** written laws
legibus: according to law; legal
legibus solutus: released from the laws (i.e., not bound by the law)
legiosus: litigious
legis actio (pl. **legis actiones**)**:** a legal or lawful action
legis pacis: conditions of peace
legis peritus or **legisperitus:** skilled or learned in the law; a legal expert (see also, **juris peritus** or **jurisperitus**)
legitima potestas: lawful power
legitimus: legitimate; lawful; legal
Legum Baccalaureus (LL.B.): Bachelor of Laws
Legum Doctor (LL.D.): Doctor of Laws
lenis: gentle
lente: slowly
leonina societas: a leonine partnership (i.e., a legally invalid partnership in which the partner shares in the losses but not in the profits)
levandae navis causa: for the sake of lightening the ship (i.e., *pro rata* compensation for goods lost at sea)
levari facias [cause to be levied]**:** a writ issued for payment of a debt from the profits of the debtor's lands and/or sale of the debtor's personal property
levis culpa [slight fault]**:** ordinary fault or neglect (see also, **culpa levis**)
levissima culpa [the slightest fault]**:** slight fault or neglect (see also, **culpa levissima**)

lex (pl. **leges**): a law or statute
lex aeterna: eternal law
lex agraria: agrarian law
lex amissa: an infamous, perjured, or outlawed person
lex apostata: a thing contrary to the law
lex apparens: apparent or manifest law (i.e., in reference to trial by battle or duel)
lex canonica: canon law
lex communis: common law
lex contractus: the law of the contract
lex domicilii: law of the domicile (i.e., laws pertaining to the person and to personal rights)
Lex Duodecim Tabularum: Law of the Twelve Tables (i.e., the ancient Roman law code)
lex fori: the law of the court (viz., the place where a suit is brought)
lex Francorum: the law of the Franks
lex Gothica: the law of the Goths
lex irrita est: a law is invalid
lex judicialis: a judicial ordeal (e.g., trial by fire, water, etc.)
lex loci: the law of the place
lex loci actus: the law of the place wherein the act is committed
lex loci contractus: the law of the place wherein the contract is made
lex loci delicti: the law of the place where the injury or crime is committed
lex loci solutionis: the law of the place of payment
lex manifesta: trial by duel or by ordeal
lex mercatoria or **lex mercatorum:** mercantile law (see also, **consuetudo mercatorum**)
lex naturale: natural law (see also, **jus naturale**)
lex non scripta (pl. **leges non scriptae**) [unwritten law]: common law
lex ordinandi: the law of the country where the action is brought
lex patriae: the law of one's country

lex rata est: a law is valid

lex salica [Salian law]: the ancient Salian law denying the French monarchy to women

lex scripta (pl. **leges scriptae**) [written law]: statute law

lex talionis: the law of retaliation (e.g., an eye for an eye)

lex terrae: the law of the land

libellus [a little book]: a letter or petition; a bill

libellus famosus [a defamatory book]: libel

liber (**l.** or **lib.**; pl. **libri**): a book

liber: free; independent; also, a free person

liber assisarum: a book of assizes or pleas

liber et legalis homo: a free and lawful person

liber homo [free man]: a free person

liber judiciarum [book of judgment]: the English Domesday book

libera batella [free boat]: fishing rights

liberatio: acquittal

liberi: children

liberis nascituris: to children yet to be born

libertas: liberty; freedom

libertas in legibus: liberty under the laws

libertus (f. **liberta**, pl. **liberti**): a freeman or freewoman

liberum arbitrium: free will; free choice

liberum maritagium: land given as a dowry to a woman and her husband

liberum servitium: free service

libitum: at pleasure; at will

libra or **libra pondo** (**lb.**): a pound by weight

licentia: license; excessive liberty

licentia loquendi: license or leave to speak

licet [it is permitted]: it is legal; it is allowed

licet saepius requisitus: although frequently requested

licitus: lawful; permitted

ligula: a court transcript; a copy of a deed or other court record

linea: line; line of descent

linea recta [a perpendicular line]: a straight or direct line of ascent and descent

linea transversalis: a transverse or oblique line of ascent and descent

lingua: tongue; speech; language

lingua Latine: in the Latin language

liquet: it is apparent; it is proven

lis: legal action; a suit

lis mota [a controversy begun]: the commencement of a suit or action

lis pendens: a pending suit

lis sub judice: a lawsuit before a judge (viz., one that has not yet been decided)

lite pendente: pending the suit; also, during the trial (see also, **pendente lite**)

litis aestimatio: the judge's estimate of damages

litis contestatio: contestation of the suit (i.e., the legal process by which a suit is brought before a judge, viz., the complaint and response by plaintiff and defendant)

litis ordinatio: the formal process by which a lawsuit is conducted

littera or **litera** (pl. **litterae** or **literae**): a letter; a letter of the alphabet; also, a record

litterae clausae: letters or papers under seal (i.e., sealed records)

litterae mortuae [dead letters]: empty or superfluous words

litterae patentes [open letters]: letters or papers not under seal (i.e., unsealed records)

litterae sigillatae: sealed letters

litura: an erasure; a correction

litus maris: ordinary tides that mark the shoreline

localiter: locally

locatio [a letting]: leasing; a lease

locatio custodiae: a deposit for safekeeping; also, a reward

locatio operis: the hiring of labor and services

locatio operis faciendi: a deposit on labor or services to be done

locatio rei: the hiring of a thing
loci communes (sing. **locus communis**): public places
loco citato (**loc. cit.** or **l.c.**): in the place cited (see also, **in loco citato**)
loco laudato (**loc. laud.**): in the place [cited] with approval
loco parentis: in place of a parent (properly, **in loco parentis**)
loco supra citato (**l.s.c.**): in the place cited above
loco tutoris: in place of a guardian
locum tenens (pl. **locum tenentes**) [holding one's place]: a placeholder; a temporary substitute or deputy, especially for a physician or a cleric
locum tenere: to hold place (i.e., to be applicable)
locus: place
locus citatus: the quoted passage
locus communis (pl. **loci communes**) [a common place]: a public place; a place of the dead
locus contractus: the place of the contract
locus criminis: the scene of the crime
locus delicti: the scene of the crime
locus in quo: the place in which (i.e., the place where something is alleged to have occurred)
locus poenitentiae: the place of repentance (i.e., the chance to withdraw from a contract before it is signed)
locus regit actum: the place governs the act (i.e., the laws of the place where the act occurs)
locus rei sitae: the place where a thing is situated
locus sigilli (**L.S.**): the place of the seal
locus standi [a place of standing]: a recognized position; the right to appear before a court (i.e., the right to be heard by a judge)
locutus: spoken
longa manu [with a long hand]: indirectly; by a long or circuitous route (see also, **manu longa**)
longe sum: I am [far] away
longus: long

loquela [imparlance]: formerly, the oral discussions between parties in a lawsuit (i.e., pleadings)

loquela sine die: an imparlance granted for an indefinite period (i.e., an indefinite postponement of an action)

loquitur (loq.): he or she speaks

luce clarius [clearer than light]: as clear as day

lucidus ordo: a clear arrangement

lucri causa: for the sake of gain

lucrum: profit

lucrum cessans: a cessation of gain (i.e., a lost opportunity for monetary gain)

lumen or **lux:** light

lusus naturae: a freak of nature

lux or **lumen:** light

luxor: to run riot

luxus: luxury; extravagance; excess

M

magis minusve: more or less

magister: master; teacher

Magister Artium (M.A.): Master of Arts

magister navis: master of a ship

magistratus: magistrate

Magna Carta or **Magna Charta:** The Great Charter signed at Runnymede by King John in 1215 C.E., granting certain civil and political liberties to nobles and, symbolically, to the English people.

magna cum cura: with great care

magna ex parte: in a great degree

magnetophonicus: a tape recording

magno cum detrimento: with great loss (of life)

magno pretio: high priced; costly

magnum opus or **opus magnum** (pl. **magna opera**) [a great work]: an author's greatest work; a masterpiece

magnus (mag.): large; great

majestus: majesty; greatness; grandeur
major: larger; greater
major domus: a master or a steward of a household (i.e., a *majordomo*)
major jus: a greater right
major pars: the majority
majores: esteemed ancestors; persons of consequence
mala or **malum:** bad; wrong
mala antiqua: old crimes; ancient offenses
mala copia: excess
mala creditus: bad credit
mala fide [in bad faith]: false or falsely; treacherously (as opposed to **bona fide**)
mala fides: bad faith
mala in se: (pl.) acts that are wrong in and of themselves (see also, **malum in se**)
mala merx: a bad lot
mala praxis or **malapraxis:** malpractice
mala prohibita (sing. **malum prohibitum**): things prohibited by law (e.g., criminal acts)
malandrinus [brigand]: a pirate; a thief
male creditus or **malecreditus:** a person of bad repute; a person not to be trusted
male gratus: ungrateful; unthankful
male positus (**m.p.** or **mal. pos.**): badly placed
maledicus: slander
malefactor: an evildoer
maleficium: injury; damage
maleficus: an evildoer (see also, **homo maleficus**)
malesuada fames: hunger that impels the crime
malevolentia: ill will; malice; spite
malevolus: malicious; spiteful
mali exempli [of bad example]: of bad precedent
malignus: hostile; malicious; wicked (as opposed to **benignus**)
malitia praecogitata: malice aforethought
malo animo: with intent to do evil

malo grato: unwillingly; in spite

malum (pl. **mala**): evil; bad; wrong

malum in se (pl. **mala in se**) [a thing evil in itself]: a thing unlawful in and of itself, regardless of statute (as opposed to **malum prohibitum**)

malum prohibitum (pl. **mala prohibita**) [a prohibited evil]: an act that is unlawful because it is forbidden by law (i.e., a legal crime though not necessarily a moral crime) (as opposed to **malum in se**)

malus animus: bad intention

managium: a dwelling; a mansion

manas mediae: persons of a mean condition; also, inferior persons

mancipatio: the ancient Roman act of emancipation

mandamus [we command]: a writ requiring that a specified action be done

mandatum: an order or command; a message or commission

mane (m.): morning; in the morning

mania: madness

mania a potu: delirium tremens

manica: manacles; handcuffs

manu aliena: by the hand of another

manu brevi [with a short hand]: briefly; summarily (see also, **brevi manu**)

manu forti [with a strong hand]: by force (e.g., a forcible entry)

manu longa [with a long hand]: indirectly; by a long or circuitous route (see also, **longa manu**)

manu propria: with one's own hand

manu scriptum or **manuscriptum (m.s.** or **ms.):** written by hand (e.g., a letter or a document)

manumissio: emancipation from slavery

manus: hand

manus dextra: the right hand

manus sinistra (or simply, **sinistra**): the left hand

manuscriptus (MS or **ms.;** pl. **manuscripta, MSS** or **mss):** a manuscript; a handwritten document

mare: the sea

mare clausum [closed sea]: a sea or other navigable body of water within the jurisdiction of a particular country that is closed to other nations

mare liberum [open sea]: a sea or other navigable body of water that is open to all nations

marginalia: marginal notes

marginalis: marginal

margo (pl. **margines**): margin; border; edge

marinarius: seaman; a sailor (see also, **nauta**)

maritimus: marine

maritus: a husband

mas or **masculus** (**m.**): male; a man

masculinus (**m.** or **masc.**): masculine; manly

mater: mother

mater familias or **materfamilias:** the mother of a family

materia: material

matertera: a maternal aunt (i.e., mother's sister) (cf., **amita**)

matima or **matrina:** a godmother (see also, **patrina**)

matrimonialiter: in the way of marriage (i.e., matrimony)

matrix: mother; the womb

maxim: an established principle

maxima cura: with the greatest care

maximus: the greatest; the largest

me absente: in my absence

me auctore: by my advice

me duce: under my leadership or direction

me indicente: without my saying a word

me invito: against my will

me judice: in my judgment; in my opinion

me libente: with my pleasure; with my goodwill

me paenitet [I regret it]: I am sorry

me vivo: in my lifetime

mea culpa [my fault]: by my own fault

mecum: with me

media nocte: in the middle of the night

media nox: midnight
media sententia: a middle view or opinion
medicina: medicine
medicinalis: medicinal
medicus: a physician; also, healing
medietatis linguae [of half-tongue]: a reference to a jury comprised of non-English-speaking persons (perhaps including non-native speakers) (see also, **de medietatis linguae**)
medio tempore: in the meantime
mediocris: mediocre; of indifferent quality
mediocritas: moderation
meditatio fugae: contemplation of flight
medius: medium; middle sized; also, intermediate
medius fidius: so help me God
melior: better
melior res: the better thing
melius inquirendum [a better inquiry]: a writ for a second inquiry
memor: mindful; remembering
memorandum (pl. **memoranda**): memorandum; memo
memoria: memory; remembrance
memoriter: from memory; by heart
mendacium: a lie
mens: mind; will; intention or intent
mens legis [the mind of the law]: the spirit or purpose of the law
mens legislatoris: legislative intent
mens rea: a guilty intent; a guilty mind
mens testatoris [mind of the testator]: the intent of those making wills
mensa: a table
mensalia: livings (e.g., a parsonage)
mensis: month
mensis vetitus: prohibited month (i.e., summer closing)
mensor: a surveyor (see also, **metator**)
menstruus: monthly; monthlong

mensularius: a money changer; a banker
mensura (mens. or **mensur.):** measure; standard; also, by measure
mente captus: captured in mind (i.e., chronically insane or suffering from a mental disorder that affects daily life)
mentiri: to lie
mentitio: lying
meo judicio: by my judgment
meo periculo [by my peril]: at my own risk
mercator: a merchant
mercatum: a market; a contract of sale
mercatus: a business or trade
merces: payment; wages; salary
meridies (M. or **m.):** midday; noon
merx: goods; merchandise
merx et pretium: goods and a price (i.e., the essential components of a sales transaction)
metator: a surveyor (see also, **mensor**)
metus perjurii: the fear of perjury
meum et tuum: mine and thine (i.e., a phrase expressing rights of property)
milliarium or **miliarium:** a milestone; a mile
minima de malis: the least of evils (viz., of evils, choose the least)
minimus: smallest; least
minor: smaller; lesser
minor aetas [lesser age]: minority; infancy
minus: less; less than
minutia (pl. **minutiae):** a trifle
minutio: a lessening; a diminution; also, a deduction
misericordia: mercy; compassion
mitior sensus or **mitiori sensu:** a milder sense (see also, **in mitiori sensu**)
mitte (mitt.): send
mitte tales (mitt. tal. or **mit. tal.):** send such
mittimus [we send]: a warrant of commitment to prison; a writ to remove records from one court to another; also, a dismissal or a discharge

mittomus: let us suppose
mixtum compositum: a hodgepodge
mobile vulgus (mob.) [the fickle masses]: a mob
mobilis (pl. **mobilia**): movable
modicus: moderate sized; middle sized
modius: an uncertain measure (e.g., of land)
modo et forma: in manner and form
modus (pl. **modi**): a mode; manner; method
modus faciendi: the mode or manner of doing something
modus operandi (m.o.): a mode of operating (e.g., the way by which a criminal commits a crime)
modus vivendi: manner of living
molliter manus imposuit [he laid his hands on gently]: a plea of non-excessive force (i.e., a justification for committing a wrong in order to prevent a greater wrong from occurring)
mora: delay; hindrance
morandae solutionis causa: for the purpose of delaying payment
moratorium [a delaying]: a legal postponement of the payment of a debt for a specified period; also, the period of such a postponement
moratur in lege: he demurs (i.e., no plea being entered)
more: after the manner of; in the fashion of
more dicto (m.d. or **more dict.):** as directed; in the manner directed (see also, **modo dicto**)
more dicto utendus (m.d.u.): to be used as directed
more solito (m.s. or **more sol.):** in the usual manner
mores (pl. **mos**) [customs; habits]: customary usages; unwritten laws
mors: death
mors immatura: an early or untimely death
mors naturalis: a natural death
mors praematura: a premature death
morsellum terrae: a morsel of earth (i.e., a small plot or parcel of land)
mortis causa [because of death]: by reason of impending death, such as in the giving of gifts or donations

mortuis testibus: the witnesses being dead

mortuum vadium or **vadium mortuum** [dead pledge]: a mortgage (viz., the land or property itself becomes the security against default, hence the term 'dead')

mortuus: dead

mortuus civiliter: civilly dead (i.e., a person deprived of civil rights)

mortuus sine prole: dead without issue

mos (pl. **mores**): custom; manner

mos majorum: ancestral custom (see also, **consuetudo majorum**)

mos pravus: a bad, evil, or illegal custom (see also, **prava consuetudo**)

motu proprio [by one's own motion]: of one's own accord

mox: soon

mox nox [soon night]: night is approaching

mulcta (mulct.): a fine or penalty

mulier: a woman

mulieratus: a legitimate son (properly, **filius mulieratus**)

multifariam: in many places

multis de causis: for many reasons

multis post annis: after many years

multus: much; many

munera publica (sing. **munus publicum**): public offices (i.e., duties)

munus (pl. **munera**): gift; grant; also, duty or service

mutanda: things to be altered

mutatis mutandis (m.m.): [with] the necessary changes being made

mutato nomine: the name having been changed

mutilus: mutilated; maimed

mutua petitio: a counterclaim

mutus et surdus: dumb and deaf

mutuum: a mutual exchange of goods or property of equivalent value

mutuus consensus: mutual consent

N

nam: for; therefore; because
narratio (narr.): a narrative; a declaration
nasciturus: yet to be born (i.e., unborn)
natale solum: native soil
natio: nation
natis et nascituris: to children born and yet to be born
natu: by birth
naturalis: natural
naturalis ratio or **ratio naturalis:** natural reason
natus (n.): born
naufragium: shipwreck
nauta: a sailor; seaman (see also, **marinarius**)
nauticus: nautical
navalis: naval; nautical
navifragus: causing shipwreck
navis or **navigium:** a ship
navis magister: a ship's captain
ne: lest; not
ne admittas: do not admit
ne exeat: let him or her not leave or depart (i.e., a writ of travel restraint)
ne exeat regno: let him or her not leave the realm (i.e., a writ of restraint forbidding a person from leaving a jurisdiction pending an action)
ne exeat republica: let him or her not leave the republic (i.e., a writ of restraint forbidding a person from leaving a country or territory pending an action)
ne multa: in brief
ne recipiatur: that it not be received
nec: neither; not
nec manifestum: not manifest
necessitas culpabilis: culpable necessity
necessitate juris: by necessity of law
nefas: unlawful; forbidden
negatum: denied

negligiens or **neglegiens:** careless; indifferent; negligent
nego: I say no (i.e., to deny or refuse)
negotia publica: public affairs
negotii causa: for the sake of business (as opposed to **animi causa**)
negotiorum gestio: management of business (i.e., the unauthorized management of another's affairs)
negotiorum gestor: manager of business (i.e., an unauthorized manager of another's affairs)
nemine contradicente (nem. con.): no one contradicting
nemine dissentiente (nem. dis.): no one dissenting (i.e., unanimous)
neminem laedere [to hurt no one]: do not harm
nemo: no one
nemo non: not no one (i.e., everyone)
nepos: nephew; grandson
neptis: granddaughter
nequam: worthless
nequiter: wickedly
neuter or **neutrum (n.)** [neither]: of neither sex; in neither direction
neutralis: neutral
nexus: tie or connection
nihil: nothing
nihil ad rem [nothing to the point]: beside the point; irrelevant
nihil capiat per billam: that [the plaintiff] take nothing by his or her bill
nihil capiat per breve: that [the plaintiff] take nothing by his or her writ
nihil debet or **nil debet:** he or she owes nothing (i.e., a plea denying a debt)
nihil dicit or **nil dicit:** he or she says nothing (i.e., a judgment by default, the defendant declining to enter a plea or answer a charge)
nihil habet: he or she has nothing
nihil non: everything

nihil obstat [nothing gives offense]: there is no objection
nihil tua refert: (fig.) it is not your business
nil: nothing
nil debet: he owes nothing
nil habuit in tenementis: he or she has no interest in tenements (i.e., a claim that the landlord had no title to the property under lease)
nil ligatum [nothing bound]: no obligation has been incurred
nimis: too much
nisi: unless; except
nisi aliud convenerit: unless it has been otherwise agreed
nisi impediatur sententia: unless the sense forbid
nisi prius [unless before then]: a civil trial held before a judge and a jury
nobili genere: of noble birth
nobilior: the more noble
nobilis: noble
nobilitas: the nobility
nocens: harmful; criminal (as opposed to **innocens**)
nocent: a guilty person
nocivus: harmful; injurious
nocte (n.): at night; in the night
noctu: by night
nocturnus: nocturnal; nightly; by night
nodus: a knot; a node
nolens volens [whether willing or not]: willy-nilly
nolle prosequi (nol. pros.): unwilling to prosecute
nolo contendere (nol. contend.) [not to contend]: a plea of 'no contest' to criminal charges by the defendant without admitting guilt
nomen (nom.; pl. **nomina):** name
nomen collectivum: a collective name or term (i.e., a class of things)
nomen generale: a general name (i.e., a genus or general class of things)
nomen juris: legal name; also, a legal designation

Latin Legal Words and Phrases 113

nomen nominandum (n.n.): a name to be named (i.e., a name supplied at a later date)

nomen proprium (N.P. or **n.p.):** proper name

nomen transcripticium: account entry transferred (i.e., the creditor's entry of an existing debt into a new account)

nominandus: to be named

nominatim: by name; expressed one by one

nomine damni [in name of damage]: on account of loss

nomine meo: in my name; on my behalf

nomine poenae: in the nature of a penalty

non: no

non acceptavit: he or she did not accept

non accrevit infra sex annos: it did not accrue within six years (i.e., it is beyond the statute of limitations)

non assumpsit [he or she did not undertake]: he or she did not promise [to do it] (i.e., a general denial in an action of *assumpsit*)

non bis in idem [not twice for the same thing]: the legal principle of double jeopardy

non causa pro causa or **non causa** [non-cause for cause]: the fallacy of false cause (i.e., a conclusion based on a false or irrelevant proposition)

non cepit: he or she did not take

non cepit modo et forma: he or she did not take in manner and form

non compos mentis: not of sound mind

non concessit: he or she did not grant

non constat: it is not settled; it is not certain or agreed (cf., **non sequitur**)

non culpabilis (non cul.): not guilty

non damnificatus: not injured

non datur tertium [no third is given]: there is no third choice

non demiset or **non demisit:** he or she did not demise (i.e., grant or convey by will or by lease)

non detinet: he or she did not detain

non ens (pl. **non entia**) [the nonexistent]: a nonentity

non est: it is not

non est factum [it is not done]: he or she did not do it

non est inventus or **non est:** he or she has not been found (i.e., a statement by a sheriff on return of a writ of arrest when the defendant is not to be found)

non est meus actus: it is not my act

non fecit: he or she did not make it (i.e., a denial in a case of *assumpsit*)

non impedivit: he or she did not impede or hinder

non infregit conventionem: he or she did not break the contract

non interfui: I was not present

non jam: no longer

non juridicus: non-judicial; not legal

non lacessitus: unprovoked

non legitimus: unconstitutional

non libet: it is not pleasing

non licet (n.l. or **non lic.):** it is not permitted

non liquet (n.l. or **non liq.):** it is not clear; it is not proven

non memini: I do not remember

non misit breve: he or she has not sent the writ

non nominatus (n.n.) [not having been named]: an unidentified person

non numeratae pecuniae: of monies not paid

non obstante (non obs.): notwithstanding

non obstante veredicto (n.o.v.): notwithstanding the verdict (i.e., a verdict for the plaintiff setting aside a verdict for the defendant)

non omittas: do not omit

non placet [it does not please]: a negative vote

non possumus: we cannot (i.e., a statement expressing inability to act in a matter)

non prosequitur (non pros.): he does not prosecute (i.e., a judgment where the plaintiff does not appear)

non sanae mentis: not of sane or sound mind

non sequitur (non seq.): it does not follow (cf., **non constat**)

non sine causa [not without cause]: with good reason
non submissit: he or she did not submit
non sui juris: not of one's own right (i.e., not of legal age or capacity)
non sum informatus: I am not informed
non tenent insimul: they do not hold together (i.e., a denial of joint tenancy)
non ultra petita: not beyond the request
non utendo: by nonuse
non valentia agere: inability to sue
non vult contendere: he or she will not contest (i.e., a plea of no contest)
nondum editus: unpublished
nondum natus: unborn
norma: pattern; rule; standard
nostro periculo: at our own risk
nostrum: ours
nota: a note; a charter or deed
nota bene (N.B. or **n.b.)** [note well]: take notice
notitia: a notice
nova debita: newly contracted debts
novae tabulae [new ledgers]: a cancellation of debts
novalis: a cultivated field
noverca: a stepmother
noverint universi per praesentes: know all men by these presents (i.e., one of the traditional opening lines of a deed) (see also, **pateat universis per praesentes**)
novissima verba [the final words]: a person's last words
novitas: newness; novelty
novus: new
novus homo: a new man (i.e., a person pardoned of a crime)
nox (pl. **noctes**): night
nuda possessio: mere possession
nudis verbis: in plain words
nudum officium: the bare office (i.e., a position without the usual emoluments)

nudum pactum: a bare pact or agreement (i.e., a pact or agreement not legally 'clothed' by law, hence unenforceable and invalid)
nudus: bare; naked
nugae: trifles; nonsense
nulla bona: no goods; no effects
nulla persona: no person
nulli secundus: second to none
nullius filius [nobody's son]: an illegitimate son; a bastard child
nullum arbitrium: no decision; no award
nullum datum: no date
nullum est erratum: there is no error (in the record)
nullum fecerunt arbitrium: they never submitted to arbitration
nullus: no; none; not any; also, no person
nullus juris: of no legal force
numerata pecunia [money counted]: money paid by count (as opposed to being weighed)
numero (No. or **no.):** in number; by number; to the number of
numerus: number
numerus clasus [closed number]: a fixed quantity; a quota
nummo sestertio: for a mere trifle (see also, **sestertio nummo**)
nummus: money (i.e., coin)
nunc: now
nunc pro tunc: now for then; retroactive (i.e., designating a delayed action that takes effect as if it were done at the proper time)
nunquam: never
nunquam indebitatus: never indebted (i.e., a plea denying indebtedness to the plaintiff)
nuntiatio: proclamation; a declaration or formal protest
nuntium: message; news
nuntius (f. nuntia): a messenger
nuper obiit: lately deceased
nupta: married
nuptiae: marriage
nuptiae secundae: a second marriage

nuptiales tabulae: a marriage record
nurus: a daughter-in-law
nutans: nodding (in approval)

O

ob: for; on account of; by reason of
ob continentiam delicti: by reason of a connection to the crime
ob contingentiam: by reason of relationship; on account of connection
ob defectum haeredis: on account of a failure (lack) of heirs
ob rem: to the purpose; with advantage; for gain
ob turpem causam: on account of a base or immoral cause (i.e., for immoral consideration)
obaeratus: burdened by debt; a debtor
obiit or **obit (ob.):** he or she died
obiit sine prole (ob. s.p.): he or she died without issue
obiter (ob.) [in passing]**:** by the way; incidentally
obiter dictum (ob. dict.; pl. **obiter dicta)** [said in passing]**:** an incidental remark; a casual comment or unofficial expression of opinion (i.e., a comment not central to or bearing directly upon the case)
objeratus: a debtor who was obliged to work for a creditor to discharge a debt or for the period of indenture
objurgatio: blaming; reproving; chiding
oblatio (pl. **oblationes**)**:** a tender of payment or performance due
obligatio: an obligation; a legal bond
obligatio civilis: a legally enforcible obligation, such as a contract obligation
obligatio ex contractu or **obligatio contractu:** a contractual obligation
obligatio ex delicto or **obligatio ex maleficio:** an obligation arising from an offense against a person or that person's property
obligatio litterarum or **obligatio litteris** or **obligatio literis:** a written contract

obligatio verborum: a verbal or spoken obligation (see also, **verborum obligatio**)
obscenus: impure; indecent; obscene
obscuro loco natus: of unknown origin
obscurus: dark; dull; obscure
observandum (pl. **observanda**): a thing to be observed
obsignator: a witness to a will
obsoletus [worn out]: obsolete; out of date
obstetrix: a midwife
obtorto collo [by the throat]: compelled to appear in court
occasio: (leg.) a hindrance or trouble; a tribute; also, vexatious litigation
occasio legis: conditions that generated the law
occidentalis: occidental; western
occupans: an occupant
occupatus: busy; engaged
octo tales [eight of such]: a summons to fill vacancies on a jury
oculatus testis: an eyewitness
odium: hatred; dislike
odor lucri [the smell of profit]: the expectation of gain
offensio: offense
officialis: official; approved
officium [sense of duty]: an office; a dutiful act
omissis omnibus aliis negotiis: laying aside all other business
omittit (**om.**; pl. **omittant**): it omits
omne or **omnis:** every; all; everything
omne die (**o.d.** or **omn. die**): all day; every day
omne quod in se erat [all that one had in his or her power]: he or she did everything that he or she could do
omne scibile: everything knowable
omnes ad unum [all to a person]: unanimous
omni ex parte: from every part (i.e., every point of view)
omni exceptione(s) major(es): beyond all exception(s); beyond all criticism
omnia performavit: he or she has done all
omnibus rebus: in every respect
omnis (**omn.**): all; every

omnium bonorum: of all goods or effects
onera realia: real burdens (i.e., an encumbrance affecting land)
onerari non: ought not to be burdened; ought not to be charged (with a crime)
oneratio: a cargo or lading
oneris ferendi: of bearing a burden
onus: a burden; an obligation
onus probandi: the burden of proof
ope et consilio: with aid and counsel (i.e., an accessory to the crime)
ope exceptionis: by force of exception
ope legis: by aid or disposition of the law
opere citato (op. cit. or o.c.): in the work cited
oportet [it behooves]: it is necessary
opposuit natura [nature has opposed]: it is contrary to nature
optato: according to one's wish
optima fide: in the best faith
optime: very well
optimo jure: with full right
optimus (opt.): the best
opus (op.; pl. opera): a work; labor; need; occasion; also, a musical composition
opus est: it is necessary
opus manificum: manual labor
opus manufactum: manufactured
oratio obliqua: an indirect speech or discourse; also, a second-hand report (i.e., hearsay)
orbis: ring; circle
orbis terrarum: the world
ordinandi lex: procedural law
ordinarius: ordinary
ordinatum est: it is ordered; so ordered
ordine [in turn]: in due order
ordinis beneficium [the benefit of order]: the right of the surety to require the creditor to exhaust the resources of the debtor first before the surety assumed liability for the debt (see also, **beneficium ordinis**)

ordo inversus (ord. inv.): inverted order (i.e., in inverse order)
ore tenus: by word of mouth; verbally
orientalis: oriental; eastern
ostiatim: from door to door (i.e., from house to house)

P

pacta conventa [the conditions agreed upon]: a diplomatic agreement
pactio: pact; contract; treaty
pactum (pact.; pl. **pacta)** [pact]: a contract or agreement
pactum de non cedendo: an agreement not to yield (i.e., transfer a right or claim)
pactum de non petendo: an agreement not to seek
pactum donationis: an agreement to give in donation
pactum illicitum: an unlawful or illegal contract or agreement
pactum vestitum: an enforceable contract or agreement
panacea: a cure-all
par: equal
par conditio creditorum: the equal treatment of creditors, prior to declaring bankruptcy (i.e., an agreement by creditors for less of what is owed in exchange for immediate payment of the debt)
par delictum: equal wrong; equal guilt
par oneri: equal to the burden
parabilis: procurable
paragium: equality of condition
paraphernalia or **bona paraphernalia:** separate goods, specifically the separate property of the wife beyond her dowry
paratum habeo [I have ready]: the defendant is ready to bring to court
paratus: prepared; ready
parens [pl. **parentes**]: a parent; a relative
parens patriae [parent of the country]: state guardianship over children and the disabled
parentalis: parental
pares: one's peers
pares cum paribus: equals with equals

pares regni: peers of the realm

pari causa: in a like or similar case; in similar conditions (see also, **in pari causa**)

pari delicto [in equal fault]: equally at fault; guilty to the same extent (see also, **in pari delicto**)

pari materia [of the same matter]: in an analogous case (i.e., as a matter of legal precedent) (see also, **in pari materia**)

pari passu [at an equal step or pace]: on equal footing; proportionally; equally; without partiality (see also, **in pari passu**)

pari ratione: for the equal reason; by a like mode of reasoning (see also, **in pari ratione**)

paries communis: a common wall

parium judicium [the judgment of equals]: the right of trial by a jury of one's peers

pars (pl. **partes**): part; a party

pars adversa: the opposite party

pars contractus: part of the contract

pars ejusdem negotii: part of the same business transaction

pars fundi: part of the ground or soil (see also, **partes soli**)

pars gravata: an aggrieved party

pars judicis: the duty of the judge

pars pro toto: a part for the whole (as opposed to **totum pro parte**)

pars rationabilis: a reasonable part

parte inaudita: one side being unheard

parte non comparente: a party not having appeared

partes aequales (p.ae. or **pt. aeq.):** in equal parts (see also, **in partes aequales**)

partes soli: parts of the ground or soil (see also, **pars fundi**)

particeps criminis: a party to the crime (i.e., an accomplice)

particeps fraudis: a partner in fraud

particula: a parcel of land

partim (p.): in part

partitio: a division; partition

partitus: divided

partus: birth; offspring; issue

parum: too little; not enough

parva proditio: petty treason

parvus (parv.): small

Pascha: Easter

passagium [passage]: a voyage

passim (pass.): here and there; throughout (as in references found throughout the pages of a book)

pateat universis per praesentes: let it be open to all men by these presents (i.e., one of the traditional opening lines of a deed) (see also, **noverint universi per praesentes**)

patens: open; accessible; manifest

pater: father

pater familias or **paterfamilias:** the father of a family; the head of a household

pater patriae: father of the nation

patiens: the patient; also, a passive party to the action

patria: native land; country

patria potestas: power of the father (e.g., exercising parental rights concerning minor children)

patrimonium: inherited property

patrina: a godmother (see also, **matima** or **matrina**)

patrinus: a godfather

patruus: a paternal uncle (i.e., father's brother) (cf., **avunculus**)

paucus: few

paulatim: little by little

pauperies: poverty; impoverishment

pax: peace

Pax Romana: Roman peace

peculium: savings; also, private property

pecunia [cattle]: money; wealth; also, property

pecunia mutua: a loan

pecunia non numerata: money not paid

pecunia numerata: counted money (i.e., money given in payment of a debt)

pede pulverosus [dusty foot]: a huckster

pedes: going by foot

pedibus: by foot; by land
pedis possessio: a foothold (i.e., actual possession)
pendens (pend.): weighing; pending; hanging
pendente lite: pending the suit; also, during the trial (see also, **lite pendente**)
pendere filo: to hang by a thread
pendulus [hanging]: undecided
pene or **paene:** almost
penes: in possession of; belonging to
penes se esse: to be in one's senses
penuria testium: a scarcity of witnesses
per: by; through
per accidens: by accident; by chance
per alluvionem: by alluvium
per ambages: in a secret manner; by evasion
per annum (p.a.) [by the year]: annually
per aversionem: by bulk (i.e., without counting or measuring)
per capita [by the head]: for each individual (as opposed to **per stirpes**)
per centum (per cent. or **p.c.** or **pct.):** by the hundred (i.e., percentage)
per consequens: by consequence; consequently
per contra: on the contrary
per corpus: by the body
per curiam: by the court as a whole
per defaltam: by default
per diem: by the day; daily (see also, **in diem**)
per eundem: by the same (viz., by the same judge)
per expressum: expressly; in direct terms
per extensum: at length
per formam doni: by the form of the gift
per fraudem: by fraud
per hominem stare: occurring through the fault of someone
per horam [by the hour]: for an hour
per incuriam [through want of care]: through carelessness; by neglect

per infortunium: by accident or misadventure
per interim: in the meantime
per jocum: in jest
per legem terrae [by the law of the land]: by due process of law
per librum: by the book
per membra curiae: by members of the court
per mensem (per mens.): by the month; monthly; for each month
per metas et bundas: by metes and bounds
per mille (per mil.): by the thousand
per minas: by threats
per modum exceptionis: by way of exception
per modum gratiae: by an act of favor
per modum justitiae: by way of justice
per modum poenae: by way of punishment (i.e., as a penalty)
per nomen: by name
per obliqua or **per obliquum:** obliquely; indirectly; sideways
per omnes (per omn.): by all; by all the judges
per os (p.o.): by mouth; orally
per pares: by one's peers
per plegium: by pledge (i.e., out on bail)
per praecepta juris: according to the rules of law
per procurationem (p.p. or **per. pro.):** by proxy; by the action of
per quod: by which; through which; whereby
per saltum (per salt.): by a leap; all at one; without an intermediate step (i.e., passing over certain proceedings)
per sceptrum [by the scepter]: by authority
per se: by or in itself; it alone; intrinsically
per singulos dies: day by day; every day
per stirpes (per stirp.) [by families]: by representation; by root and stock (i.e., property in relation to inheritance) (as opposed to **per capita**)
per subsequens matrimonium: by subsequent marriage
per tacitam reconventionem: by a tacit renewal of the contract

per testes: by witnesses
per totam curiam (per tot. cur.): by the full court (i.e., unanimously)
per universitatem: by the whole; in its entirety
per vadium: by pledge
per verba de futuro: by words of the future (i.e., a promise)
per verba de praesenti: by words of the present (i.e., a declaration)
per viam: by way of
per vicem: by turns; alternately
per vices: by retaliation; reciprocally
per vim: by force; forcibly
per vim legis: by force of law
per visum juratorum: by the viewing of the jury
percepti sed non consumpti: fruits gathered but not consumed
periculum: peril; risk; danger
peritus: skilled
perjurium [false swearing]**:** perjury
perjurosus: perjured
permissu: by permission
persona [a mask worn by stage players]**:** a person or personality
persona designata: a person individually not as a member of a class
persona dignior: the more worthy or suitable person
persona ficta: a fictitious person
persona grata (p.g.): an acceptable person
persona non grata (p.n.g.): an unacceptable person
persona proposita: the person proposed (see also, **propositus**)
personae miserabiles: poor and destitute persons
personali exceptione: by personal exception
personali objectione: by personal objection
personam: in the person (see also, **in personam**)
pessima fides: the worst faith
pessimi exempli: of the worst example
petitio principii: begging the question

petitor: a plaintiff
Philosophiae Doctor (Ph.D.): Doctor of Philosophy
phrenesis: madness; frenzy
pietas: piety; filial affection
pignus: a pledge
pinxit (pinx. or **pxt.):** he or she painted it
pirata (pl. **piratis):** pirate
pius: pious; reverent; dutiful
placebo: I will please (i.e., a prescription given to please a patient)
placet [it pleases]: it is agreed
placita communia: common pleas (i.e., civil actions between individuals) (see also, **communia placita**)
placitum (pl. **placita):** a plea; a decree; also, a judicial decision
planum facere: to make plain; to explain
plaustrum: wagon; cart
plebs: people
plena aetas: of full age
plena fides: full faith; full credit
plena forisfactura: complete forfeiture (of one's possessions)
plena potestas: full or plenary power
plena probatio: full proof (i.e., proof by two or more witnesses) (see also, **probatio plena**)
plena sensu: a fuller sense
plene administravit: he or she has fully administered
plene administravit praeter: he or she has fully administered, except
plene computavit: he or she has fully accounted
pleno jure: with full right or authority
plenum dominium: full dominion (i.e., the right of owners to use their property as they deem fit)
plenus: plenty; full; complete
plexus: a network
pluralis (pl.): plural
pluris petitio: a claim for more than is due
plus: more

plus petitio: requesting too much (i.e., a claim for more than is due)

plus quam tolerabile: more than can be endured

poena [pain]**:** penalty; punishment

poena arbitraria: arbitrary punishment (i.e., left to the discretion of the judge)

poena corporalis: corporal punishment

poena extraordinaria: unusual punishments (i.e., those set at the discretion of the judge)

poena ordinaria: usual punishments (i.e., those fixed or attached to specified crimes)

poena pecuniaria: a pecuniary punishment

poenalis: penal

pondere, numero, et mensura: by weight, number, and measure

ponderosus: heavy; weighty

popularis: popular (i.e., belonging to the people)

porta: a gate

portentus: indicated; predicted; foretold

portio: part; portion; section

portorium circumvectionis: port customs; transit duties

positus: position; place

posse [possibility]**:** to be able; to be possible

posse comitatus [the power of the county]**:** a sheriff's posse

possessio: possession; detention

possessio bona fide: possession in good faith

possessio mala fide: possession in bad faith

possessio pedis: possession by occupation

possidere: to possess a thing

possumus: we can; we are able

post (p.): after; later; also, a later page or line of text

post causam cognitam [after the cause has been made known]**:** after investigation

post contractum debitum: after debt has been contracted

post diem: after the (appointed) day

post disseisin: after being dispossessed (i.e., for a second time)

post facto: after the fact (see also, **ex post facto**)
post factum or **postfactum** [after the fact]: an act done after something else has already taken place
post funera natus: a posthumous child
post hoc: after this; subsequently
post hoc ergo propter hoc [after this, therefore because of this]: a fallacy of cause and effect
post litem motam: after the litigation began
post meridianus: after midday; in the afternoons
post meridiem (P.M. or **p.m.):** after noon
post mortem or **postmortem:** after death
post natus: born after
post obitum (post obit.): after death; also, taking effect after someone's death
post partum or **postpartum:** after birth
post postscriptum (P.P.S. or **PPS):** an additional postscript
post prolem suscitatam: after issue is born
post quem: after which (i.e., the starting point, as opposed to **ante quem**) (see also, **ad quem**)
post scriptum or **postscriptum (P.S.** or **PS):** written after; a postscript
post tantum tempus: after so long a time
post terminum: after the term
postea: thereafter; afterward (i.e., a statement giving an account of the proceedings)
posterior: at the rear; the rear part
postulatio actiones: a petition to bring a legal action or suit
postulatus: a legal complaint or suit
potens: strong; powerful
potentatus: political power
potenter: powerfully
potentia: power; might
potestas: power; dominion
potestas gladii: the power of the sword
potestas maritalis: powers vested by virtue of marriage
potestas res cognoscendi: the power of the recognition of things

prae manu: at hand; on hand

praecepta: precepts; commands; also, maxims

praecipe [a command]: a writ commanding a person to do some act or to show cause to be excused from acting

praecipe quod reddat: command him or her to return

praeclarus: bright; illustrious; splendid; noble; also, famous

praecox: premature

praeda: plunder; booty

praeda bellica: spoils of war (i.e., goods or property seized during war)

praedictus (praed. or **praedict.):** aforementioned; aforesaid

praedium [land]: landed property; a farm; an estate

praedium rusticum: a country estate

praedium urbanum: an urban tenement; a business estate

praedo (pl. **praedones**): a robber

praefatus (praef. or **praefat.):** aforesaid

praefectus urbi: an urban prefect (i.e., a Roman senator charged with keeping law and order in Rome)

praejudicium: an objection

praemium or **premium:** a reward

praemunire: to forewarn

praenomen: a first name

praeparatus (praep.): prepared

praepositus negotiis: a person who manages the business of another

praescriptio longi temporis: an objection on the grounds of prescriptive right (i.e., long-term possession)

praescriptis verbis: in the words before written (i.e., the words defining the issue at hand)

praesens in curia: present in court

praesentia animi: presence of mind

praeses: a provincial governor; the president of a college or university

praestare: to perform an obligation

praeter dotem: over and above the dowry

praeter intentionem: beyond the intention

praeter jus: beyond the law

praeter legem: beyond the law (i.e., the use of equity to fill gaps in the law)

praeteritus: past; former

prava consuetudo: a bad, evil, or illegal custom (see also, **mos pravus**)

pravus: crooked; depraved

precarium: permission to occupy or use property, such as in a lease

precludi non debet: he or she ought not to be barred

premium or **praemium:** a reward

presumptio juris: a legal presumption

presumptus: taken for granted; presumed

pretermit: to disregard or omit

pretium: a price

pretium affectionis [the price of affection]: the sentimental value of a thing distinct from its market value

pretium periculi: an insurance premium

pretium puellae [the price of a maiden]: the marriage price demanded by a young woman's guardian

pridie: on the previous day

prima facie [at first appearance]: at first glance (i.e., a judgment based on the first impression)

prima luce (prim. luc.): at first light (i.e., early in the morning)

primae impressionis: of the first impression (i.e., a case without precedent)

primitiae: the first fruits

primo [in the first place]: first; first of all

primo fronte: at first sight

primo intuiti: at the first glance

primo loco: in the first place

primo venienti: to the person who comes first

primogenitus: the firstborn; also, the eldest child (see also, **anecius**)

primum (prim.): first

primum non nocere: first, to do no harm

primus: the first

primus inter pares: first among equals

princeps: principal; first; also, a prince

principia: principles; maxims

principium: the beginning

prior: coming before; ahead (in time)

prior petens: the person first applying

priori petenti: to the first person applying

pristinus: former; earlier

prius: coming before, prior, previous

privati juris: of private right (see also, **juris privati**)

privatim: privately; in private; also, in private life (as opposed to **publice**)

privilegium: a special right or privilege

privilegium clericale: clerical privilege (see also, **clericale privilegium**)

privilegium de non appellando: the privilege of not appealing

pro: for; before; on behalf of; according to

pro bono et malo: for good and ill

pro bono publico [for the public good]: legal services provided free of charge (also known as **pro bono**)

pro confesso [for the confession]: as confessed; also, as if confessed

pro consilio impenso: for counsel given

pro convicto: as convicted

pro defectu justitiae: for want of justice

pro defendente (pro def.): for the defendant

pro domo: for home (i.e., for one's family)

pro donato: as a gift

pro dote: as a dowry

pro et contra: for and against

pro et durante: for and during

pro forma: as a matter of form; formally

pro hac vice (p.h.v.): for this occasion

pro homine: in or on behalf of humanity; also, in favor of a specific person

pro illa vice: for that turn
pro indefenso: as undefended (i.e., making no defense)
pro indiviso: as undivided (i.e., in common or held jointly)
pro interesse suo: to the extent of his or her interest
pro laesione fidei: for breach of faith
pro loco et tempore: for the place and time
pro mea parte [for my part]**:** to the best of my ability
pro modo admissi: according to the manner of the offense
pro mutuum: as if a loan
pro non scripto: as though not written
pro nunc: for now
pro opera et labore: for service and labor
pro parte: partly; in part
pro parte virili: for one's own share (see also, **pro virili**)
pro patria: for one's country
pro portione: in proportion
pro posse suo: to the extent of his or her own power or ability
pro praemio: for a recompense; for a reward
pro privato commodo: for private convenience
pro querente (pro quer.): for the plaintiff
pro rata [according to rate]**:** in proportion; proportionally
pro rata itineris: for the proportion of the voyage or journey
pro ratione aetatis (pro rat. aet.): according to age
pro re: according to circumstance
pro re nata (p.r.n.): according to the present circumstance(s); as needed (see also, **e re nata**)
pro salute animae: for the safety of the soul
pro salute animarum: for the safety of their souls
pro se: for oneself; personally; in person
pro socio: on behalf of a partner
pro solido: for the whole; as one
pro sua parte: to the best of one's ability
pro suo: for one's own
pro tanto: for so much; to that extent
pro tempore (p.t. or **pro tem.):** for a time; temporarily; for the time being

pro tribunali: before the judge

pro verbo [according to the word]: literally

pro veritate: for the truth; as true

pro virili: for one's own share (see also, **pro parte virili**)

proavia: a great-grandmother

proavus: a great-grandfather

probabilis causa litigandi: a probable ground for legal action

probatio [a proving]: trial; examination; also, proof (by demonstration)

probatio mortua [dead proof]: proof by writings, deeds, objects, etc.

probatio plena: full proof (i.e., proof by two or more witnesses) (see also, **plena probatio**)

probatio probata [a proved proof]: a proof not open to further debate

probatio semiplena [half proof]: proof by one witness only

probatio viva [living proof]: proof by the mouth or testimony of living witnesses

probatum est: it has been proven

probatus: approved; commended; proved

probi et legales homines: good and lawful men (i.e., persons competent to serve on a jury)

probus et legalis homo: a good and lawful man (i.e., a person competent to serve on a jury)

procax: shameless

procedendo: proceeding

procurator: a proctor (i.e., an agent or other designated person acting on one's behalf, such as an attorney)

procurator in rem suam: the proctor in his own affair (i.e., the attorney in one's own case)

procurator negotiorum: a proctor, such as an agent or attorney, who manages another's business affairs

profert: he produces

profundus: profound; deep-seated

prope: near; close by

prolicidum: the destruction of human offspring

propinquitas: closeness

propositum: resolution

propositus (pl. **propositi**): an ancestor through whom descent is traced to establish a person's right or legal claim, such as an inheritance (see also, **persona proposita**)

propria or **proprius:** one's own; also, proper; appropriate; suitable

propria manu: by one's own hand

propria persona: in one's own person (see also, **in propria persona**)

proprietas: property

propriis manibus: by one's own hands

proprio jure: by one's own right

proprio motu: by one's own initiative

proprio nomine: in one's own name

proprio vigore: by its own power or force

proprius or **propria:** one's own; also, proper; appropriate; suitable

propter: for; on account of

propter affectum: on account of disposition or interest (i.e., a challenge to a juror because of potential bias)

propter commodum curiae: for the advantage of the court

propter curam et culturam: for care and cultivation

propter defectum: on account of a defect or incapacity

propter defectum sanguinis: on account of a lack of blood kin (i.e., a lack of heirs)

propter delictum: for offense; on account of a crime (viz., the dismissal of a juror because of a past felony conviction)

propter hoc: on account of this

propter impotentiam: by reason of impotence

propter majorem securitatem: for the sake of greater security

propter privilegium: on account of privilege

prospectus [outlook]: a document that outlines a proposed business venture or investment opportunity

prosum: to be useful; to benefit someone or something

protestando: protesting

provisio [foresight]: a condition or stipulation
provisione legis: by provision of the law
provisione tenus: to the extent of the provision
proviso [it being provided]: condition, limitation, or stipulation
provocatio: an appeal to a higher court
proximo (prox.): the next; of or in the following [month]
proximo mense (prox. m.): the next month; in the following month
proximus: closest or nearest; also, neighbor; neighboring
proximus pubertati: nearing puberty
prudentia: prudence; discretion
puberes: minors having attained the age of puberty
pubertas: puberty
publica vindicta: the defense of the public
publice: publicly; in public; also, in public life (as opposed to **privatim**)
publici juris: of public right (i.e., according to common or public use) (see also, **juris publici**)
publicus: public
puella: girl; a female youth
puer: boy; a male youth
pueritia: childhood
puerperium: childbirth; labor
pugna: a fight
punctatim: point for point
punctum (pl. **puncta**): a point or spot; a moment
punctum temporis: a point of time; the shortest space of time
Punica fides [Punic faith]: treachery
pusillus: puny; petty
pyritegium [cover fire]: curfew; the curfew bell (see also, **ignitegium**)

Q

qua: which; as; as far as; also, in the character of
quacumque: in whatever way

quacumque via data: whichever way it is taken
quadrans: a quarter; a fourth part
quadruplex: quadruple
quae est eadem: which is the same
quae plura: what more
quae sequuntur personam: which follow the person
quae supra scripta est: which was written above (i.e., previously written)
quae vide (qq.v.): (pl.) which see
quaeque: each; every
quaere or **quare (qu.)** [wherefore]: why; for what reason; also, query; inquire; a question
quaerens or **querens:** the plaintiff or complainant
quaeritur [it is sought]: the question arises
quaesta: an inquest or inquiry
quaestio or **questio:** a question; an inquiry; also, a problem
quaestio facti: a question of fact
quaestio juris: a question of law
quaestio perpetua (pl. **quaestiones perpetuae**): perpetual inquiry (i.e., a standing court of justice)
quaestio vexata (pl. **quaestiones vexatae**): a vexed or vexing question (i.e., a point often debated though never resolved) (see also, **vexata quaestio**)
quaestio voluntatis: a question of intention
quaestus [what is acquired]: profit; gain; also, land acquired through labor or purchase, not through hereditary right (as opposed to **haereditas**)
quam: as much as; than
quamdiu: as long as; so long as; also, how long
quamdiu se bene gesserit: as long as one conducts him- or herself properly (i.e., during good behavior)
quamprimum [forthwith]: as soon as possible
quando acciderint: when assets come into hand
quandocunque: at whatever time; at any time
quandocunque defecerit: at whatever time he or she died

quanti minoris [how much lesser]: an action to reduce retroactively the price of a thing sold that was found to be somehow defective

quantum [as much as]: how much; of what size or amount

quantum damnificatus: how much damage?

quantum et quale: how much and of what kind? (i.e., the extent and quality)

quantum meruit: as much as it is worth (i.e., the amount that is deserved)

quantum nunc valent: how much are they now worth? (e.g., lands or properties) (see also, **quid valet nunc**)

quantum scio: as far as I know

quantum valebant: as much as they were worth

quantus: how much; how great; how many; also, as much as

quaque (qq.): each; every

quare or **quaere (qu.)** [wherefore]: why; for what reason; also, query; inquire; a question

quare clausum fregit (q.c.f.) [wherefore he or she broke the close]: the charge of trespassing

quare ejecit infra terminum: wherefore he ejected [a tenant] during or within the term

quare executionem non (q.e.n.): why execution should not be issued

quare impedit?: why does he or she hinder?; also, because he or she hinders

quare obstruxit?: why does he or she obstruct?; also, because he or she obstructs

quarta pars: a quarter part; one-quarter

quarto die post: the fourth day after

quartus: the fourth

quarum or **quorum:** of which; of whom (i.e., the minimum number of members legally present to transact business or a legal proceeding)

quasi: as if; as though; as it were; almost

quasi dicas: as though you were to say

quasi dicat (q.d.): as if one should say; also, as much as to say

quasi dictum (q.d.): as if stated; as if said

quasi dixisset: as if he or she had said

quasi in rem: as if against a thing (i.e., legal action regarding property not persons)

quatuor pedibus currit [it runs on four feet]: it is an analogous case (i.e., the principle applies here as well)

querela or **querella** (pl. **querelae** or **querellae**): bill of complaint; also, a court action

querens or **quaerens:** the plaintiff or complainant

querimonia: a grievance or complaint

querulus: plaintive; complaining

questa: an inquest or inquiry

questus: a complaint

questus est nobis: he or she has complained to us (i.e., regarding nuisance or damage caused by a neighbor)

qui: who

qui tam (q.t.): who so; who as well (i.e., an action to recover, as brought by an informer in conjunction with the state)

quia: because; whereas

quia ita lex scripta est: because the law is so written (viz., the text of a law or statute)

quia non possum: that I cannot; because I cannot

quia possum: that I can; because I can

quia timet: because he or she fears

quicquid praecipies: whatever you may enjoin

quid actum est: what has been done

quid ergo?: why then?

quid faciendum: what is to be done

quid juratum est or **quid juravit:** what has been sworn

quid juris?: what is the law?

quid pro quo [this for that]: something given in return for a favor

quid valet nunc: what it is now worth (see also, **quantum nunc valent**)

quidam [somebody]: a person known though unnamed

quiete clamantia: a quitclaim

quietus: (leg.) freed or acquitted; also, a written discharge or release

quietus redditus: a quit rent (i.e., paid in lieu of military service)

quilibet: whoever will

quo: by what?; with what?

quo animo? [with what mind?]: with what spirit or intent?

quo jure?: by what right?

quo modo? or **quomodo?:** by what means?; in what way?

quo modo et quando [in what mode and time]: by what manner and time

quo warranto [by what warrant]: by what right or authority

quoad: as far as

quoad hoc [as to this]: as far as this goes; as regards this particular matter

quoad maritum: as concerns the husband

quoad minus: as to the lesser matter

quoad mobilia: as concerns the movables

quoad potest: to the extent of one's powers

quoad reliquum: as regards the remainder (i.e., the remaining balance)

quoad valet seipsum [as regards its real value]: so far as it is worth

quoad valorem [as regards the value]: to the extent of the value

quod: which; that; because

quod billa cassetur or **billa cassetur** [that the bill be quashed]: let the bill or case be set aside (i.e., discontinued) (see also, **cassetur billa**)

quod computet: that he or she account (i.e., an audit of the books)

quod curia concessit: which the court granted

quod erat demonstrandum (Q.E.D. or **q.e.d.**): which was to be demonstrated or shown

quod erat faciendum (Q.E.F. or **q.e.f.**): which was to be done

quod est (q.e.): which is

quod nota (q.n.): which note; which mark

quod plerumque fit: what usually happens

quod recuperet: that the plaintiff recover (e.g., debt or damages)
quod sciam: as far as I know
quod superest [what is left over]: as to what remains; as for the rest
quod ultra: as to the rest
quod vide (q.v.): (sing.) which see
quodlibet [what you please]: a subtle or debatable point
quomodo: in what manner or way
quondam [former]: formerly; at times
quoque (qq.): also; too
quorum or **quarum:** of which; of whom (i.e., the minimum number of members legally present to transact business or a legal proceeding)
quota: a share or proportion
quotannis: annually
quotidie or **quotidianus** (**quot.** or **quotid.**): daily; every day
quousque: how long; how far
quovis modo: in whatever manner

R

rapina: robbery
raptus: rape
rata [rate]: an individual share
ratio: reason; rationale; also, ratio; proportion
ratio agendi: the reason or rationale for acting
ratio cognoscendi: the reason for or means of knowing
ratio decidendi: the reason or rationale for deciding (i.e., the argument or logical process)
ratio essendi: the reason for the existence of a thing
ratio juris: judicial reason
ratio legis: legal reason (i.e., the reason for a law or statute)
ratio naturalis or **naturalis ratio:** natural reason
ratio pertinens: a reason pertaining to the question
ratio scripta: written reason (viz., a document that explains a ruling)

ratio summa: supreme reason
ratiocinatio: reasoning
rationabile estoverium: reasonable necessaries (i.e., alimony)
rationabilis: reasonable
rationarium: a statistical account
ratione contractus: on account of the contract
ratione delicti: on account of the crime
ratione domicilii: by reason or on account of domicile
ratione loci: by reason of locality
ratione materiae: by reason of the matter at hand
ratione personae: by reason of the person
ratione privilegii: on account of privilege
ratione soli: by reason or on account of land or soil
ratione suspecti judicis: on account of the judge being suspected
ratione tenurae: by reason of tenure
ratum: deemed as valid
re: in the matter of; regarding; concerning (see also, **in re**)
re infecta: the business being unfinished
re vera or **revera:** in truth; in fact
rebus ipsis et factis: by the facts and circumstances themselves
rebus sic stantibus: things thus standing (i.e., the circumstances being what they are)
recto folio or **recto (r.):** on the right-hand page of a book (i.e., the right-hand page)
rectus: straight; right; correct
rectus in curia: upright in court (i.e., blameless)
reddendo singula singulis: each term being rendered singly
reddendum: a clause in a lease that concerns rent or payment
redditus or **reditus** [a thing rendered or returned]: rent (variously paid)
redemptiones: ransom; redemption; also, heavy fines
reditus albi [white rent or return]: rent payable in money
reditus mobilis [movable rent or return]: a variable rent or return
reditus nigri [black rent or return]: rent payable in service or in kind; also, blackmail

reductio: a reduction

reductio ad absurdum: reduction to the absurd (in logic, to point out the falsity of an opponent's argument by showing the absurdity of its logical conclusions)

referendum [being referred]: a legislative decision referred to the voters for approval

reformatio in melius: reform or change for the better

reformatio in pejus: reform or change for the worse

regalia: royal rights (see also, **jura regalia**)

regalis or **regius:** royal

regia via: a royal highway; a public road (see also, **via regia**)

regimen: guidance; direction

regina (R.): a queen

registrarius: a notary public

regium donum: a royal gift or grant

regius or **regalis:** royal

regula: rule; pattern; standard

regulae juris: rules of law (i.e., a collection of general legal principles)

rei: of a thing

rei publicae causa: for political reasons

relicta or **relictus:** widowed (i.e., a surviving spouse)

relicta verificatione: his or her plea being abandoned

reliqua: a balance of account

reliquum or **reliquus (reli.** or **reliq.):** the rest; the remaining; the remainder

remittitur: it is remitted or sent back (e.g., a lessening of the judgment for damages to avoid further appeal) (see also, **additur**)

remittitur damnum: the damage is remitted

remotis testibus: the witnesses being absent

renovo: to renew

reo absente: the defendant being absent (see also, **absente reo**)

reo praesente: the defendant being present

repertorium (pl. **repertoria**): a catalog

res (pl. **res**): a thing, matter, or circumstance; a cause or action

res adjudicata [a matter adjudged]: a judgment; a decided case (see also, **res judicata**)

res aliena: the property belonging to another

res alienari prohibita: a thing that cannot be alienated

res caduca [a fallen thing]: an escheat (i.e., property that has been lost or abandoned and therefore fallen into the possession of the state)

res communes: things held for common or public use

res controversa (pl. **res controversae**): a controversial matter; a point in question

res corporales [corporeal things]: tangible things

res derelicta: abandoned or lost things

res discrepat: disagreement; discord; nonagreement

res expedit: it is useful, expedient, or advantageous

res familiaris: family estate; also, family heritage or inheritance

res fessae: distress; misery; misfortune; also, weary of matters; tired of life (see also, **fessi rerum**)

res fit inempta: the item is regarded as unbought (i.e., the sale is off)

res fungibiles or **fungibiles res:** fungible things (i.e., commercially interchangeable)

res gestae [things done]: deeds; transactions; the material facts; also, exploits in war

res hereditaria: an heirloom

res in cardine est [the matter is on the hinge]: the matter is hanging in the balance

res incorporales [things incorporeal]: non-tangible things

res integra or **res integra est** [a whole or untouched matter]: a case or matter without precedent; also, an undecided point

res inter alios: a matter between others

res inter alios acta: a thing done between others (viz., contracts that only affect the signing parties)

res ipsa loquitur: the thing or matter speaks for itself (i.e., in tort law, when evidence is lacking, a defendant's guilt can be inferred from the nature of the accident, such as in cases of negligence)

res judicata [a matter adjudged]: a judgment; a decided case (see also, **res adjudicata**)

res litigiosae: things that are in litigation (whether property or rights)

res mancipi: things that might be sold (e.g., animals or lands)

res mobiles: movable things

res non est integra: the matter has changed from its original state or position

res nova: a new case or matter; a question not before decided

res nullius: things which are the property of no one

res perit domino or **res periit domino:** the thing is lost to the owner

res privitae: private property

res publica or **respublica** [public things]: state; commonwealth; also, public affairs; the common good

res publicae: public property

res quotidianae: everyday matters

res religiosae: religious or sacred things (viz., burial places)

res repetundae: extortion

res sacrae: consecrated things

res sanctae: sacred things (i.e., things not to be harmed or violated)

res singulorum: individual or personal property

res sua: one's own property

res universitatis [universal things]: those things belonging to the community for the public purposes

rescissio (pl. **rescissiones**): a rescending or annulment of a judicial act

residuum: residue

respectus: respite; delay

respondeat: let him or her respond (i.e., answer)

respondentia: an official response or answer

respondere non debet: ought not to answer (i.e., a claim of privilege by a defendant)

responsa prudentum: the opinions of legal experts

responsalis: a proctor; an attorney

responsio or **responsum** or **responsura:** answer; response

respublica or **res publica** [republic]: state; commonwealth; also, public affairs; the common good

restitutio in integrum: restoration to the original condition (i.e., the rescinding of a contract or transaction to restore the parties to their original position)

retenta possessione: possession being retained

retineatur: let it be retained

retinendus: to be kept or retained

retractatio: a refusal; a denial; also, a reconsideration, reexamination, or correction

retraxit: he or she has withdrawn (i.e., the withdrawal by the plaintiff of a suit that results in a dismissal with prejudice)

reus [an accused person]: a defendant

revocatur: it is revoked or set aside (i.e., the annulment of a judgment because of an error in fact)

rex (R.): a king

rogatio: a request; a demand

rogatio testium: calling upon a witness to testify, as in the case of an oral will or testament

rubramentum: red ink

rubrica [red earth]: a law with its title written or printed in red ink

rudera: rubbish; debris

ruri: in the county

rus: the country (as opposed to **urbs**)

rustica et urbana: rural and urban

rusticus: rustic; rural

S

saccularii: pickpockets
sacramentum: an oath or pledge
salus: health; safety; well-being; welfare
salutarius: healthful; beneficial

salva conscientia [with safety to one's conscience]: without compromising one's conscience

salva dignitate [with safety to one's dignity]: without compromising one's dignity

salva fide [with safety to one's faith]: without breaking one's word

salva res est: the matter is safe

salvo jure [saving the right or rule]: without prejudice to one's rights; also, without infraction of law

salvo pudore: without offense to modesty

salvo sensu: without violation of sense

salvus: safe; unharmed; preserved

salvus plegius: a safe-pledge (e.g., bail)

sanae mentis: of sound mind

sanae mentis et bonae memoria: of sound mind and good memory

sanctio: a sanction (i.e., a clause in a law defining the penalty for breach)

sanctus: sacred; holy; sainted

sanguinarius: bloodthirsty

sanguis: blood

sanus: sane; healthy

satis: enough

scandalum magnatum (scan. mag.): defamation or slander of notable or high-ranking persons

scelus: an evil deed; a crime

sciendum est: it is to be known or understood; also, be it remarked

sciens et prudens: full knowledge and understanding; wittingly

scienter: knowingly; willfully; (leg.) guilty knowledge

scilicet (sc. or **scil.)** or **scire licet** [that is to say]: namely; to wit (see also, **videlicet**)

scintilla: a spark or trace; a small fragment (of evidence)

scintilla juris: a small spark or particle of right or interest

scire facias (sci. fa.) [cause it to be known]: make it known (i.e., a writ to enforce, annul, or vacate a judgment, patent, charter, or other matter of record)

scire feci: I have given notice

scire fieri: a writ of inquiry

scire licet or **scilicet** (**sc.** or **scil.**) [that is to say]: namely; to wit (see also, **videlicet**)

scripsit: he or she wrote it

scripto: by written documents

scripto vel juramento: by writ or oath

sculpsit (**sc.** or **sculpt.**): he or she sculpted, carved, or engraved it

se defendendo: in defending oneself; in self-defense

secundum (**sec.**): according to; in favor of

secundum actorem: in favor of the plaintiff

secundum aequum et bonum: according to what is equitable and good

secundum allegata et probata: according to the things alleged and proved

secundum artem (**sec. art.**): according to practice; scientifically; artificially

secundum bonum et aequum: according to what is good and equitable

secundum formam chartae: according to the form of the charter

secundum formam doni: according to the form of the gift or grant

secundum formam statuti: according to the form of the statute

secundum gustum: according to taste

secundum legem (**sec. leg.**): according to law

secundum legem communem: according to common law

secundum materiam subjectam: according to the subject matter

secundum naturam (**sec. nat.**): according to nature; naturally

secundum normam legis: according to the rule of law

secundum ordinem: according to order; in an orderly manner

secundum quid [according to some one thing]: with limitations

secundum regulam (**sec. reg.**): according to the rule

secundum subjectam materiam: according to the subject matter

secundum usum: according to usage
secundum veritatem: according to truth (i.e., what is universally true)
secundus: the second
securitate pacis: security of the peace
secus: otherwise; to the contrary
sed: but
sed non allocatur: but it is not allowed
sed per curiam: but by the court (it was held)
sedato animo: with settled purpose
sedes honoris: seat of honor
semel: once
semper: always
senectus: old age
senex: an old man
senilis: aged; senile
senior: older
sensu bono: in a good sense
sensu lato (s.l. or sen. lat.): in a broad sense
sensu malo: in a bad sense
sensu stricto (s.s. or sen. str.): in a strict sense
sententia: opinion
sententiae judicum: the finding of the jury
separaliter: separately (i.e., multiple defendants being charged with separate offenses); also, separately or apart from anything already pled
separatim: separately; severally
separatio a mensa et thoro [separation from room and board]: legal separation
separatio a vinculo matrimonii [separation from the bond of marriage]: divorce
septimana: a week
sepultus (S.): buried
sequens (s or s. or seq.): the following
sequente luce: the following day
sequentes (ss or ss.): (pl.) the following

sequentia (seqq.): the following things
sequester or **sequestra:** a mediator
sequestrum: a deposit (usually held by a third party)
sequitur (seq.): it follows (i.e., a logical inference)
seriatim: in a series; successively; also, severally
serus: late; too late
servatis servandis: the necessary service being rendered
serviens narrator: sergeant-at-law (i.e., an English barrister of the highest standing)
servitus (pl. servitutes): servitude; bondage; also, an easement
servus (f. serva): a servant; a slave
sestertio nummo: for a mere trifle (see also, **nummo sestertio**)
sexus: sex (i.e., gender)
sexus muliebris: the female sex
sexus virilis: the male sex
si: if; supposing that
si aliquid sapit: if he or she knows anything
si deprehendatur: if apprehended
si ita est: if it is so
si opus sit (s.o.s. or **si op. sit):** if necessary
si prius: if before
si quis: if anyone
si sine liberis decesserit: if he shall have died without children
si sit legitimae aetatis: if he or she is of lawful age
sic: thus; so (usually found in brackets following a doubtful word in a quotation to indicate that the original passage is being followed *verbatim*)
sic hic: thus here
sic in originali: thus in the originals
sic passim [thus in passing]: thus throughout
sic utere tuo: use yours thus
sicarius: assassin
sicut: as; just as; as it were
sicut alias: as at another time; heretofore
sicut ante: as before
sicut me Deus adjuvet: so help me God

sigillum: a seal

signator (f. **signatrix**): signatory (i.e., a witness to a will or other legal document)

signatura: signature (see also, **subscriptio** and **subscriptum**)

signum: sign; mark; signet or seal

silva caedua: the wood being cut (i.e., every manner of wood that can be cut down and that will grow back within a year)

similis: similar; like

similiter: in like manner

simplex: simple

simpliciter: plainly or in a simple manner; also, without reservation or reserve

simplum (simp.): the single value of something (see also, **duplum**)

simul [at once]: together; at the same time (see also, **in simul**)

simul cum: together with

simul et semel: at one and the same time

sincerus: sincere; genuine; also, morally upright

sine: without

sine actione agis: no cause of action (i.e., a denial of the complaint)

sine animo remanendi: without the intention of remaining

sine animo revertendi: without the intention of returning

sine anno (s.a.): without date

sine auxilio: unaided

sine consideratione curiae: without the consideration of the court

sine controversia: without dispute

sine cura or **sinecura:** without care (i.e., all the benefits of office without its responsibilities)

sine cura et cultura: without care or culture (i.e., natural)

sine decreto: without a decree

sine die (s.d.): without a day; indefinitely (i.e., an adjournment without fixing a day for future action)

sine dilatione: without delay

sine dubio: without doubt

sine fraude: without deceit; without harm

sine hoc: without this

sine joco: without jesting; seriously
sine judico: without judgment (i.e., without a judicial sentence)
sine lege: without law; without restraint
sine legitima prole (s.l.p.): without legitimate issue
sine loco (s.l.): without place
sine loco, anno, vel nomine (s.l.a.n.): without place, year, or name
sine loco et anno (s.l.a.): without place and year
sine mascula prole (s.m.p.): without male issue
sine mora: without delay
sine nomine (s.n.): without name; anonymous
sine numero: without number
sine pacto: without an agreement
sine pari: without equal
sine prole (s.p.): without issue (i.e., offspring)
sine prole femina (s.p.f.): without female issue
sine prole mascula (s.p.m.): without male issue
sine prole supersite (s.p.s.): without surviving issue
sine qua non [without which not]: an indispensable condition
sine quo non [without whom not]: an indispensable person
sine testibus (s. test. or **sine test.):** without witnesses
sine ulla querela or **sine ulla querella:** without any complaint
sine vi aut dolo: without force or fraud
sinecura or **sine cura:** without care (i.e., all the benefits of office without its responsibilities)
singillatim: singly; separately; one by one
singularis (sg. or **sing.):** singular; each; individual
singuli in solidum: each for the whole (i.e., each person is responsible for the entire amount, not merely a portion of it)
singulorum (sing.): of each
sinister (sinist.): left
sinistra: left hand; left side
sit venia verbis: pardon my words
situs: situation; location
sobrietas: sobriety
socer: father-in-law

societas: partnership or association
socius (pl. **socii**): partner; associate; also, an ally
socius criminis: a partner or associate in crime
sodalis: companion; also, a member of a secret society
sola vestura: an exclusive right of pasturage
solacium or **solatium** [solace]: consolation; relief (viz., compensation for loss of pleasure or comfort)
solarium: a sundial
solidum: a whole, an entire or undivided thing
solo animo: by mere intention or design
solum: land; soil
solus: by oneself; alone
solutio: payment; settlement
solutus: freed; released; unbound; unrestrained
solvere poenas: to pay the penalty
solvit ad diem: he or she paid at or on the day
solvit post diem: he or she paid after the day
solvit vel non: whether he or she has paid or not
soror: sister
sortitio: the casting of lots
sparsium: scattered about; here and there
spatium: space; interval
speciali gratia: by special favor
species: a particular sort, type, or kind
specimen: a sample; an example
spes: hope
splendide mendax: nobly mendacious (i.e., untruthful for a good purpose)
spoliatio [forcible deprivation]: robbing, plundering; also, dispossessing
spondeo: I promise
sponsalia: a betrothal; a mutual promise to marry (properly, **stipulatio sponsalitia**)
sponsio: a pledge; solemn promise; an engagement (e.g., of marriage)
sponsus (f. **sponsa**): spouse

sponte: spontaneously; voluntarily; by choice

sponte oblata: freely offered (i.e., usually in reference to a gift to the Crown)

sponte sua or **sua sponte** [of one's own accord]: voluntarily; without prompting; without being solicited

sportula (pl. **sportulae**) [a small basket]: a present; a gratuity; also, largess

spreta authoritate judicis: despite the authority of the judge

stagnum [standing water]: a pond or marsh

stare decisis [to stand by things decided]: to abide by legal precedent

stare in judico: to appear before a court or tribunal, either as plaintiff or defendant

statarius: standing firm; steady

statim (stat.): immediately; on the spot; at once

statu quo: as things were before

statua: statue; image; also, a statute

status: state; condition; also, a position or posture

status quo or **status in quo** [the state in which]: an existing condition or unchanged position

stent (sing. **stet**): let them stand

sterilis: sterile; barren

stet (st.): let it stand (i.e., to leave something as it stands, such as a word or phrase)

stigma: a mark; a mark on the skin

stilus or **stylus:** a pencil

stirpes [the root or stem]: the person from whom a family is descended

stirpitus [root and branch]: thoroughly; entirely

stratum super stratum (S.S.S. or **s.s.s.):** layer upon layer

stricti juris: according to strict law

strictissimi juris: of the strictest law (i.e., to be interpreted and applied in the strictest manner)

stricto sensu: in a strict sense (as opposed to **lato sensu**)

strictum juris: the rigor of the law

strictum jus or **jus strictum:** strict law (i.e., interpreted according to the strict letter of the law)

stultus: foolish; silly

stylus or **stilus:** a pencil

sua sponte or **sponte sua** [of one's own accord]: voluntarily; without prompting; without being solicited

suae potestatis: a person free from any restraint

sub: under; beneath; up to

sub audi (sub aud.): what is not expressed; (fig.) to read between the lines

sub colore juris: under color of law

sub conditione: on condition

sub cura mariti: under the care of her husband

sub curia: under the court; under the law

sub disjunctione: in the alternative

sub divo: in the open air

sub idem tempus: about the same time

sub judice: under a judge (i.e., under judicial consideration); before the court

sub modo: under a condition, restriction, or qualification

sub nomine (sub nom.): under the name of (i.e., referring to a change in case names)

sub pede sigilli [under foot of seal]: under seal

sub poena or **subpoena** [under penalty]: a subpoena (i.e., a legal summons to appear in court under penalty for failure to comply)

sub potestate: under the power or protection of another

sub potestate parentis: under the authority of a parent

sub rosa [under the rose]: confidentially

sub salvo et securo conducto: under safe and secure conduct

sub sigillo: under seal (i.e., in the strictest confidence)

sub silentio [in silence]: privately; also, without notice being taken

sub spe rati: in the hope of a decision

sub spe reconciliationis: under the hope of reconciliation

sub suo periculo: at one's own risk

sub verbis (s.vv.): under the words or headings; under the entries

sub verbo (s.v.): under the word or heading; under the entry
sub vino: under the influence of wine
sub voce (s.v.): under the word or heading; under the entry
sub vocibus (s.vv.): under the words or headings; under the entries
subaudi (sub. or **subaud.):** what is not expressed; (fig.) to read between the lines
subinde: now and then; repeatedly
subitarius: improvised
subito: suddenly
subitum: an emergency
subpoena ad testificandum: a subpoena to appear in court to give testimony
subpoena duces tecum: a subpoena to appear in court with the specified records or documents (see also, **duces tecum**)
subscriptio [a writing beneath]**:** a signature (see also, **signatura**)
subscriptum [signed]**:** a signature (see also, **signatura**)
subter: under
sufficiens: sufficient
sufficit (pl. **sufficiunt**): it is enough
suffragium [a voting tablet]**:** the right to vote
suggestio falsi [suggestion of a falsehood]**:** an indirect lie or misrepresentation
sui generis [of its own kind]**:** unique; one of a kind; something in a class by itself
sui juris [in one's own right]**:** of full legal capacity (as opposed to **alieni juris**)
sumendus: to be taken
summa diligentia: with the utmost diligence
summa injuria: the greatest injury
summa necessitate: in extreme necessity
summa potestas: the highest or ultimate power; the final authority
summa vitae or **vitae summa:** lifespan
summoneas: a writ of summons ordering a party to appear in court

summum jus: the highest law; also, the rigor of the law

summus: the greatest; the highest; the utmost (as opposed to **infimus** or **infumus**)

sumptu publico: at the public expense

suo jure: in one's own right

suo loco: in its proper place

suo nomine: in one's own name

suo periculo: at one's own peril or risk

super: above; upon

super aliquam partem fundi: upon any part of the land

super altum mare: upon the high seas

super eisdem deductis: upon the same grounds

super visum corpore: upon view of the body

superficies: the surface of the ground; also, a building or other improvements

superior: higher (in position or grade) (as opposed to **inferior**)

superoneratio: overstocking a pasture or meadow used for grazing (i.e., a form of trespass)

superplusagium: a surplus; a remainder

supersedeas [you shall desist]: a stay or suspension of judgment, usually pending appeal

superus: above; higher (as opposed to **inferus**)

supplementum (suppl.): a supplement; something added later

supplicatio: petition to pardon a first offense or to reverse a judgment

supplicavit: a surety; a bond to keep the peace

supplicium [atonement]: a punishment of death (see also, **ultimum supplicium**)

suppressio veri: the suppression of the truth (i.e., a willful concealment of facts)

supra (sup.): above (i.e., an author or work cited previously in the text)

supra vires: beyond one's powers

suprema potestas: supreme power or authority (viz., superior to all others)

suprema voluntas: a last will

surdus: deaf

sursum reddere: to render up or surrender

suspendatur per collum (sus. per col.) [let him be hanged by the neck]: the sentence of death by hanging

suspensio per collum [hanging by the neck]: execution by hanging

suus: one's own

syllabus (syl. or **syll.):** an abstract or written summary (e.g., the main points in a precedent case)

T

tabellarius: letter carrier

taberna: a shop

tabernarius: a shopkeeper

tabula [table]: record book; register; also, bill of indictment

tabula in naufragio [plank from a shipwreck]: an item or argument added to a lawsuit on appeal, often as a last-ditch effort

tabula rasa: blank tablet; clean slate

tabulae: written documents (e.g., contracts or wills)

tabulae nuptiales: a marriage record

tabulae publicae: public archives

tabularius: a notary

tacit: it is silent

tacitus [silent]: unspoken; implied; inferred

tallagium or **talagium:** a tax; a toll

tales de circumstantibus [such of the bystanders]: a sufficient number of persons present to supply a deficiency in a panel of jurors

talis (tal.): such; also, a tales (i.e., a juror summoned to fill a vacancy)

talis qualis (tal. qual.): such as it is

taliter: in such a manner

tandem: at length

tanquam alter idem or **tamquam alter idem:** as if a second self (i.e., a completely trustworthy person)

tanquam optimum maximum: at its best and greatest
tantum: so much; as much
tantus: so much; so great
tardus: slow; late
te judice [you being the judge]: in your judgment
tecum: with you
tempestas mala: bad weather
temporalis exceptio: a temporary exception
temporarius: temporary; adapted to time and circumstance
tempore (temp. or **t.):** in the time of
tempore pacis: in time of peace
tempus: time; a season
tempus continuum: time running on without interruption
tempus deliberandi: time for deliberation
tempus instat: this is the time; this is the moment
tempus me deficit: I have no time
tempus semestre: six months; a six-month period
tenebra: darkness
tenendum: to be held (i.e., a clause in a deed stating tenure)
tenet: he or she holds
ter [thrice]: three times
terminus (pl. **termini**): a boundary; a limit either of space or of time
terminus a quo [the point from which]: the beginning or starting point
terminus ad quem [the point to which]: the ending point
terminus ante quem [time before which]: the earliest possible date or period
terminus post quem [time after which]: the latest possible date or period
terra: earth; land
terra culta: cultivated land
terra firma: solid land
terra non secta: untilled earth
terra nova: newly cleared land
tertius: the third

testamentum: a will or testament
testatio mentis [testator's mind]: a testament or will
testator (f. **testatrix**): a person who makes a will
testatum: attested (i.e., the witness section of a deed)
teste: by the evidence or witness of
teste me ipso or **teste meipso** [I myself being a witness]: by my own witness
testimonium de auditu [testimony by hearing]: secondhand testimony; hearsay
testis (pl. **testes**): a witness
testis gravis: an important witness
thesaurus or **thesaurium:** a treasure or treasury; a storehouse
thesaurus inventus: a treasure trove (i.e., hidden treasure)
timidus: fearful
titulus [title]: a label or inscription
tortum: crooked; twisted; wrong
totidem verbis: in so many words
toties quoties (tot. quot.): as often as; repeatedly; on each occasion
toto genere: in every respect
totum: total; the whole
totum pro parte: the whole for a part (as opposed to **pars pro toto**)
tractim: in managed bits; by degree
traditio rei: delivery of a thing
tragicus: tragic
trans: through; across
transeat in exemplum: let it become an example or a precedent
transfugium [going across]: desertion
transitus: transit; transition; also, passage (from one place to another)
transitus vetitus: no trespassing
transmarinus [from beyond the sea]: foreign
transversum digitum: a finger's breadth
tributum: tribute; tax; taxation
trifur [a threefold thief]: a notorious thief
trifurciter: a notorious rogue
trimestrium: a quarter of the year (i.e., a three-month period)

trinoda necessitas: the threefold necessity (i.e., in reference to land taxes)

tripartitus: divided into three parts (e.g., a contract or deed which names three distinct parties)

triplex: triple

tu quoque [you as well]: a statement accusing the accuser of the same misdeed

tum: at that time

tunc: then

turpis: base; foul; also, immoral

turpis causa: an immoral cause or consideration

turpis contractus: an immoral contract

tuta: safe; secure

tutamen (pl. **tutamina**): protection; a protective pact

tutela: guardianship (i.e., legal protection of a minor)

tutor (f. **tutrix**): a guardian; a tutor; an instructor

typographum: typewritten

typus: type; a mold or pattern

U

uberrima fides: superabundant faith (i.e., implicit trust)

ubi: where

ubi infra (i.s.) [where below]: in the place mentioned below

ubi supra (u.s.) [where above]: in the place mentioned above

ulterius concilium: further consideration

ultimatum: a final proposal

ultime: finally; at last

ultimo (ult.): the last or previous [month]

ultimo loco: in the last place

ultimo mense (ult. m.): the last or previous month

ultimum (ult.): finally; for the last time; also, the ultimate or extreme

ultimum supplicium: the death penalty (see also, **supplicium**)

ultimus (ult.): the last; the final; the most distant

ultimus haeres [the last of the heirs]: the final heir

ultra: beyond; above
ultra fines mandati: beyond the limits of the mandate
ultra licitum: beyond the legal limit
ultra mare: beyond the sea
ultra petita: beyond that which was sought
ultra valorem: beyond the value
ultra vires: beyond one's power; beyond legal authority (see also, **extra vires**)
una cum: together with
una voce [with one voice]**:** unanimously
unde nihil habet: whereof one has nothing (e.g., a widow without a dower)
unde petit judicium: whereof one demands a judgment
undique: everywhere; from all sides; in every respect
unico contextu: in one connection; in one transaction; by one and the same act
uno actu: in a single act; by one and the same act
uno animo [with one spirit]**:** unanimously
uno consensu: in one accord; unanimously
uno flatu [with one breath]**:** at the same moment
uno ictu: at one blow; at once
uno ore [one mouth]**:** unanimously
uno tempore: at the same time
uno verbo: in a word
urbani: townsfolk
urbs: city or town (as opposed to **rus**)
usque (usq.): as far as
usque ad: up to; as far as
usque ad filum aquae: as far as the thread or the center of the stream
usque ad sententiam: until the pronouncing of judgment
usucapio: title or acquisition of land by prescription (i.e., lengthy possession)
usura: usury; interest
usura manifesta: open usury or interest
usura veleta: veiled or hidden usury or interest
usus: use

usus bellici: use in warfare
usus et fructus or **usus fructus** [use and the fruit]: deriving a benefit (i.e., the use or enjoyment of the property of another)
usus loquendi: usage in speaking; customary language
ut: in order that; so that; as
ut ante or **ut antea:** as before
ut antiquum: as in ancient times
ut assolet: as is customary
ut audivi: as I have heard
ut credo: as I believe
ut dictum (ut dict.): as directed
ut fit: as is commonly the case
ut infra (ut inf. or **u.i.)** [as below]: as stated or cited below
ut ne quis utatur: that no one make use of it
ut supra (ut sup. or **u.s.)** [as above]: as stated or cited above
utatur: let him or her make use (i.e., benefit)
utendus: to be used
uterque: both of them
uti possidetis: as you now possess (i.e., with the possessions held at the present time)
uti possidetis jure: as possessed according to law
uti rogas (u.r.) [as you ask]: as requested (i.e., an approval)
utilis: useful
utilitas: utility; usefulness
utitur jure suo: one exercises his or her right
utrius libet: of whichever [the client] pleases
uxor (ux.): wife

V

vacat (vac.; pl. **vacant):** empty; missing (e.g., the missing part of an inscription)
vacatio: freedom; exemption; immunity
vacatis bona: goods without an owner (i.e., the goods of someone who dies without a successor)
vacuo: in a vacuum

vacuum: a vacuum; an empty space

vacuum domicilium: an empty dwelling space; an empty house

vadium mortuum or **mortuum vadium** [dead pledge]: a mortgage (i.e., the land or property itself becomes the security against default, hence the term 'dead')

vadium vivum or **vivum vadium** [live pledge]: a security by which money borrowed is repaid out of profits gained from the fruits of the land against which it is borrowed

vectigal: duty; tax

vehiculum (vehic.): vehicle; any means of transport or conveyance

vel non: whether or not

velum: a veil; a screen; a curtain

venalis [for sale]: capable of being bribed (i.e., corrupt bargaining)

venatio: hunting

venditio: selling

venditioni exponas: that you expose for sale (i.e., a writ directing the sale of seized property)

venire facias [to make to come]: a writ from a judge ordering the sheriff to summon a jury

venire facias ad respondendum [to make to come to respond]: a summons to answer an indictment

venire facias de novo [to make to come anew]: a second writ from a judge ordering the sheriff to summon another jury for a new trial

venit et defendit: he or she comes and defends

venit et dicit: he or she comes and says

venter: the belly; the womb

ventre inspiciendo or **de ventre inspiciendo:** examining the womb (historically, a writ commanding a sheriff to examine a woman, in the presence of 12 male jurors and 12 women, to determine if she truly is with child and, if so, when the child is likely to be born)

verax: truthful

verba: words (i.e., those spoken as opposed to written); also, language

verba jactantia [boastful words]: words spoken in exaggeration or jest (i.e., statements that are not taken as legally binding upon the person or persons speaking them)

verba precaria: precatory words (i.e., words of request)

verba solennia or **verba solemnia:** solemn words; formal words (i.e., words essential to validity)

verbatim: word for word; literally

verbatim et literatim: word for word and letter for letter (i.e., an exact copy)

verbi causa: for instance

verbi gratia (v.g.): for example

verborum obligatio: a verbal obligation (see also, **obligatio verborum**)

verbum (pl. **verba**): word

verbum sapienti (verb. sap.): a word to the wise (sometimes spoken by way of caution)

verecundia: modesty; shame

veredictum: a verdict

vergens ad inopiam: verging on poverty (i.e., tending toward insolvency) (see also, **ad inopiam**)

veritas: truth

veritas convicii: the truth of the accusation

verso folio or **verso (v.):** on the left-hand page of a book (i.e., the left-hand page)

versus (v. or **vs.)** [facing]: toward; against (see also, **adversus**)

versus (v. or **vs.)** [turning]: a verse; a line of writing

verum: the truth; reality; also, truly

verus: true; genuine

vesania: madness; insanity

vesper (vesp.): evening

vestigium [footprint]: a vestige; a trace

vestimentum [vestment]: clothing; garment; also, investiture

vetera statua: ancient statutes

veterinus: a beast of burden

vetitum (est): it is forbidden
veto [I forbid]: the refusal of a chief executive to execute an order
vetus: old
vetustas: antiquity
vetustus: ancient; old-fashioned
vexata quaestio: a vexed or vexing question (i.e., a point often debated though never resolved) (see also, **quaestio vexata**)
vi aut metu: by force or fear
vi et armis: with force and arms
via: way; highway; road
via actionis: by means of an action
via alta: a highway (see also, **alta via**)
via amicabili: in a friendly way
via iniqua: a bad road
via juris: by means of law
via publica: a public way
via regia: a royal highway; a public road (see also, **regia via**)
viagium: a voyage
vice versa (V.V. or v.v.) [with the position or order reversed]: conversely
vicecomes or **vice comes:** a sheriff
vicinus: neighbor; neighboring
vicissim: alternately
victus: means of living or support
vicus: district
vide (v.): see
vide ante (v.a.): see before (i.e., above)
vide infra (v.i.): see below
vide post (v.p.): see after (i.e., below)
vide supra (v.s.): see above
videlicet (viz.) [that is to say]: namely; to wit (see also, **scillicet**)
vidimus: we have seen (see also, **inspeximus**)
vidua: a widow
vigore cujus: by the force of which
viis et modis: by ways and means

vilis: cheap; inferior; worthless
vinculum: a bond or tie; a relation or connection
vinculum matrimonii: the bond of matrimony
vindex injuriae: an avenger of wrong
vir: man; husband
vir et uxor: husband and wife
vires corporis: bodily strength
virtus: virtue; strength
virtute cujus: by virtue of which
virtute officii: by virtue of office
vis (pl. **vires**): strength; power; force
vis a tergo: a force or power from behind
vis armata: armed force (as opposed to **vis inermis**)
vis divina: an act of God (see also, **vis major**)
vis et metis: force and fear
vis fluminis: the force of a river or stream (i.e., the current)
vis impressa: direct or immediate force (see also, **vis proxima**)
vis inermis: an unarmed force (as opposed to **vis armata**)
vis inertiae: the force of inertia
vis major: superior or irresistible force; act of God (i.e., an inevitable accident) (see also, **vis divina**)
vis proxima: direct or proximate force (see also, **vis impressa**)
vis vel metus: force or fear
vis vitae or **vis vitalis:** vital power; life-force
visus: view; inspection
vita: life
vitae summa or **summa vitae:** lifespan
vitium: error; a fault or crime
vitium clerici: a clerical error
vitium scriptoris: a scribal error (i.e., an error in a copy or transcription)
vitricus: a stepfather
viva voce [by a living voice]: orally; by word of mouth; also, by oral examination
vivax: long-lived
vivos or **vivus:** alive; living

vivum vadium or **vadium vivum** [live pledge]: a security by which money borrowed is repaid out of profits gained from the fruits of the land against which it is borrowed
vivus or **vivos:** alive; living
vix: with difficulty; with effort
vixit... annos (v.a.): he or she lived... years
vocare ad curiam: to summon to court
vocatio in jus: a summoning to court
vociferatio: an outcry (i.e., hue and cry)
voluntas: will; volition; intention
voluntas legis: the spirit of the law
voluntas pro facto: the will for the deed
voluntas testatoris: the will of the testator
vox (pl. **voces**): voice
vox populi (pl. **voces populi**): the voice of the people
vulgaris: common
vulgi opinio: public opinion
vulgo concepti or **vulgo quaesiti** [commonly conceived]: illegitimate children of unknown paternity
vulnus: an injury; a wound

Selected Latin Maxims and Legal Principles

A

A verbis legis non est recedendum: From the words of the law there is no departure.

Ab abusu ad usum non valet consequentia: The usefulness of something is not invalidated by the consequences of its abuse.

Ab actu ad posse valet illatio: It is possible to infer the future from the past.

Ab assuetis non fit injuria: From that which is customary no injury can arise.

Ab communi observantia non est recedendum: From common observance (or usage) there is no departure.

Ab uno disce omnes: From one learn all (i.e., from one example we judge the rest).

Absens haeres non erit: The absent one will not be heir (i.e., out of sight, out of mind).

Abundans cautela non nocet: Abundant caution does no harm.

Abusus non tollit usum: Abuse does not take away use (i.e., abuse is no argument against use).

Accessorius sequitur naturam sui principalis: The accessory follows the nature of his principal (i.e., the accessory is not guilty a crime higher than that of the principal).

Accusare nemo se debet: No one is compelled to accuse him- or herself.

Acta exteriora indicant interiora secreta: External actions indicate internal secrets (i.e., inward intent).

Actio non datur non damnificato: No action is given for one not injured.

Actio personalis moritur cum persona: A personal action (or right) dies with the person.

Actio semel extincta non reviviscit: An action once extinguished does not revive.

DOI: 10.4324/9781003255369-2

Actor incumbit probatio, reus excipiendo fit actor: It is incumbent upon the plaintiff to prove, upon the defendant to present exceptions.

Actor sequitur forum rei: A plaintiff follows the court of the defendant.

Actori incumbit onus probandi: The burden of proof falls on the plaintiff.

Actus Dei nemini nocet: Acts of God bring injury to no one.

Actus legis nemini facit injuriam: A legal act of the court injures no one.

Actus me invito factus, non est meus actus: An act that I commit against my will is not my act.

Actus non facit reum nisi mens sit rea: The act does not make a person guilty unless the mind is also guilty (i.e., unless there is intent).

Ad acta atra peracta sunt facta atta patrata: For dark acts are prepared dark jails.

Ad impossibilia nemo tenetur: No one is held to the impossible (i.e., no one is expected to perform an impossible task).

Adversus solem ne loquitor: Neither speak against the sun (i.e., do not dispute with what is obvious).

Aedificare in tuo proprio solo non licet quod alteri noceat: It is not permitted to build on your own land that which may harm another.

Aedificatum solo, solo cedit: That which is built on the land goes with the land.

Aequitas agit in personam: Equity acts upon the person (not the property).

Aequitas est quasi aequalitas: Equity is as it were equality.

Aequitas nunquam contravenit leges: Equity never contravenes the laws.

Aequitas sequitur legem: Equity follows the law.

Aestimatio praeteriti delicti ex post facto nunquam crescit: The evaluation of a past crime is never increased by what subsequently happens.

Affirmanti incumbit probatio: Proof is incumbent upon the one who alleges a fact (i.e., the one who makes the allegation).

Affirmanti non neganti incumbit probatio: The proof does not lie with the one who denies the charge.

Agentes et consentientes pari poena plectentur: Acting and consenting are liable to the same punishment.

Aliena negotia exacto officio gerunter: Great care should be taken when carrying out the business of another.

Alieni appetens, sui profusus: Greedy for another's property, wasting one's own.

Alienatio rei praefertur juri accrescendi: The law favors alienation over accumulation.

Aliquis non debet esse judex in propria causa: One ought not to be a judge in his or her own case.

Alitur vitium vivitque tegendo: The crime is nourished and lives by being concealed (i.e., vice lives and thrives by secrecy).

Aliud est celare, aliud tacere: It is one thing to conceal, another to be silent.

Aliud est possidere, aliud esse in possessione: It is one thing to possess, another to be in possession.

Aliud est punire, aliud vindicare: It is one thing to punish, another to vindicate.

Alius peccat, alius plectitur: One sins, the other is punished.

Allegans contraria not est audiendus: A person making contradictory allegations is not to be heard.

Allegari non debuit quod probatum non relevat: That which, if proved but not relevant, ought not to be alleged.

Ambiguitas contra stipulatorem est: An ambiguity is taken against the party using it.

Ambulatoria est voluntas defuncti usque ad vitae supremum exitum: The will of the deceased is movable (or revocable) until the actual moment of death.

Animus ad se omne jus ducit: It is to the spirit (or intention) that all law applies.

Animus hominis est anima scripti: The will (or intent) of the person is the will (or intent) of the written instrument.

Annus inceptus pro completo habetur: A year begun is held as completed.

Apices juris non sunt jura: The subtleties (or adornments) of the law are not the law.

Applicatio est vita regulae: Application is the life of the rule.

Aqua cedit solo: The water passes with the soil (i.e., the water goes with the ground).

Arbitramentum aequum tribuit cuique suum: Just arbitration renders to each what is his or hers.

Arbitrium est judicium: An award is a judgment.

Arbor dum crescit; lignum dum crescere nequit: It is a tree while it is growing; wood when it is unable to grow.

Argumentum ab inconvenienti plurimum valet in lege: An argument from inconvenience (or hardship) is very forcible by law.

Arma in armatos sumere jura sinunt: The law allows persons to take up arms against the armed (viz., the right to defend oneself).

Assignatus utitur jure auctoris: The assignee is possessed of the rights of the one he or she represents.

B

Beati possidentes: Blessed are they who possess (i.e., possession is nine-tenths of the law).

Bello parta cedunt republicae: Things acquired in war go to the state.

Beneficium invito non datur: A benefit (or privilege) is not granted against one's will.

Bis dat qui cito dat: He or she gives twice who gives quickly.

Bona fides exigit ut quod convenit fiat: Good faith requires that what is agreed upon shall be done.

Boni judicis est lites dirimere: A good judge is one who prevents litigation.

C

Cassis tutissima virtus: Virtue is the safest helmet.
Causa causae est causa causati: The cause of the cause is the cause of the effect.
Causa ecclesiae publicis aequiparatur: The cause of the church is equal to that of the public.
Causa et origo est materia negotii: The cause and origin is the material of business.
Causa proxima non remota spectatur: The immediate not the remote cause is to be considered.
Causa vaga et incerta non est causa rationabilis: A vague and uncertain cause is not a reasonable cause.
Certum est quod certum reddi potest: That which can be made certain is certain.
Cessante causa, cessat effectus: The cause ceasing, the effect ceases.
Cessante ratione legis, cessat ipsa lex: The reason for the law ceasing, the law itself ceases.
Charta de non ente non valet: A charter (or deed) concerning a thing not in existence holds no value.
Charta est legatus mentis: A charter (or deed) is the legatee (or representation) of the mind.
Clausulae inconsuetae semper inducunt suspicionem: Unusual clauses always lead to suspicion.
Cogitationis poenam nemo meretur: No one deserves punishment for a thought.
Communis error facit jus: Common error makes law.
Compromissarii sunt judices: Arbitrators are judges.
Confessio facta in judicio omni probatione major est: A confession made in court is of greater effect than any proof.
Confessus in judicio pro judicato habetur: The one who confesses in court is held to have been adjudged.
Conscientia mille testes: Conscience is as a thousand witnesses.
Consensus facit legem: Consent makes the law.
Consensus tollit errorem: Consent takes away error.

Consentientes et agentes pari poena plactantur: Those consenting and those perpetrating are liable to equal punishment.

Constructio legis non facit injuriam: The making of the law does no injury (or, law should be made to do no injury).

Consuetudo debet esse certa: Custom ought to be certain.

Consuetudo est optimus interpres legum: Custom is the best interpreter of the law.

Consuetudo loci observanda est: The custom of the place is to be observed.

Consuetudo pro lege servatur: Custom is held as law.

Contra factum non valet argumentum: There is no valid argument against a fact.

Contra testimonium scriptum, testimonium non scriptum non fertur: (fig.) Oral testimony that runs counter to the written record is inadmissible.

Contractus contra bonos mores nullus est: A contract that runs counter to good morals is null and void.

Contractus ex turpi causa nullus est: A contract arising from base causes is null and void.

Contrariorum contraria est ratio: The reason of contrary things is contrary.

Corruptio optimi pessima: The corruption of the best is the worst.

Corruptissima re publica plurimae leges: In the most corrupt state exist the most laws.

Crimen omnia ex se nata vitiat: Crime vitiates all that arises from it.

Crimina morte extinguuntur: Crimes are extinguished by the death of the criminal.

Cui prodest scelus, is fecit: Who benefits from the crime, he committed it.

Cujus est commodum, ejus est onus: The person who has the benefit (or opportunity) has also the burden.

Cujus est dare ejus est disponere: Whose it is to give, his it is to dispose.

Cujus est instituere ejus est abrogare: The one who institutes may also abrogate.

Cujus est solum, ejus est usque ad coelum: The one who owns the land owns the sky above it.

Culpa poena par esto: Let the punishment equal the crime.

Culpa tenet suos auctores: A fault binds its author.

Culpa vacare maximum est solacium: To be relieved of guilt is the greatest solace.

Culpam poena premit comes: Punishment presses hard on the heels of crime.

Cum confitente sponte mitius est agendum: One confessing willingly should be dealt with leniently.

Cum finis est licitus etiam media sunt licita: When the end is lawful, the means are likewise lawful.

Cum libertate justitiaque omnibus: With liberty and justice for all.

Cum tacent, clamant: When they are silent, they cry loudest (i.e., silence speaks louder than words).

Currit tempus contra desides: Time runs against those who are slow.

Cursus curiae est lex curiae: The practice of the court is the law of the court.

D

Da mihi factum, dabo tibi jus: Give me the facts, and I will give you law.

Damnum non facit qui jure suo utitur: The one who exercises his or her rights harms no one.

Damnum sentit dominus: The master (of the house) suffers the loss.

Damnum sine injuria esse potest: Loss without injury is deemed possible.

Dans et retinens nil (or **nihil**) **dat:** Giving and retaining [possession] gives nothing.

De facto jus oritur: The law arises out of fact.

De fide et officio judicis non recipitur quaestio: Concerning the good faith and duty of the judge, no quesion can be allowed.

De gustibus non [est] disputandum: There is no disputing about tastes.

De jure judices, de facto juratores, respondent: Judges answer concerning law, jurors concerning fact.

De majore et minore non variant jura: Of greater and lesser the laws do not vary.

De minimis non curat lex: The law does not concern itself with trifles.

De minimis non curat praetor: A magistrate does not concern himself with trifles.

De morte hominis nulla est cunctatio longa: No delay is long when it concerns the death of a man.

De similibus idem est judicium: In similar cases, the judgment is the same.

Debet esse finis litium: There ought to be an end to litigation.

Debile fundamentum fallit opus: A weak foundation destroys the work.

Debita sequuntur personam debitoris: Debts follow the person of the debtor.

Decipit frons prima multos: The first appearance deceives many.

Degeneres animos timor arguit: Fear betrays ignoble souls.

Delegatus non potest delegare: A delegate cannot delegate.

Delicatus debitor est odiosus in lege: A luxuriant debtor is odious in the [eye of the] law.

Derivativa potestas non potest esse major primitiva: The power derived cannot be greater than that from which it is derived.

Deus solus haeredem facere potest: Only God can make someone an heir.

Dies dominicus non est juridicus: The Lord's Day is not a day for legal proceedings.

Dies inceptus pro completo habetur: A day begun is held as complete.

Dilationes in leges sunt odiosae: Delays in the law are odious.

Dissimulatione tollitur injuria: Injury is removed by reconciliation (i.e., by forgiveness).

Dolo malo non videtur habere qui suo jure utitur: The one who exercises his or her rights is not thought to do so with evil intent.

Dolo malo pactum se non servabit: A pact made with evil intent (or induced by fraud) will not be upheld.

Dolosus versatur in generalibus: A deceiver deals in generalities.

Dolus auctoris non nocet succesori: The fraud of a predecessor harms not the successor.

Dolus circuitu non purgator: Fraud is not purged by circuity (viz., circuitous means).

Dona clandestina sunt semper suspiciosa: Clandestine gifts are always suspicious.

Donatio non praesumitur: A gift is not presumed.

Dormiunt aliquando leges nunquam moriuntur: Laws sometimes sleep [but] never die.

Duo non possunt in solido unam rem possidere: Two cannot each possess [the same] thing in its entirety.

Dura lex, sed lex: The law is hard, but it is the law.

Durum et durum non faciunt murum: Hard and hard do not make a wall (i.e., to lay bricks without mortar).

E

Eadem est ratio, eadem est lex: The same reason, the same law.

Effectus sequitur causam: The effect follows the cause.

Ei incumbit probatio, qui dicit, non qui negat: The burden of proof lies upon the one who asserts, not upon the one who denies.

Ejus est non nolle qui potest vale: (fig.) The one who consents expressly also consents tacitly.

Errare humanum est: To err is human.

Error juris nocet: An error of law injures.
Error qui non resistitur approbatur: An error that is not resisted is approved.
Est modus in rebus: There is a measure (or limit) to things.
Ex desuetudine amittuntur privilegia: It is out of disuse that rights are lost.
Ex dolo malo non oritur actio: A legal action does not arise from fraud.
Ex facto jus oritur: The law arises out of fact.
Ex maleficio non oritur contractus: A contract cannot arise from malfeasance (or misconduct).
Ex malis moribus bonae leges natae sunt: From bad usages, good laws have sprung.
Ex turpi causa non oritur actio: A legal action does arise from an immoral cause.
Ex uno disce omnes: From one learn all (i.e., from one case we judge the rest).
Exceptio firmat regulam (in casibus non exceptis): The exception affirms the rule (in cases not excepted).
Exceptio probat regulam: The exception proves the rule.
Exceptio semper ultima ponenda est: An exception is always to be put last.
Exempla illustrant non restringunt legem: Examples illustrate but do not restrain the law.
Expedit reipublicae ne sua re quis male utatur: It is for the public good that a person not make bad use of his or her property.
Expedit reipublicae ut sit finis litium: It is for the public good that there be an end to litigation.
Experientia docet: Experience teaches.
Expressio unius est exclusio alterius: The express mention of the one is the exclusion of the other.
Expressum facit cessare tacitum: What is expressed makes what is silent cease.
Extra legem positus est civiliter mortuus: An outlaw is civilly dead.

F

Facilis est lapsus juventutis: Youth is liable to err.

Facio ut des: I do that you may give.

Facio ut facias: I do that you may do.

Facta sunt potentiora verbis: Deeds are more powerful than words.

Factum infectum fieri nequit: What is done cannot be undone.

Factum negantis nulla probatio: No proof is incumbent upon a person who denies a fact.

Factum unius alteri necere non debet: The deed of the one should not harm another.

Facultas probationum non est angustanda: The opportunity (or right) of offering proof is not to be narrowed.

Falsa causa non nocet: A false motive does no injury (or harm).

Falsa demonstratio non nocet: A false description does no injury (or harm).

Falsa grammatica non vitiat chartam: False grammar does not vitiate a charter (or deed).

Falsus in uno, falsus in omnibus: False in one thing, false in everything.

Fama nihil est celerius: Nothing is swifter than rumor.

Fatetur facinus qui judicium fugit: To flee the law is to confess one's guilt.

Festina lente: Make haste slowly.

Fiat justitia, ruat coelum: Let justice be done, though the heavens fall.

Fictio cedit veritati: Fiction yields to truth.

Fictio legis neminem laedit: A fiction of the law injures no one.

Fide, sed cui vide: Trust, but be careful whom.

Fieri non debet sed factum valet: It ought not be done but once done it is valid.

Finem respice: Look to the end (i.e., consider the outcome).

Finis finem litibus imponit: The end puts an end to litigation.

Finis unius diei est principium alternis: The end of one day is the beginning of another.

Flamma fumo est proxima: Flame is near smoke (i.e., where there is smoke, there is fire).

Foedum inceptu, foedum existu: Foul beginning, foul ending.

Forma dat esse: Form gives being.

Fortior est custodia leges quam hominis: The custody of the law is stronger than man's.

Fractionem diei non recipit lex: The law takes no notice of the fraction of a day (i.e., the entire day is allowed for a thing to be done).

Fraus est celare fraudem: It is fraud to conceal fraud.

Fraus latet in generalibus: Fraud hides in generalities.

Fronti nulla fides: There is no trusting appearances.

Frustra probatur quod probatum non relevat: It is useless to prove that which, when proved, is not relevant.

Fundamentum est justitiae fides: The foundation of justice is good faith.

Furiosi nulla voluntas est: An insane person has no free will.

Furiosus absentis loco est: An insane person is like one who is absent.

Furiosus solo furore punitur: An insane person is punished by madness alone.

G

Generale nihil certi implicat: A general expression implies nothing certain.

Generalia specialibus non derogant: General things do not derogate from specific things.

Generalia verba sunt generaliter intelligenda: General words are to be taken generally.

Generalis regula generaliter est intelligenda: A general rule is to be understood generally.

Grammatica falsa non vitiat chartam: Grammatical error does not invalidate a charter (or deed).

Gravissimum est imperium consuetudinis: The power of custom is most weighty.

H

Habemus opimum testem confidentem reum: We hold the best witness to be the defendant who confesses.

Haereditas nunquam ascendit: Inheritance never ascends.

Haeres est nomen juris, filius est nomen naturae: Heir is a name given by law, son is a name given by nature.

Haeres est pars antecessoris: An heir is a part of the ancestor.

Haeres haeredis mei est meus haeres: The heir of my heir is my heir.

Honestum non est semper quod licet: That which is lawful is not always honorable.

Humani nihil alienum: Nothing that relates to humankind is alien to me.

Humanum est errare: To err is human.

Hypotheses non fingo: I frame no hypothesis (i.e., I deal entirely with the facts).

I

Idem non esse et non apparere: It is the same thing not to exist and not to appear.

Ignorantia facti excusat: Ignorance of fact excuses.

Ignorantia judicis est calamitas innocentis: The ignorance of a judge is calamitous to an accused person.

Ignorantia juris non excusat: Ignorance of the law does not excuse.

Ignorantia legis neminem excusat: Ignorance of the law excuses no one.

Ignorantia legis nocet: Ignorance of the law is harmful.

Immovilia situm sequuntur: Immovables follow the law of their locality.

Impossibilium nulla obligatio est: There is no obligation to do impossible things.

Impotentia excusat legem: Powerlessness (or inability) excuses the law.

Impunitas semper ad deteriora invitat: Impunity is always an invitation to a greater crime.

In aequali jure melior est conditio possidentis: Where rights are equal, the condition of the possessor is better.

In alternativis electio est debitoris: In alternatives, the debtor has the option.

In consimili casu, consimile debet esse remedium: In similar cases, the remedy should be similar.

In contractibus tacite insunt quae sunt moris et consuetudinis: In contracts, matters of custom and general usage are implied.

In criminalibus probationes debent esse luce clariores: In criminal cases proofs ought to be clearer than light.

In dubiis benigniora semper praeferenda sunt: In doubtful cases, the more liberal [construction] is always to be preferred.

In dubio contra proferentem: When in doubt, [rule] against the one who made the offer (i.e., the one who wrote the contract).

In dubio pars melior est sequenda: When in doubt, the gentler course is to be followed.

In dubio pro reo: When in doubt, favor the accused.

In dubio sequendum quod tutius est: When in doubt, the safer course is to be followed.

In fictione juris semper nequitas existit: In legal fictions, equality always exists (i.e., equality is always inherent).

In generalibus latet error: In generalities hides error.

In generalibus versatur error: In generalities dwells error.

In judiciis minori aetati succurritur: In judicial proceedings, infancy is favored.

In judicio non creditur nisi juratis: In a trial only sworn witnesses are believed.

In jure, non remota causa sed proxima spectatur: In law, the proximate not the remote cause is to be regarded.

In jure omnis definitio periculosa est: In every law definition is dangerous.

In maleficiis voluntas spectatur non exitus: In malicious acts the intention is to be regarded not the result.

In maxima potentia, minima licentia: In the greatest power exists the least liberty.

In medio virtus: Virtue lies in the mean (i.e., in the middle course).

In nocte consilium: In the night is counsel (i.e., sleep on it).

In odium spoliatoris omnia praesumuntur: All things despised are presumed against a despoiler (viz., one who destroys evidence).

In pari delicto potior est conditio defendentis: Where both parties are equally at fault, the defender holds the better position.

In pari delicto potior est conditio possidentis: Where both parties are equally at fault, the possessor holds the better position.

In poenam sectatur et umbra: For punishment even a shadow is pursued.

In propria causa nemo judex: One should not be judge in his or her own cause.

In re communi potior est conditio prohibentis: In a partnership, the one who prohibits [a change] has the better right.

In toto et pars continetur: In the whole the part is also contained.

In vino veritas: In wine is truth (i.e., under wine's influence, the truth is told).

Incerta pro nullis habentur: Things uncertain are held for nothing.

Inclusio unius est exclusio alterius: The inclusion of one is the exclusion of another.

Incolas domicilium facit: Residence makes domicile.

Incommodum non servit argumentum: Inconvenience does not serve as an argument.

Incommodum non solvit argumentum: Inconvenience does not destroy as an argument.

Index animi sermo est: Speech is an indicator of thought.
Indignante invidia florebit justus: The just will flourish in spite of envy.
Injuria non excusat injuriam: One wrong does not justify another.
Injuria non praesumitur: Injury is not to be presumed.
Insanus omnis furere credit ceteros: Every madman thinks all others insane.
Intentio caeca mala: A hidden intention is an evil one.
Inter arma leges silent or **inter arma silent leges:** In time of war, the laws are silent.
Interdum vulgus rectum videt: Sometimes the common folk see correctly.
Interest reipublicae ut sit finis litium: It is in the interest of the public good that there be an end of litigation.
Invito beneficium non datur: A benefit cannot be forced upon an unwilling person.
Ipsae leges cupiunt ut jure regantur: The laws themselves desire that they should be ruled by right.
Ira furor brevis est: Anger is a brief madness.

J

Judex aequitatem semper spectare debet: A judge ought always to aim at equity.
Judex damnatur cum nocens absolvitur: The judge is condemned when a guilty person is acquitted.
Judex est lex loquens: A judge is the law speaking.
Judex non potest esse testis in propria causa: A judge cannot be a witness in his or her own case.
Judex non potest injuriam sibi datam punire: A judge cannot punish an injury done to him- or herself.
Judicandum est legibus, non exemplis: One is to judge by laws, not by examples (i.e., precedents).
Judicia posteriora sunt in lege fortiora: Later decisions are stronger in law.

Judicis est judicare secundum allegata et probata: A judge is to judge according to what is alleged and what is proven.

Judicis est jus dicere non jus dare: A judge is to declare the law not make the law (note: a supposed pun on the words *judicis* and *jus dicere*).

Judicium est quasi juris dictum: A judgment is as if a command of the law.

Judicium semper pro veritate accipitur: A judgment is always accepted as the truth.

Juncta juvat: Things joined together are helpful (i.e., in union there is strength).

Jura naturae sunt immutabilia: The laws of nature are immutable.

Jura publica anteferenda privatis: Public rights are to be preferred before private rights.

Jurare est Deum in testem vocare: To swear is to call God to witness.

Juratores sunt judices facti: Jurors are the judges of fact.

Jure non dono: By right, not by gift.

Juris et de jure: Of law and by law.

Jus descendit et non terra: A right descends and not the land.

Jus est ars boni et aequi: Law is the art of the good and the just.

Jus et fraus nunquam cohabitant: Justice and fraud never dwell together.

Jus ex injuria non oritur: A right cannot arise from injury.

Jus publicum privatorum pactis mutari non potest: A public right cannot be altered by the agreements of private persons.

Jus respicit aequitatem: Law regards equity.

Jus vendit quod usus approbavit: The law recommends what use has approved.

Justitia et fortitudo invincibilia sunt: Justice and fortitude are invincible.

Justitia nec differenda nec neganda est: Justice is neither to be deferred nor delayed.

Justitia nemini neganda est: Justice is to be denied to no one.

Justitiae soror fides: Faith is the sister of justice.
Justo geminantur anni: The years are doubled for the just.

L

Legem enim contractus dat: The contract gives the law.
Leges mori serviunt: Laws are subservient to custom.
Leges non verbis sed rebus sunt impositae: Laws are imposed on things, not words.
Leges posteriores priores contraria abrogant: Later laws abrogate prior contrary laws.
Leges vigilantibus non dormientibus subveniunt: The laws aid the vigilant not those who sleep.
Legis interpretatio legis vim obtinet: The interpretation of the law obtains the force of law.
Lex de futuro, judex de praeterito: The law provides for the future, the judge for the past.
Lex dilationes semper exhorret: The law always abhors delays.
Lex est dictamen rationis: Law is the dictate of reason.
Lex est norma recti: Law is a rule of right.
Lex est summa ratio: Law is the highest reason.
Lex judicat de rebus necessario faciendis quasi re ipsa factis: The law judges of things, which must be done, as if actually done.
Lex neminem cogit ad impossibilia: The law compels no one to do what is impossible.
Lex nil facit frustra, nil jubet frustra: The law does nothing in vain, commands nothing in vain.
Lex non a rege est violanda: The law is not to be violated by the king.
Lex non curat de minimis: The law does not care about trifling matters.
Lex non favet delicatorium votis: The law favors not the wishes of the dainty (viz., those given to complaints).
Lex posterior derogat priori: A later law repeals an earlier one.

Lex prospicit non respicit: The law looks forward not backward.

Lex punit mendacium: The law punishes a lie.

Lex reprobat moram: The law disapproves delay.

Lex respicit aequitatem: The law regards equity.

Lex semper dabit remedium: The law provides a remedy.

Lex spectat naturae ordinem: The law regards the course of nature.

Lex succurrit minoribus: The law assists minors.

Lex uno ore omnes alloquitur: The law speaks to all with the same mouth (i.e., in the same way).

Libra justa justitiam servat: A just balance preserves justice.

Linea recta semper praefertur transversali: A direct line is always preferred to a transverse (or oblique) line.

Lis litem generat: Strife begats strife.

Littera scripta manet: The written letter remains.

Locus contractus regit actum: The place of the contract governs the act.

Locus regit actum: An act is governed by the laws of the place.

Longa patientia trahitur ad consensum: Long-suffering is taken as consent.

Longa possessio jus parit: Long possession gives birth to a right.

Lupus pilum mutat, non mentem: The wolf changes its coat, not its disposition.

M

Magna culpa dolus est: Gross negligence is [equivalent to] fraud.

Major continet in se minus: The greater contains in itself the less.

Majus dignum trahit ad se minus dignum: The more worthy draws to itself the less worthy.

Mala grammatica non vitiat chartam: Grammatical error does not invalidate the charter.

Maleficia propositis distinguuntur: Evil deeds are distinguished from evil purposes.

Malitia supplet aetatem: Malice supplies the place of age (viz., crimes committed by minors).

Malum non praesumitur: Evil is not presumed.

Malus usus est abolendus: An evil custom ought to be abolished.

Maris et feminae conjunctio est de jure naturae: The union of male and female is founded on the law of nature.

Mater artium necessitas: Necessity is the mother of invention.

Melior est conditio possidentis: Better is the condition of the one who possesses.

Melior est petere fontes: It is better to go to the fountainhead (i.e., to the source).

Mendacem memorem esse oportet: A liar should have a good memory.

Mens sana in corpore sano: A sound mind in a sound body.

Mens testatoris in testamentis spectanda est: In wills, the intention of the testator is to be regarded.

Merx est quidquid vendi potest: Merchandise is whatever can be sold.

Minatur innocentibus qui parcit nocentibus: He threatens the innocent who spares the guilty.

Minor jurare non potest: A minor cannot swear.

Misera est servitus ubi jus est vagum aut incertum: Wretched is the servitude (or slavery) where the law is changeable and uncertain.

Mobilia non habent situm: Movable things have no fixed location or place.

Mobilia sequuntur personam: Movable things follow the person.

Modus et conventio vincunt legem: The manner of the agreement and the consent of the parties overrule the law.

Modus legem dat donationi: The manner gives law to a gift.

Mors dicitur ultimum supplicium: Death is reserved for ultimate punishment.

Mors omnia solvit: Death dissolves all things.

Mortui non mordant: The dead do not bite (i.e., dead men tell no tales).

Mortuo leoni et lepores insultant: Even hares insult a dead lion.

Mortuus sasit vivum: The dead ancestor invests the living heir.

Mos majorum ut lex valet: Ancestral custom has the force of law.

Mos pro lege: Custom for law (i.e., usage has the force of law).

Mos retinendus est fidelissimae vetustatis: A custom of the truest antiquity is to be retained.

Multa fidem promissa levant: Many promises lessen confidence.

Multa non vetat lex quae tamen tacite damnavit: The law does not forbid many things that it has silently condemned.

Multas cautiones habet: One must take many precautions.

Multi multa, nemo omnia novit: Many people know many things; no one knows everything.

Mundus vult decipi: The world wishes to be deceived.

Murus aeneus conscientia sana: A sound conscience is a wall of brass.

N

Natura appetit perfectum, ita et lex: Nature aspires to perfection, so does the law.

Naturae vis maxima: The highest force is that of nature.

Ne fronti crede: Trust not to appearances.

Ne judex ultra petita partium: A judge may not award beyond what the parties ask.

Ne procedat judex ex officio: A judge shall not proceed on his or her own.

Ne puero gladium: Do not entrust a sword to a boy.

Ne quis judex in propria causa: No one is judge in his or her own cause.

Selected Latin Maxims and Legal Principles 189

Nec ultra petita nec infra petita: Being neither more than nor less than what is requested.

Necessitas facit licitum quod alias non est licitum: Necessity makes lawful what otherwise is not lawful.

Necessitas inducit privilegium quoad jura privata: Necessity induces a privilege with respect to private rights.

Necessitas non habet legem: Necessity knows no law.

Necessitas publica major est quam privata: Public necessity is greater than private.

Necessitas quod cogit defendit: Necessity defends what it compels.

Necessitas vincit legem: Necessity conquers the law.

Negligentia semper habet infortuniam comitem: Negligence always has misfortune for a companion.

Neminem laedit qui jure suo utitur: The one who uses his or her own rights harms no one.

Nemo agit in se ipsum: No one takes action against him- or herself.

Nemo bis punitur pro eodem delicto: No one is punished twice for the same crime.

Nemo cogitationis poenam patitur: No one suffers punishment on account of one's thoughts.

Nemo dat quod non habet: No one gives what he or she does not have.

Nemo de domo sua extrahi potest: No one can be dragged out of his or her home.

Nemo debet bis puniri pro uno delicto: No one ought to be punished twice for the same offense.

Nemo debet esse judex in propria causa: No one may be judge in his or her own cause.

Nemo debet locupletari (ex) aliena jactura: No one ought to be enriched at another person's expense.

Nemo est haeres viventis: No one is an heir of the living.

Nemo est supra leges: No one is above the law.

Nemo ex consilio obligatur: No one is liable for the advice he or she gives.

Nemo gratis mendax: No one is a liar for free.

Nemo inauditus condemnari debet: No one ought to be condemned without being heard.

Nemo plus juris ad alienum transferre potest quam ipse haberet: No one can transfer to another a greater right than what he or she might have.

Nemo potest esse simul actor et judex: No one can be at once plaintiff and judge.

Nemo potest esse tenens et dominus: No one can be both tenant and landlord.

Nemo potest sibi debere: No one can be in debt to himself.

Nemo praesumitur ludere in extremis: No one is presumed to trifle (or make light) at the point of death.

Nemo praesumitur malus: No one is presumed to be bad (i.e., guilty).

Nemo punitur pro alieno delicto: No one is punished for the crime of another.

Nemo repente fuit turpissimus: No one ever became suddenly wicked.

Nemo tenetur ad impossibile: No one is held to do the impossible.

Nemo tenetur divinare: No one is bound to foretell the future.

Nemo tenetur edere instrumenta contra se: No one is forced to produce writings (viz., evidence) against him- or herself.

Nemo tenetur seipsum accusare: No one is bound to accuse him- or herself (i.e., to incriminate oneself).

Nescit vox missa reverti: The word once spoken can never be recalled.

Nihil (or **Nil**) **consensui tam contrarium est quam vis atque metus:** Nothing is so contrary to consent as force and fear.

Nihil dat qui non habet: He gives nothing who has nothing.

Nihil habet forum ex scena: The court has nothing to do with that which is not before it.

Nihil quod est inconveniens est licitum: Nothing that is inconvenient is allowed (i.e., legal).

Nil consuetudine majus: Nothing is greater than custom.

Nil dictum quod non dictum prius: Nothing is said that has not been said before.

Nil ligatum: Nothing is bound.

Nil novi sub sole: There is nothing new under the sun.

Nimia subtilitas in jure reprobatur: Too much subtlety in the law is reprehensible.

Nimium altercando veritas amittitur: By too much debate, truth is lost.

Nocet empta dolore voluptas: Pleasure bought by pain is injurious.

Nomina sunt mutabilia, res autem immobiles: Names are mutable, but things are immutable.

Nomina sunt notae rerum: Names are the marks of things.

Non debet cui plus licet, quod minus est non licere: To one allowed the greater should not be disallowed (or prohibited) the lesser.

Non decipitur qui scit se decipi: One is not deceived who knows him- or herself to be deceived.

Non est regula quin fallat: There is no rule that may not fail (i.e., every rule has an exception).

Non est vivere, sed valere, vita: Life is not mere living but the enjoyment of health.

Non facias malum ut inde veniat bonum: You may not do evil that good may come of it.

Non nobis solum: We live not for ourselves alone.

Non omne damnum inducit injuriam: Not all damage (or loss) leads to injury.

Non omne quod licet honestum: Not everything that is legal is honorable.

Non quod dictum est, sed quod factum est, inspicitur: Give regard not to what is said but to what is done.

Non remota causa sed proxima spectatur: The immediate, not the remote, cause is to be considered.

Non valet donatio nisi subsequatur traditio: A gift is not valid unless there is subsequent possession.

Non videntur qui errant consentire: Those who err are not seen to consent.

Nosce te ipsum or **nosce teipsum:** Know thyself.

Noscitur a sociis: He is known by his associates (i.e., the meaning of a word is determined by its textual context).

Novus rex, nova lex: New king, new law.

Nudum pactum ex quo non oritur actio: No action arises from a naked promise.

Nulla crimen sine lege: No crime without law.

Nulla emptio sine pretio esse potest: There can be no sale without a price.

Nulla poena sine lege: No punishment without law.

Nullum commodum capere potest de injuria sua propria: No one can obtain advantage by his or her own wrong.

Nullum simile est idem nisi quatuor pedibus currit: No comparison is the same unless it runs on all fours (i.e., unless there is a resemblance).

Nullum tributum sine lege: No tax without law.

Nuptias non concubitus sed consensus facit: Consent, not cohabitation, makes a marriage.

O

Obedientia est legis essentia: Obedience is the essence of the law.

Occasio furem facit: Opportunity makes the thief.

Odiosa et inhonesta non sunt in lege praesumenda: Odious and dishonest acts are not to be presumed in the law.

Omissio nihil operatur: What is omitted has no operative effect.

Omne crimen ebrietas et incendit et detegit: Drunkenness both kindles and discloses every crime.

Omne majus continet in se minus: Every greater thing contains the lesser within itself.

Omne quod solo inaedificatur solo cedit: Everything that is built upon the soil belongs to the soil.

Omne verum vero consonat: All truth with truth accords.

Omnem movere lapidem: To leave no stone unturned.

Omnia praesumuntur contra proferentem: Everything is presumed against the one who made the offer.

Omnis amans amens: Every lover is demented.

Omnis indemnatus pro innoxio legibus habetur: Everyone who has not been found guilty is deemed innocent by the laws.

Omnis ratihabitio retrotrahitur: Every ratification has a retroactive effect.

Optima legum interpres est consuetudo: Custom is the best interpreter of the law.

Optimi consiliarii mortui: The best counselors are the dead.

Optimus interpres rerum usus: Usage is the best interpreter of things.

P

Pacta privata non derogant juri communi: Private contracts cannot adversely affect (or restrict) the public law (or right).

Par in parem imperium non habet: An equal has no authority over an equal.

Parendo legibus ordo servatur: By obeying the laws is order preserved.

Paribus sententiis reus absolvitur: Where opinions are equal, a defendant is absolved (i.e., acquitted).

Partus sequitur ventrem: The offspring follows its mother (e.g., the calf belongs with the cow).

Pater (is) est quem nuptiae demonstrant: The father is (he,) the one whom the marriage indicates.

Peccata contra naturam sunt gravissima: Crimes against nature are the gravest.

Pecunia non olet: Money does not smell.

Pecunia obediunt omnia: All things are obedient to money.

Pendente lite nihil innovetur: Nothing must be altered during pending litigation.

Per fas et nefas: By proper and improper means (i.e., by fair means or foul).

Periculum in mora: There is danger in delay.

Permittiur quod non prohibetur: What is not prohibited is permitted.

Plena et celeris justitia fiat partibus: Let the parties have full and speedy justice.

Posito uno oppositorum negaur alterum: To affirm one position is to negate the other opposing position.

Post factum nullum consilium: Counsel is of no effect after the fact.

Potentia non est nisi ad bonum: Power is not given except for the public good.

Potior est conditio defendentis: The position of the defendant is stronger.

Potior est conditio possidentis: The position of the one who possesses is stronger.

Praestat cautela quam medela: Caution is better than cure.

Presumendum est pro libertate: The presumption is in favor of liberty.

Prior tempore, potior jure: First in time, stronger in right.

Privatum commodum publico cedit: Private convenience must yield to the public good.

Probandi necessitas incumbit illi qui agit: The necessity of proving rests upon the one who begins the action.

Probatis extremis, praesumitur media: The extreme being proved, the mean is presumed.

Probum non poenitet: An honest person does not repent.

Q

Quae fuerunt vitia mores sunt: What were once vices are now customs.

Quae non valeant singula, juncta juvant: Things that may not avail singly are effective when joined.

Quae propter necessitatem recepta sunt, non debent in argumentum trahi: What is admitted by necessity ought not be drawn into argument.

Qualis pater, talis filius: Like father, like son.

Quaestio fit de legibus, non de personis: The question must refer to the laws, not to persons.

Quasi agnum committere lupo: As though handing the lamb over to the wolf.

Qui approbat non reprobat: The one who accepts cannot also reject.

Qui bene interrogat bene docet: The one who questions well teaches well.

Qui destruit medium destruit finem: The one who destroys the means also destroys the end.

Qui facit per alium facit per se: The one who acts through another acts by him- or herself.

Qui haeret in litera, haeret in cortice: The one who lingers at the letter lingers at the bark (i.e., fails to get at the substance of the law).

Qui jure suo utitur nullum damnum facit: The one who uses his or her own rights causes harm to no one.

Qui male agit odit lucem: The one who acts badly hates the light.

Qui mandat ipse fecisse videtur: The one who orders the act is seen as the one who does the act.

Qui nimium probat nihil probat: The one who proves too much proves nothing.

Qui non improbat, approbat: The one who does not disapprove, approves.

Qui parcit nocentibus innocentes punit: The one who spares the guilty punishes the innocent.

Qui peccat ebrius luat sobrius: Let the one who sins when drunk be punished when sober.

Qui prior est tempore, potior est jure: The one who is first in time is stronger in law.

Qui tacet consentire videtur: The one who is silent is seen to consent.

Qui tacet consentit: The one who is silent consents.

Qui vult decipi decipiatur: Let the one who wishes to be deceived be deceived.

Quia ita lex scripta est: Because the law is written thus.

Quicquid plantatur solo, solo cedit: Whatever is planted in the soil is ceded with the soil.

Quid leges sine moribus vanae proficiunt?: What good are laws when there are no morals?

Quidquid agas prudenter agas: Whatever you do, do so with caution.

Quieta non movere: Not to move quiet things (i.e., to let sleeping dogs lie).

Quis custodiet ipsos custodes?: Who shall guard the guards?

Quisque sibi proximus: Everyone is nearest to himself.

Quisque suos patimur manes: Everyone suffers from the spirits of his or her own past.

Quo ligatur eo dissolvitur: What is bound by contract is dissolved by contract.

Quod cito fit, cito perit: What is done quickly, perishes quickly.

Quod contra legem fit pro infecto habetur: What is done contrary to the law is considered as not done.

Quod datum est ecclesiae datum est Deo: What is given to the church is given to God.

Quod dubitas, ne feceris: Where you doubt, then neither do.

Quod est inconveniens et contra rationem non est permissum in lege: Whatever is inconvenient and contrary to reason is not permitted in law.

Quod est necessarium est licitum: What is necessary is legal.

Quod initio non valet, tractu temporis non valet: What is invalid from the outset cannot be made valid over time.

Quod necessitas cogit, defendit: What necessity forces, it justifies.

Quod necessitas cogit, excusat: What necessity forces, it excuses.

Quod non legitur non creditur: What is not read is not believed.

Quod nullius est, est domini regis: What belongs to no one belongs to the lord the king.

Quod nullius est, fit occupantis: What belongs to none becomes the property of the occupier.
Quod nullum est, nullum effectum producit: That which is null produces no effect.
Quod omnis tangit ab omnibus approbetur: That which touches all should be approved by all.
Quod per me non possum, nec per alium: What I cannot do in person, I cannot do by proxy.
Quod pure debetur praesenti die debetur: That which is due unconditionally is due immediately.
Quod tibi fieri non vis, alteri ne feceris: What you do not want done to you, do it not to another.
Quod vanum et inutile est, lex non requirit: The law does not require the vain and the useless.
Quod voluit non dixit: What one says is not (always) what one intends.

R

Ratihabitio mandato aequiparatur: Ratification is equivalent to a mandate.
Ratio est legis anima: Reason is the spirit and soul of the law.
Ratio non clauditur loco: Reason is not confined to place.
Recte quod honeste: That is rightly done which is honestly done.
Res amicos invenit: Fortune finds us friends.
Res communes omnium (jure naturali): Common things belong to everyone.
Res derelicta, primi occupantis: Abandoned things belong to the first one who finds or occupies them.
Res est misera ubi jus est vagum et incertum: It is a wretched state of affairs where the laws are vague and uncertain.
Res humanae in summo declinant: At their height, human affairs decline.
Res inter alios acta, aliis nec nocet nec prodest: A thing done between some neither harms nor benefits others.

Res inter alios judicatae nullum praejudicium faciunt: A matter adjudged does not prejudice those who are not party to it.

Res ipsa loquitur, sed quid in infernos dicit?: The thing speaks for itself, but what the devil does it say?

Res judicata pro veritate accipitur: An adjudicated matter is accepted as true.

Res nolunt diu male administrari: Things refuse to be mismanaged long.

Res nullius fit primi occupatis: A thing with no owner belongs to the first one who finds it.

Res perit suo domino or **Res periit suo domino:** The loss falls upon its owner.

Res sua nemini servit: No one may have an easement over his or her property.

Res sunt humanae flebile ludibrium: Human affairs are a jest to be wept over.

Respice, adspice, prospice: Examine the past, examine the present, examine the future.

Respice finem: Look to the end (i.e., consider the result).

Respondeat superior: Let the superior answer.

Rex non potest peccare: The king can do no wrong.

Risus abundat in ore stultorum: Laughter abounds in the mouth of fools.

S

Salus populi est suprema lex: The welfare of the people is the supreme law.

Salus respublica suprema lex: The welfare of the state is the supreme law.

Salus ubi multi consiliarii: There is safety in many advisers.

Satius est petere fontes quam sectari rivulos: It is better to seek the source than follow the rivelet.

Scientia est potentia: Knowledge is power.

Scire debes cum quo contrahis: You ought to know with whom you are dealing.

Scire et scire debere aequiparantur in lege: Knowledge and the duty to know are regarded the same in the law.

Scribere est agere: To write is to act.

Scriptum jus est lex: Written law is the law.

Semel heres, semper heres: Once an heir, always an heir.

Semper in dubiis benigniora praeferenda sunt: In doubtful matters the more benevolent resolution is always to be preferred.

Semper praesumitur pro matrimonio: The presumption always favors valid marriage.

Semper praesumitur pro negante: The presumption always favors the negative.

Sensus verborum est anima legis: The meaning of words is the soul of the law.

Sententia non fertur de rebus non liquidis: Judgment is not given on matters that are not clear.

Sequi debet potentia justitiam, non praecedere: Power should follow justice, not precede it.

Sermon index animi: Speech is the index of the mind.

Si judicas, cognosce: If you judge, understand.

Si sic omnes: If all did thus.

Sic utere tuo ut alienum non laedas: Use your own [property] in such a way as not to harm others.

Silent leges inter arma: The laws are silent during war.

Simplex commendatio non obligat: A simple recommendation does not infer an obligation.

Sine justitia, confusio: Without justice, confusion.

Sit pro ratione voluntas: Let will stand for reason.

Societas delinquere non potest: A society cannot commit crime.

Socii mei socius meus socius non est: The partner of my partner is not my partner.

Solo cedit, quicquid solo plantatur: What is affixed to the soil belongs to the soil.

Solve et repete: Pay and seek again (i.e., settle now, then appeal later).

Solventur risu tabulae: The indictments are dismissed with a laugh.

Specialia generalibus derogant: The specific derogates from the general (i.e., takes precedent).

Spectemur agendo: Let us be judged by our actions.

Spoliatus debet ante omnia restitui: The one who has been robbed ought first to have his or her goods restored.

Stabit praesumptio donec probetur in contrarium: A presumption stands until the contrary is proved.

Stare decisis et non quieta movere: To abide by precedent and not to unsettle things established.

Sua cuique sunt vitia: Everyone has his or her own vices.

Summum jus, summa injuria: Extreme law, extreme injury.

Superflua non nocent: Superfluous things do no harm.

Suppressio veri suggestio falsi: Suppression of the truth is the suggestion of falsehood.

T

Tam facti quam animi: As much in deed as in intention.

Tempora mutantur nos et mutantur in illis: Times change and we change with them.

Tempus anima rei: Time is the essence of the contract.

Tempus omnia revelat: Time reveals all things.

Tempus omnia terminat: Time ends all things.

Terra transit cum onere or **Transit terra cum onere:** Land passes with its burdens.

Testamentum omne morte consummatum: Every will (or testament) is consummated by death.

Testes ponderantur non numerantur: Witnesses are weighed not numbered (i.e., counted).

Testis unus, testis nullus: One witness is no witness.

Traditio loqui facit chartam: Delivery makes a charter speak (i.e., go into effect).

Transeat in exemplum: Let it stand as an example.

Tutius erratur ex parte mitiori: It is safer to err on the milder side.

U

Ubi eadem ratio, ibi eadem lex: Where the same reason, there the same law.

Ubi jus, ibi remedium: Where there is law, there is remedy.

Ubi jus incertum, ibi jus nullum: Where the law is uncertain, there is no law.

Ubi lex non distinguit, nec nos distinguere debemus: Where the law does not distinguish, neither should we distinguish.

Ubi lex voluit, dixit; ubi non voluit, tacuit: Where the law wills, it speaks; where the law wills not, it remains silent.

Ubi mel, ibi apes: Where there is honey, there are bees.

Ubi non est principalis, non potest esse accessorius: Where there is no principal, there can be no accessory.

Ultra posse nemo obligatur: No one is obligated to do more than he or she is able.

Universitas non moritur: The university does not die (i.e., a corporation outlives the death of those who founded it).

Unus vir nullus vir: One man is no man.

Usus est tyrannus: Custom is a tyrant.

Usus fit ex iteratis actibus: Usage arises from repeated acts.

Uti non abuti: It is to use, not to abuse.

Uti possidetis, ita possideatis: As you possess, so may you possess.

Utile per inutile non vitiatur: What is useful is not vitiated by what is useless.

V

Vacare culpa magnum est solatium: A great solace it is to be free of fault.

Vel faciendo vel delinquendo: Either by doing something or by leaving something undone (i.e., by act or omission).

Venalis populus venalis curia patrum: The people and the senators are equally venal.

Venia necessitati datur: (fig.) Necessity knows no law.

Venire contra factum proprium non valet: To go against one's own fact is not allowed (also known as the principle of *estoppel*).

Verba aliquid operari debent: Words ought to have some effect.

Verba generalia generaliter sunt intelligenda: General words are to be understood generally.

Verba intentioni debent inservire: Words ought to be made subservient to intent.

Verba sunt indices animi: Words are the indices of the mind.

Verba volant, scripta manent: Spoken words fly away, written words remain.

Verbum sat sapienti: A word to the wise is sufficient.

Veritas demonstrationis tollit errorem nominis: The truth of the description removes the error of the name.

Veritas est justitiae mater: Truth is the mother of justice.

Veritas nihil veretur nisi abscondi: Truth fears nothing save concealment.

Veritas nimium altercando amittitur: By too much altercation truth is lost.

Veritas nunquam perit: Truth never perishes.

Veritas omnia vincit: Truth conquers all things.

Veritas praevalebit: Truth will prevail.

Veritatem dies aperit: Time reveals the truth.

Veritatis simplex oratio est: The language of truth is simple.

Vetustas pro lege semper habetur: An old custom is ever regarded as law.

Via antiqua via est tuta: The old way is the safe way.

Via trita est tutissima: The trodden path is the safest.

Via trita via tuta: The trodden path the safe path.

Vicarius non habet vicarium: A delegate cannot have a delegate.

Vidi scivi et audivi: I saw, I knew, and I heard (viz., to notarize).

Vigilantibus non dormientibus jura subveniunt: Laws aid the vigilant not those who sleep.

Vir sapit qui pauca loquitur: Wise is the person who talks little.

Selected Latin Maxims and Legal Principles 203

Vis legibus est inimica: Force is the enemy of the law.

Vita mutatur non tollitur: Life is changed not taken away.

Volenti non fit injuria: No harm is done by those who willingly act.

Voluntas in delictis non existus spectatur: In crimes, the intent, not the consequence, is considered.

Voluntas in mente retenta, voluntas non est: An intent retained in the mind is not an expression of intent.

Voluntas non potest cogi: The will cannot be forced.

Voluntas pro facto reputatur: The will is to be taken for the act.

Voluntas reputatur pro facto: The will is to be taken for the deed.

Voluntatis non necessitatis: A matter of choice, not of necessity.

Vox audita perit, litera scripta manet: The voice that is heard perishes, the letter that is written remains.

Vox emissa volat, litera scripta manet: Spoken words fly, written words remain.

Vox volat, scripta manet: Spoken things fly, written things remain.

Vulgus amicitias utilitate probat: The common crowd seeks friendships for their usefulness.

A Sampling of Latin Quotations Related to Law and Life

Adeo in teneris consuescere multum est: So much depends upon habit in the tender years (Virgil).

Æquum est peccatis veniam poscentem reddere rursus: The one who asks pardon for faults should grant the same in return (Horace).

Alia tendanda via est: Another way must be tried (Virgil).

Alter alteris auxilio eget: One requires the aid of the other (Sallust).

Aut inveniam viam aut faciam: Either I will find a way or I will make one (attributed to Hannibal).

Beneficium accipere libertatem est vendere: To accept a favor is to sell one's freedom (Publilius Syrus).

Bibamus, moriendum est: Let us drink, death is certain (Seneca the Elder).

Bonis nocet quisquis pepercerit malis: Whoever spares the bad injures the good (Publilius Syrus).

Bonis quod bene fit haud perit: A kindness done for the good is never done in vain (Plautus).

Certum voto pete finem: Set a definite limit to your desire (Cicero).

Corpus non animae domicilium sed diversum est: The body is not the abode of the soul but its enemy (Willett's *Emblem Book*, no. 87, after St. Paul).

Crede mihi, miseris coelestia numina parcunt; nec semper laesos et sine fine, premunt: Believe me, the gods spare the afflicted, and do not always oppress those who are unfortunate (Ovid).

Doctrina est ingenii naturale quoddam pabulum: Learning is a kind of natural food for the mind (Cicero).

Dolendi modus, timendi non autem: There is a limit to grief, but not to fear (Francis Bacon, after Pliny the Younger).

DOI: 10.4324/9781003255369-3

Dubiam salutem qui dat afflictis, negat: The one who offers the afflicted a doubtful deliverance denies all hope (Seneca).

Dubitando ad veritatem pervenimus: By way of doubting we arrive at the truth (Cicero).

Ducis ingenium, res adversae nudare solent, celare secundae: Disasters are wont to reveal the abilities of a leader, good fortune to conceal them (Horace).

Ducunt volentem fata, nolentem trahunt: Fate leads the willing and drags the unwilling (Seneca, after Cleanthes).

Dulce bellum inexpertis: War is delightful to the inexperienced (Erasmus).

Dum vitant stulti vitia, in contraria currunt: While fools try to avoid one error, they hasten into its opposite (Horace).

Durate et vosmet rebus servate secundis: Carry on and preserve yourselves for better times (Virgil).

Errare humanum est: To err is human (Pope, after Cicero).

Felix qui potuit rerum cognoscere causas: Happy is the one who knows (or understands) the causes of all things (Virgil).

Fit erranti medicina confessio: Confession is as healing medicine to one who has erred (Cicero).

Fundamentum justitiae primum est ne cui noceatur: The foundation of justice is first not to harm others (after Cicero).

Fures privatorum in nervo atque in compedibus aetatem agunt; fures publici in auro atque in purpura: Thieves guilty of private thefts spent their lives in shackles and chains; thieves of the public treasury spent their lives in gold and purple (attributed to Cato the Elder).

Furor arma ministrat: Rage supplies arms (Virgil).

Hac urget lupus, hac canis: On one side a wolf besets you, on the other a dog (Horace).

Haud semper errat fama; aliquando et elegit: Fame does not always err; sometimes it chooses well (Tacitus).

Homo homini lupus est: Man is a wolf to man (Plautus).

Honesta mors turpi vita potior: An honorable death is better than an ignominious life (Tacitus).

Honesta quaedam scelera successus facit: Success makes some wicked deeds honorable (Seneca).

Honeste vivere, alterum non laedere, suum cuique tribuere: To live honorably, not to injure another, and to give each his or her due (Domitius Ulpianus, defining the three precepts of the law).

Honestus rumor alterum patrimonium est: A good name is a second inheritance (Publilius Syrus).

Humiles laborant ubi potentes dissident: The lowly suffer when the powerful disagree (Phaedrus).

Injuriarum remedium est oblivio: The remedy for wrongs is to forget them (Publilius Syrus).

Interdum vulgus rectum videt, est ubi peccat: Sometimes the common people see what is right, at other times they err (Horace).

Judex damnatur ubi nocens absolvitur: The judge is condemned when the guilty is acquitted (Publilius Syrus).

Judicis est innocentiae subvenire: It is the duty of the judge to support innocence (Cicero).

Juravi lingua, mentem injuratam gero: I have sworn with my tongue, but I have a mind unsworn (Cicero).

Jurisprudentia est divinarum atque humanarum rerum notitia, justi atque injusti scientia: Jurisprudence is knowledge of things human and divine, knowledge of what is just and what is not just (from the *Corpus Juris* of Justinian).

Jus summum saepe summa malitia est: Extreme law is often extreme wrong (Terence).

Justae causae facilis est defensio: The defense of a just cause is easy (Cicero).

Justitia autem praecipit suum cuique reddere: Justice enjoins us to return to each his own (Cicero).

Justitia suum cuique distribuit: Justice distributes to each his or her due (Cicero).

Justum ab injustis petere insipientia est: It is folly to expect justice at the hands of the unjust (Plautus).

Levis est dolor qui capere consilium potest: Light is the pain (or grief) that is able to take counsel (Seneca).

Levius fit patientia quicquid corrigere est nefas: Patience lightens that which it is impossible to change (Horace).

Lex citius tolerare vult privatum damnum quam publicum malum: The law will sooner tolerate a private loss than a public evil (Coke).

Liberatem natura etiam mutis animalibus datam: Liberty is given by nature even to mute animals (Tacitus).

Libertas inaestimabile res est: Liberty is a thing of inestimable worth (from the *Corpus Juris* of Justinian).

Maximum remedium est irae mora: Delay is the greatest remedy for anger (Seneca).

Mens agitat molem: Mind moves the mass (i.e., mind moves matter) (Virgil).

Mens sibi conscia recti: A mind conscious of its own uprightness (Horace).

Mille mali species, mille salutis erunt: There are a thousand forms of evil; there will be a thousand remedies (Ovid).

Mors laborum ac miseriarum quies est: Death is repose from all our toils and miseries (Cicero).

Mors sola fatetur quantula sint hominum corpuscula: Death alone reveals how small men's bodies are (Juvenal).

Multas cautiones habet: One must take many precautions (after Cicero).

Multitudo (autem) sapientium sanitas orbis terrarum: A multitude of the wise is the health of the world (Holbein, after Wisdom of Solomon 6:26).

Multo majoris alapae mecum veneunt: (fig.) I sell freedom at a much higher price (Phaedrus).

Nihil [enim] semper floret; aetas succedit aetati: Nothing flourishes forever; age succeeds age (Cicero).

Nihil honestum esse potest, quod justitia vacat: Nothing can be honorable where justice is absent (Cicero).

Nihil inimicius quam sibi ipse: (fig.) Man is his own worst enemy (Cicero).

Nil agit exemplum litem quod lite resolvit: That example (precedent) does nothing which, in resolving one dispute, introduces another (Horace).

Nomina debent naturis rerum congruere: The names of things ought to agree with their natures (St. Thomas Aquinas).

Non ignara mali, miseris succerrere disco: Not unacquainted with misfortune, I learn to give aid to those in misery (Virgil).

Nosce tempus: Know your time (after Erasmus).

Nulli negabimus, nulli differemus justitiam: We shall not negate, nor delay, the justice that is due (from the Magna Carta).

Nuptiae sunt coniunctio maris et feminae et consortium omnis vitae, divini et humani juris communicatio: Marriage is the unity of husband and wife and a consortium of all life, a community of human and divine law (Modestino).

O dulce nomen libertatis, O jus eximium nostrae civitatis: O sweet the name of freedom, our right of eminent civility (Cicero).

Omne ignotum pro magnifico est: Everything unknown is thought to be magnificent (Tacitus).

Omni aetati mors est communis: Death is common to every age (Cicero).

Omnia bona bonis: All things are good to the good (a heraldry motto, after St. Paul).

Omnia orta occident: All things that rise also set (Sallust).

Optanda mors ets, sine metu mortis mori: To die without fear of death is to be desired (Seneca).

Orandum est ut sit mens sana in corpore sano: You should pray to have a sound mind in a sound body (Juvenal).

Pax optima rerum quas homini novisse datum est: Peace is the best thing that men may know (Silius Italicus).

Per scelera semper sceleribus certum est iter: The way to wickedness is always through wickedness (Seneca).

Post cineres gloria sera venit: Glory comes too late after death (Martius).

Posteri dies testes sunt sapientissimi: Succeeding days are the wisest evidences (attributed to Virgil).

Princeps major singulis, minor universis: The prince is greater than one, lesser than all (after Aristotle).

Quanti est sapere!: What a great thing it is to be wise! (Terence).

Quid rides? Mutato nomine de te fabula narratur: Why do you laugh? Change the name and the tale is told of you (Horace).

Quod semper aequum ac bonum est: What is always equitable and good (Julius Paulus, in defining natural law).

Quot homines, tot sententiae: So many men, so many opinions (Terence).

Repente dives nemo factus est bonus: No good person ever became suddenly rich (Publilius Syrus).

Repente nemo fuit turpissimus: No one became extremely wicked all at once (Juvenal).

Res est profecto stulta nequitiae modus: (fig.) It is surely folly to stop midway through the crime (Seneca).

Res humanas ordine nullo Fortuna regit: Without order doth Fortune rule human affairs (Seneca).

Rivalem patienter habe: Bear patiently with a rival (Ovid).

Scientia est lux lucis: Knowledge is the light of light (attributed to Leonardo da Vinci).

Semita certe tranquillae per virtutem patet unica vitae: The only path to a tranquil life is through virtue (Juvenal).

Sic habeto, non esse te mortalem, sed corpus hoc: Be sure that it is not you that is mortal but only your body (Cicero).

Singula de nobis anni praedantur euntes: As the years pass, they rob us of one thing after another (Horace).

Societatis vinculum est ratio et oratio: Reason and speech are the bond of society (Cicero).

Spiritus intus alit: The spirit within nourishes (Virgil).

Summum bonum appertere est bene vivere: To seek the highest good is to live well (St. Augustine).

Suum cuique tribuere, ea demum summa justitia est: To give everyone his due, that is supreme justice (Cicero).

Tempus molestiis medetur omnibus: Time heals all wounds (figuratively, after Euripides).

Tempus omnia revelat: Time reveals all things (an adage, after Erasmus).

Ut saepe summa ingenia in occulto latent: How often it is that great genius is hidden by obscurity (Plautus).

Varia vita est: Life is changeable (Plautus).

Virtus hominem jungit Deo: Virtue unites man with God (Cicero).

Vitia nobis sub virtutum nomine obrepunt: Vices steal upon us under the name of virtues (Seneca).

Vivimus aliena fiducia: We live by trusting one another (Pliny the Elder).

Latin Abbreviations

A

a. [ante]: before; ahead of
a.a. [ad acta]: to the archives; shelved (i.e., to close the case or the matter)
A.A.S. [anno aetatis suae]: in the year of his or her age
A.B. or **B.A.** [Artium Baccalaureus]: Bachelor of Arts
A.D. [anno Domini]: in the year of our Lord
a.d. [ante diem]: before the day
a.h.d. [ad hunc diem]: to or at this day
a.h.l. [ad hunc locum]: to or at this place
a.h.v. [ad hanc vocem]: to or at this word
a.m. [alia manu]: by another hand
A.M. or **a.m.** [ante meridiem]: before noon
A.M. or **M.A.** [Artium Magister]: Master of Arts
A.R. [Anno Regni or anno regni]: in the year of the reign
A.S. [aetatis suae]: of his or her age; of his or her lifetime
a.v. [ad valorem]: according to the value
a.v. [annos vixit]: he or she lived (so many years)
ab init. [ab initio]: from the beginning; from the start
abs. re. [absente reo]: the defendant being absent
actio. non [actionem non habere]: a denial of a plaintiff's charge
ad 2nd vic. [ad secundum vicem]: for the second time
ad eund. [ad eundem gradum]: to the same degree or standing
ad fin. [ad finem]: to or at the end; finally
ad inf. or **ad infin.** [ad infinitum]: to infinity; endless; without limit
ad init. [ad initium]: at the beginning
ad int. or **ad inter.** [ad interim]: in the meantime; temporarily
ad lib. [ad libitum]: at will; to improvise
ad loc. [ad locum]: to or at the place
ad sec. vic. [ad secundum vicem]: for the second time
ad ter. vic. [ad tertiam vicem]: for the third time

ad us. [ad usum]: according to custom or usage
ad val. [ad valorem]: according to the value
ads. or **adsm.** [ad sectam]: at the suit of
adv. [adversum or adversus]: against
adv. bon. mor. [adversus bonos mores]: contrary to or against good morals
aeq. [aequalis]: equal
aet. or **aetat.** [aetatis]: of the age; of one's lifetime
al. man. [alia manu]: by another hand
alt.... alt.... [alter ... alter ...] : the one ... and the other ...
alt. anni. [alternis annis]: every other year
alt. die. [alternis diebus]: every other day
alt. hor. [alternis horis]: every other hour
ann. [annales]: records; chronicles
app. [apparatus]: equipment; also, a set of materials summarizing textual evidence
arg. [arguendo]: in arguing; in the course of arguing; by way of argument
ats. [ad sectam]: at the suit of
austr. [australis]: southern

B

b. [beatus]: blessed; deceased
b.i.d. [bis in die]: twice a day
B.M. [beatae memoriae]: of blessed memory
b.p. [bonum publicum]: the common good
b.v. [bene vale]: farewell
bon. pub. [bonum publicum]: the common good
bor. [borealis]: northern

C

c̄ [cum]: with
C. [centum]: 100
c. or **ca.** [circa]: around; about; near

c. or **circ.** [circiter]: around; about; almost
c. or **circ.** [circum]: around; about; near
c.a.v. [curia advisari vult]: the court wishes to be advised or to consider the matter
c.c. [cepi corpus]: I have taken a body
c.d. or **cet. d.** [cetera desunt]: the rest is lacking
c.m.a. [cum multis aliis]: with many others
c.n. [cras nocte]: tomorrow night
C.R. [custos rotulorum]: custodian of rolls
c.v. [cras vespere]: tomorrow evening
c.v. [curriculum vitae]: a résumé
ca. ad re. [capias ad respondendum]: a writ of arrest intended to keep the defendant safely in custody until trial
ca. ad sa. or **ca. sa.** [capias ad satisfaciendum]: a writ of arrest to present a defendant in court to satisfy a plaintiff's complaint
ca. re. or **ca. res.** [capias respondendum]: a writ of arrest intended to keep the defendant safely in custody until trial
Cantab. [Cantabrigiensis]: of Cambridge
cas. fortuit. [casus fortuitus]: a case of fortune; a chance happening; an accident
cent. [centum]: 100
cet. par. [ceteris paribus]: other things being equal
cf. [confer]: compare
chart. [charta]: paper; charter; deed
coll. vit. [colluvies vitiorum]: a den of iniquity
con. or **conj.** [conjunx or conjux]: wife; spouse
con. or **cont.** [contra]: against
cont. bon. mor. [contra bonos mores]: contrary to good morals
cotid. [cotidianus or cotidie]: daily
crast. [crastinus]: of tomorrow; on the morrow
crepus. [crepusculum]: twilight; in the evening
cuj. [cujus or cuius]: of which or whose
cuj. lib. [cujus libet]: of whatever pleases
cul. [culpabilis]: culpable; guilty
cur. [curia]: a court of justice

cur. adv. vult [curia advisari vult]: the court wishes to be advised or to consider the matter

D

d. [decretum]: a decree; an ordinance
d.c. or **d. cet.** [desunt cetera]: the rest is wanting (e.g., the missing part of a quotation)
d.d. [dono dedit]: given as a gift
d. ex d. [diem ex die]: from day to day
D.P. or **d.p.** [directione propria]: with proper directions
d.s.p. [decessit sine prole]: died without issue
d.s.p.s. [decessit sine prole supersite]: died without surviving issue
D.T. [delirium tremens]: trembling delirium caused by alcohol poisoning
D.V or **d.v.** [Deo Volente]: God willing
de d. in d. [de die in diem]: from day to day
del. [delineavit]: he or she drew it
dext. [dexter]: right
di. et fi. [dilecto et fideli]: to his or her beloved and faithful
dieb. alt. [diebus alternis]: every other day
diluc. [diluculum]: the break of day; in the morning
div. [dividatur]: let it be divided
div. [divide]: divide
don. [donec]: until
dub. [dubitatur]: it is doubted
dub. [dubitavit]: it has been doubted
dup. [duplum]: twice as much; double the price

E

e.g. [exempli gratia]: for example
e.o. [ex officio]: by virtue of office
ead. [eadem]: the same
ejusd. [ejusdem]: of the same

et al. [et alia]: and other things
et al. [et alibi]: and elsewhere
et al. [et alii or et aliae]: and others
et conj. [et conjunx]: and spouse
et seq. [et sequens]: and the following
et seq. [et sequente]: and in what follows
et seq. [et sequentes]: and what follows
et seq. [et sequitur]: and the one following
et seq. pag. [et sequentes paginae]: and the following page(s)
et seqq. [et sequentes or et sequentia]: and what follows
et ux. [et uxor]: and wife
etc. [et cetera]: and the rest; and so on; and so forth
ex dem. [ex demissione]: on the demise
ex err. [ex errore]: in error
ex rel. [ex relatione]: from relation; by information
ex. gr. [exempli gratia]: for example
exc. [excudit]: he or she printed or engraved it
exhib. [exhibeatur]: let it be exhibited or given

F

f. [femina]: female; a woman
f. [folium]: a leaf of a book or a manuscript
f. or **fem.** [femina]: female; a woman
f. or **fem.** [femininum]: feminine
f. or **ft.** [fiat]: let it be so; let it be made or done
f.r. [folio recto]: on the front of the page (i.e., the right-hand page)
f.v. [folio verso]: on the back of the page (i.e., the left-hand page)
fec. [fecit]: he or she made or did it
ff. [fecerunt]: they made or did it
ff. [folia]: pages
fi. fa. [fieri facias]: cause it to be done
fi. fe. [fieri feci]: I have caused it to be done
fin. [finis]: the end

fl. or **flor.** [floruit]: flourished
fol. [folium]: a leaf; a page of a book
freq. [frequenter]: frequently
frust. [frustillatim]: bit by bit; in small bits
ft. [fiat or fiant]: let it be made; let them be made

G

grad. [gradatim]: step by step; gradually or by degrees
grat. [gratus]: pleasant; agreeable

H

H. [hora]: hour
h.a. [hoc anno]: in this year
h.c. [honoris causa]: for the sake of honor
H.I. [hic iacet or hic jacet]: here lies
H.I.S. [hic iacet sepultus]: here lies buried
h.l. [hoc loco]: in this place
h.m. [hoc mense]: in this month
H.M.P. [hoc monumentum posuit]: he or she erected this monument
h.n. [hoc nomine]: in this name
h.o. [hoc ordine]: in this order
h.q. [hoc quaere]: look for this
H.S. [hic sepultus]: here [lies] buried
h.s. [hoc sensu]: in this sense
H.S.E. [hic sepultus est]: here lies buried
h.t. [hoc tempore]: at this time
h.t. [hoc titulo]: under this title
h.v. [hoc voce]: under this word or phrase
hab. corp. [habeas corpus]: that you have the body (i.e., a writ to determine the legality of a person's arrest or imprisonment)
haer. [haeres]: an heir
hebdom. [hebdomada]: a week; a seven-day period
her. [heres]: an heir
hor. [hora]: hour

I

i.a. [in absentia]: in absence
i.e. [id est]: that is; that is to say
i.l.c. [in loco citato]: in the place cited
i.q. [idem quod]: the same as
ib. or **ibid.** [ibidem]: in the same place (e.g., in a book)
id. [idem]: the same; the same as above
ign. [ignotus]: unknown
illeg. [illegibilis]: illegible
illic. [illico]: immediately
impr. [imprimis]: first of all; first in order
in d. [in dies]: daily; from day to day
in lim. [in limine]: on the threshold; in or at the beginning
in litt. [in litteris]: in correspondence
in loc. cit. [in loco citato]: in the place cited
in pr. [in principio]: in the beginning
in trans. [in transitu]: in transit; on the way
in ut. [in utero]: in the womb
in vit. [in vitro]: in a glass; in a test tube or petri dish
incert. [incertus]: uncertain; doubtful
ind. [indies]: daily; from day to day
indet. [indeterminans]: unidentified
inf. [infra]: below; under; within
inf. dig. [infra dignitatem]: beneath one's dignity
init. [initio]: in or at the beginning (referring to a passage in a book)
inscr. [inscriptio]: an inscription; a heading
int. [internus]: inward; internal
inter noct. [inter noctem]: during the night
inv. [invenit]: he or she designed it
iux. [iuxta]: near; next to; close by

J

J.D. [Juris Doctor]: Doctor of Law
J.U.D. [Juris Utriusque Doctor]: Doctor of Canon and Civil Law
jux. [juxta]: near; next to; close by

L

l. or **lib.** [liber; pl. libri]: a book
L.B. [lectori benevolo]: to the gentle reader
l.c. [loco citato]: in the place cited
L.H.D. [Litterarum Humaniorum Doctor]: Doctor of Humanities
L.S. [lectori salutem]: greetings to the reader
L.S. [locus sigilli]: the place of the seal
l.s.c. [loco supra citato]: in the place cited above
lac. [lacuna]: gap; deficiency (e.g., missing words in a text or manuscript)
laev. [laevus]: left
lb. [libra or libra pondo]: a pound by weight
Litt.D. [Litterarum Doctor]: Doctor of Letters
LL.B. [Legum Baccalaureus]: Bachelor of Laws
LL.D. [Legum Doctor]: Doctor of Laws
loc. cit. [loco citato]: in the place cited
loc. laud. [loco laudato]: in the place [cited] with approval
loq. [loquitur]: he or she speaks

M

m. [mane]: morning; in the morning
m. [mas or masculus]: male; a man
m. [masculinus]: masculine; manly
M. or **m.** [meridies]: midday; noon
m. seq. [mane sequenti]: on the following morning
M.A. [Magister Artium]: Master of Arts
M.D. [Medicinae Doctor]: Doctor of Medicine
m.d. [more dicto]: as directed; as prescribed
m.d.u. [more dicto utendus]: to be used as directed
m.m. [mutatis mutandis]: [with] the necessary changes being made
m.o. [modus operandi]: a mode of operating
m.p. [male positus]: badly placed
m.s. [more solito]: in the usual manner

m.s. or **ms.** [manu scriptum or manuscriptum]: written by hand
M.V. [Medicus Veterinarius]: Doctor of Veterinary Science
mag. [magnus]: large; great
mal. pos. [male positus]: badly placed
masc. [masculinus]: masculine; manly
mens. or **mensur.** [mensura]: measure; standard; also, by measure
mitt. [mitte]: send
mitt. tal. or **mit. tal.** [mitte tales]: send such
mob. [mobile vulgus]: the fickle masses; a mob
more dict. [more dicto]: as directed; in the manner directed
more sol. [more solito]: in the usual manner
MS or **ms.** [manuscriptus]: manuscript; a handwritten document
MSS or **mss.** [manuscripta]: manuscripts; handwritten documents
mulct. [mulcta]: a fine or penalty

N

n. [natus]: born
n. [neuter or neutrum]: neuter; neither; of neither sex
n. [nocte]: at night; in the night
N.B. or **n.b.** [nota bene]: note well; take notice
n.l. [non licet]: it is not permitted
n.l. [non liquet]: it is not clear; it is not proven
n.n. [nomen nominandum]: a name to be named (i.e., supplied at a later date)
n.n. [non nominatus]: an unidentified person
n.o.v. [non obstante veredicto]: notwithstanding the verdict
N.P. or **n.p.** [nomen proprium]: proper name
narr. [narratio]: a narrative; a declaration
nem. con. [nemine contradicente]: no one contradicting
nem. dis. [nemine dissentiente]: no one dissenting (i.e., unanimous)
No. or **no.** [numero]: in number; by number
nol. contend. [nolo contendere]: not to contend (i.e., a plea of 'no contest' to criminal charges)

nol. pros. [nolle prosequi]: unwilling to prosecute
nom. [nomen; pl. nomina]: name
non cul. [non culpabilis]: not guilty
non lic. [non licet]: it is not permitted
non liq. [non liquet]: it is not clear; it is not proven
non obs. [non obstante]: notwithstanding
non pros. [non prosequitur]: he does not prosecute (i.e., the plaintiff does not appear)
non seq. [non sequitur]: it does not follow

O

o.c. [opere citato]: in the work cited
o.d. [omne die]: all day; every day
ob. [obiit or obit]: he or she died
ob. [obiter]: by the way; incidentally; in passing
ob. dict. [obiter dictum; pl. obiter dicta]: an incidental remark; a casual comment or unofficial expression of opinion
ob.s.p. [obiit sine prole]: he or she died without issue
om. [omittit or omittunt]: it omits or they omit
omn. [omnis]: all; every
omn. die [omne die]: all day; every day
op. [ope]: by means of
op. [opus]: a work; also, a musical composition
op. cit. [opere citato]: in the work cited
opt. [optimus]: the best
ord. inv. [ordo inversus]: inverted order (i.e., in inverse order)
Oxon. [Oxoniensis]: of Oxford
oz. [uncia]: an ounce

P

p. [pagina]: the page of a book or letter
p. [partim]: in part
p. [post]: after; later; also, a later page or line of text
p.a. [per annum]: by the year; annually

p.ae. [partes aequales]: in equal parts

p.c. [per centum]: by the hundred (i.e., percentage)

p.g. [persona grata]: an acceptable or welcome person

p.h.v. [pro hac vice]: for this occasion

P.M. or **p.m.** [post meridiem]: after noon

P.M. or **p.m.** [post mortem]: after death

p.n.g. [persona non grata]: an unacceptable or unwelcome person

p.o. [per os]: by mouth; orally

p.p. [per procurationem]: by proxy; by the action of

P.P.S. or **PPS** [post postscriptum]: an additional postscript

p.r.a. [pro ratione aetatis]: according to age

p.r.n. or **P.R.N.** [pro re nata]: according to the present circumstance; as needed

P.S. or **PS** [post scriptum or postscriptum]: written after; a postscript

p.t. [pro tempore]: for a time; temporarily; for the time being

pact. [pactum; pl. pacta]: pact; a contract or agreement

parv. [parvus]: small

pass. [passim]: throughout; here and there

pct. [per centum]: by the hundred (i.e., percentage)

pedet. [pedetentim]: step by step; by degrees

pend. [pendens]: weighing; pending; hanging

per cent. [per centum]: by the hundred (i.e., percentage)

per mens. [per mensem]: by the month; monthly; for each month

per mil. [per mille]: by the thousand

per omn. [per omnes]: by all; by all the judges

per pro. [per procurationem]: by proxy; by the action of

per salt. [per saltum]: by a leap; all at once; without an intermediate step

per stirp. [per stirpes]: by families; by representation; by root and stock

per tot. cur. [per totam curiam]: by the full court (i.e., unanimously)

Ph.B. [Philosophiae Baccalaureus]: Bachelor of Philosophy

Ph.D. [Philosophiae Doctor]: Doctor of Philosophy
pinx. [pinxit]: he or she painted it
pl. [pluralis]: plural
post obit. [post obitum]: after death; also, taking effect after someone's death
pp. [paginae]: the pages of a book or letter
PPS [post postscriptum]: an additional postscript
praed. or **praedict.** [praedictus]: aforementioned; aforesaid
praef. or **praefat.** [praefatus]: aforesaid
praep. [praeparatus]: prepared
prim. [primum]: first
prim. luc. [prima luce]: at first light; early in the morning
pro def. [pro defendente]: for the defendant
pro quer. [pro querente]: for the plaintiff
pro rat. aet. [pro ratione aetatis]: according to age
pro tem. [pro tempore]: for a time; temporarily; for the time being
prox. [proximo]: the next; of or in the following [month]
prox. m. [proximo mense]: the next month; in the following month
PS [post scriptum or postscriptum]: a postscript
pt. aeq. [partes aequales]: in equal parts
pxt. [pinxit]: he or she painted it

Q

q.c.f. [quare clausum fregit]: the charge of trespassing
q.d. [quasi dicat]: as if one should say; as much as to say
q.d. [quasi dictum]: as if stated; as if said
q.e. [quod est]: which is
Q.E.D. or **q.e.d.** [quod erat demonstrandum]: which was to be demonstrated or proven
Q.E.F. or **q.e.f.** [quod erat faciendum]: which was to be done
q.e.n. [quare executionem non]: wherefore execution should not be issued
q.n. [quod nota]: which note; which mark

q.t. [qui tam]: who as well (i.e., an action to recover)
q.v. [quod vide]: (sing.) which see
qq. or **Qq.** [quaque]: each; every
qq. or **Qq.** [quoque]: also; too
qq.v. [quae vide]: (pl.) which see
qu. [quaere or quare]: a question or query
quot. or **quotid.** [quotidie or quotidianus]: daily; every day

R

r. [recto (folio)]: on the right hand (of the page)
R. [regina]: queen
R. [rex]: king
R.I.P. [requiescat in pace]: may he or she rest in peace
R.I.P. [requiescit in pace]: he or she rests in peace
reli. or **reliq.** [reliquum or reliquus]: the rest; the remaining; the remainder

S

s or **s.** [sequens]: (sing.) the following
S. [sepultus]: buried
S. [signa]: write or mark thus
s. [signetur]: let it be written; label it thus
s.a. [sine anno]: without date
s.d. [sine die]: without a day; indefinitely
s.l. [sensu lato]: in a broad sense
s.l. [sine loco]: without place
s.l.a. [sine loco et anno]: without place and year
s.l.a.n. [sine loco, anno, vel nomine]: without place, year, or name
s.l.p. [sine legitima prole]: without legitimate issue
s.m.p. [sine mascula prole]: without male issue
s.n. [sine nomine]: without name; anonymous
s.o.s. [si opus sit]: if necessary
s.p. [sine prole]: without issue

s.p.f. [sine prole femina]: without female issue
s.p.m. [sine prole mascula]: without male issue
s.p.s. [sine prole supersite]: without surviving issue
s.s. [sensu stricto]: in a strict sense
S.S.S. or **s.s.s.** [stratum super stratum]: layer upon layer
s. test. [sine testibus]: without witnesses
s.v. [sub verbo]: under the word or heading; under the entry
s.v. [sub voce]: under the word or heading; under the entry
s.vv. [sub verbis]: under the words or headings; under the entries
s.vv. [sub vocibus]: under the words or headings; under the entries
Sal. or **S.** [Salutem dicit!]: Greetings!
sc. [scilicet]: that is to say; namely; to wit
sc. [sculpsit]: he or she sculpted, carved, or engraved it
sci. fa. [scire facias]: cause it to be known; make it known
scil. [scilicet]: that is to say; namely; to wit
sculpt. [sculpsit]: he or she sculpted, carved, or engraved it
sec. [secundum]: according to
sec. art. [secundum artem]: according to practice
sec. leg. [secundum legem]: according to law
sec. nat. [secundum naturam]: according to nature
sec. reg. [secundum regulam]: according to rule
sen. lat. [sensu lato]: in a broad sense
sen. str. [sensu stricto]: in a strict sense
seq. [sequens]: (sing.) the following
seq. [sequitur]: it follows
seqq. [sequentia]: (pl.) the following (things)
sg. [singularis]: singular; each; individual
si op. sit [si opus sit]: if necessary
Sig. [signa]: write or mark thus
sig. [signetur]: let it be written; label it thus
sigill. [sigillum]: seal; signet
simp. [simplum]: the single value of something
sine test. [sine testibus]: without witnesses
sing. [singularis]: singular; each; individual
sing. [singulorum]: of each

sinist. [sinister]: left
ss or **ss.** [scilicet]: that is to say (indicating the venue)
ss or **ss.** [sequentes]: (pl.) the following
st. [stet]: let it stand
stat. [statim]: immediately; on the spot; at once
sub aud. [sub audi]: to read between the lines
sub nom. [sub nomine]: under the name of
sub. or **subaud.** [subaudi]: to read between the lines
sup. [supra]: above (i.e., an author or work cited previously in the text)
sup. cit. [supra citato]: cited above
suppl. [supplementum]: a supplement; something added later
sus. per col. [suspendatur per collum]: let one be hanged by the neck
syl. or **syll.** [syllabus]: an abstract or written summary

T

t. [tempore]: in the time of
tal. [talis]: such
tal. qual. [talis qualis]: such as it is
temp. [tempore]: in the time of
tot. quot. [toties quoties]: as often as; repeatedly; on each occasion

U

u.i. [ubi infra]: in the place mentioned below
u.i. [ut infra]: as stated or cited below
u.r. [uti rogas]: as requested
u.s. [ubi supra]: in the place mentioned above
u.s. [ut supra]: as stated or cited above
ult. [ultimo]: the last or previous [month]
ult. [ultimum or ultimus]: the last; to the last; the final; the most distant; the ultimate or extreme
ult. m. [ultimo mense]: the last or previous month
usq. [usque]: as far as
ut dict. [ut dictum]: as directed

ut inf. [ut infra]: as stated or cited below
ut sup. [ut supra]: as stated or cited above
ux. [uxor]: wife

V

v. [verso (folio)]: on the left hand (of the page)
v. [versus]: toward; against
v. [versus]: verse
v. [vide]: see
v. or **vo.** [verso]: reverse side
v. or **vol.** [volumen]: volume
v.a. [vide ante]: see before (i.e., above)
v.a. [vixit ... annos]: he or she lived ... years
v.g. [verbi gratia]: for example
v.i. [vide infra]: see below
v.p. [vide post]: see after (i.e., below)
v.s. [vide supra]: see above
V.V. or **v.v.** [vice versa]: with the position or order reversed; conversely
vac. [vacat or vacant]: empty; missing (e.g., the missing part of an inscription)
vehic. [vehiculum]: vehicle; any means of transport or conveyance
verb. sap. [verbum sapienti]: a word to the wise
verb. sat or **verb. sat sap.** [verbum sat sapienti (est)]: a word to the wise is sufficient
vesp. [vesper]: evening
vet. [veteres]: the ancients; forefathers
viz. [videlicet]: that is to say; namely; to wit
vs. [versus]: toward; against
vs. [versus]: verse
vss. [versa]: verses

Miscellanea (Miscellaneous)

Some Common Prepositions and Particles

a or **ab**: from; by
ad: to; at; up to
ambo: both
ante: before
anti: against; opposed to

apo: from; away from
apud: at; near; by; next to
bis: twice
circa: about; near; around
circum: around; about
cis or **citra**: this side of; within
contra: against
coram: before; in the presence of
cui: to whom
cum: with
de: of; concerning; from
donec: until
dum: while
durante: during
e or **ex**: from; out of
ergo: therefore

et: and; also
extra: without; outside of; in addition to
hic, **hac**, **hoc**: this
ibi: there

in: in; into
infra: below; beneath
inter: between; among
intra: inside; within
juxta (iuxta): near; next to; according to
ne: lest; not
nec: neither; not
nihil or **nil**: nothing
nisi: unless
non: no; not
ob: for; on account of

omne (omnis): all
ope: by means of

per: by; through
pone: behind
post: after
prae (pre): before
praeter: in front of; beyond
pro: for; before; on behalf of
prope: near
propter: because of; on account of
qua: as
quasi: as if
re: regarding; concerning
retro: behind; backward
secundum: according to

semis: half; one half
semper: always
si: if; supposing that
sic: thus; so
sine: without
sub: under
super: over; above
supra: over; above

totus: all; the whole
trans: across; through
ubi: where
ultra: beyond
usque ad: up to; as far as
ut: as; so that
vel: or

Some Common Prefixes

a- or **an-** without
ab- away from
ad- toward; near
ante- before
anti- against
auto- self
bi- two, twice
bis- two; twice
bin- two
circum- around
contra- against
di- twice; two
dia- through
dis- twice; two
duo- two
epi- on; upon
eu- good
ex- out of
extra- outside of
hemi- one-half
hepta- seven; seventh
hetero- other
hexa- six; sixth
homo- same
hyper- above; beyond

hypo- below; under
inter- between; among
intra- within
macro- large
mega- large
meta- beyond; altered
micro- small
mon- one
mono- one
multi- many
neo- new
non- not
ortho- correct; straight
para- beyond
penta- five; fifth
per- through; beyond
peri- around
poly- many
post- after
prae- (pre-) before
proto- before; first; lower
pseudo- false
pyro- changed by heat
quadra- four; fourth
quadri- four; fourth

retro- backward; behind
semi- half
sesqui- one and one half
sub- below; under
super- above
supra- above
sym-/syn- with; together

ter- three
tetra- four
toxi- poisonous
tri- (tris-) three; three times
ultra- beyond
un- one
uni- single

The Latin Calendar

The Calendar Year (Mensis)

Januarius: January
Februarius: February
Martius: March
Aprilis: April
Maius: May
Iunius: June
Quinctilis or **Iulius:** July (after Julius Caesar)
Sextilis or **Augustus:** August (after Caesar Augustus)
September: September
October: October
November: November
December: December

Januarii: in January
Februarii: in February
Martii: in March
Aprilis: in April
Maii: in May
Junii: in June
Julii: in July

Augusti: in August

Septembris: in September
Octobris: in October
Novembris: in November
Decembris: in December

The Calendar Month

Idus [the Ides]: the fifteenth day in March, May, July, and October; the thirteenth day in all other months
Kalendae or **Calendae** [the Kalends or Calends]: the first day of a Roman month
Nonae [the Nones]: the seventh day in March, May, July, and October; the fifth day in all other months

The Days of the Week (Septimana)

Dies Dominica or **Dies Solis:** Sunday
Dies Lunae: Monday
Dies Martis: Tuesday
Dies Mercurii: Wednesday
Dies Iovis/Jovis: Thursday
Dies Veneris: Friday
Dies Saturni: Saturday
Dies Sabbati: the Sabbath day

Die Soli: on Sunday
Die Lunae: on Monday
Die Martis: on Tuesday
Die Mercurii: on Wednesday
Die Iovis/Jovis: on Thursday
Die Veneris: on Friday
Die Saturni: on Saturday
Die Sabbati: on the Sabbath Day

The Seasons of the Year

Aestas: Summer
Autumnus: Autumn; Fall
Bruma: Winter Solstice
Hiems: Winter
Solstitium: Summer Solstice
Ver: Spring

Roman Numerals

Cardinals

unus (I): one
duo (II): two
tres (III): three
quattuor/quatuor (IIII, IV): four
quinque (V): five
sex (VI): six
septem (VII): seven
octo (VIII): eight
novem (VIIII, IX): nine
decem (X): ten

Ordinals

primus: first
secundus, alter: second
tertius: third
quartus: fourth

quintus: fifth
sextus: sixth
septimus: seventh
octavus: eighth
nonus: ninth
decimus: tenth

undecim (XI): eleven
duodecim (XII): twelve
tredecim (XIII): thirteen
quattuordecim (XIIII, XIV): fourteen
quindecim (XV): fifteen
sedecim (or **sexdecim**) (XVI): sixteen
septendecim (XVII): seventeen
duodeviginti (or **octodecim**) (XVIII): eighteen

undeviginti (or **novemdecim**) (XIIII, XIX): nineteen

viginti (XX): twenty
unus et viginti (XXI) (or **viginti unus**): twenty-one
duo et viginti (or **viginti duo**) (XXII): twenty-two

duodetriginta (XXVIII): twenty-eight
undetriginta (XXIX): twenty-nine
triginta (XXX): thirty
duodequadraginta (XXXVIII): thirty-eight
undequadraginta (XXXIX): thirty-nine
quadraginta (XL): forty
duodequinquaginta (XLVIII): forty-eight
undequinquaginta (XLIX): forty-nine

undecimus: eleventh
duodecimus: twelfth
tertius decimus: thirteenth
quartus decimus: fourteenth

quintus decimus: fifteenth
sextus decimus: sixteenth

septimus decimus: seventeenth

duodevicesimus (or **octavusdecimus**): eighteenth

undevicesimus (or **novemdecimus**): nineteenth

vicesimus: twentieth
vicesimus primus (or **unus et vicesimus**): twenty-first
vicesimus secundus (or **duo et vicesimus** or **alter et vicemus**): twenty-second
duodetricesimus: twenty-eighth
undetricesimus: twenty-ninth
tricesimus: thirtieth
duodequadragesimus: thirty-eighth
undequadragesimus: thirty-ninth
quadragesimus: fortieth
duodequinquagesimus: forty-eighth
undequinquagesimus: forty-ninth

quinquaginta (L): fifty
sexaginta (LX): sixty
septuaginta (LXX): seventy
octoginta (LXXX): eighty
nonaginta (XC): ninety
centum (C): one hundred
centum (et) unus (CCI): one hundred and one
ducenti (CC): two hundred

ducenti quinquagenta (CCL or E): two hundred and fifty
trecenti (CCC): three hundred
quadringenti (CD): four hundred
quingenti (D): five hundred

sescenti (DC): six hundred
septingenti (DCC): seven hundred
octingenti (DCCC): eight hundred
nongenti (DM): nine hundred
mille (M): one thousand
duo milia (MM): two thousand

quinquagesimus: fiftieth
sexagesimus: sixtieth
septuagesimus: seventieth
octogesimus: eightieth
nonagesimus: ninetieth
centesimus: the hundredth
centesimus (et) primus: hundred and first
ducentesimus: two hundredth

ducentesimus (et) quinquagesimus: two hundredth and fiftieth
trecentesimus: three hundredth
quadringentesimus: four hundredth
quingentesimus: five hundredth

sescentesimus: six hundredth
septingentesimus: seven hundredth
octingentesimus: eight hundredth
nongentesimus: nine hundredth
millesimus: one thousandth
bis millesimus: two thousandth

English-Latin Index

A

abatement: **abatamentum**
abortion: **aborticidum**
abortive: **abortivus**
above: **supra** or **superus**
abridgment: **compendium**
absence of justice: **jus nullum**
absent: **absens**
according to: **secundum**
according to age: **pro ratione aetatis**
according to circumstance: **pro re**
according to custom: **ex more** or **ad usum**
according to equity: **ex aequitate**
according to fact: **ex facto**
according to justice: **ex justitia**
according to law: **de jure** or **secundum legem**
according to lineage: **in stirpes**
according to nature: **ex natura** or **secundum naturam**
according to taste: **ad gustum** or **secundum gustum**
according to the law(s): **ex legibus** or **in jure**
according to the law of nature: **ex jure naturae**
according to the value: **ad valorem** or **in valorem**
according to time and circumstance: **ex re et ex tempore**
according to truth: **secundum veritatem**
according to usage: **secundum usum**
accusation: **accusatio**
accused: **accusatus**
accused person: **homo reus**
acre of land: **ager**
across: **trans**
act: **actus** or **gestum**
act of God: **actus Dei** or **vis divina** or **vis major**
act of war: **casus belli**
action (legal): **actio**
actions of good faith: **actiones bonae fidei**
acts: **acta**
additions: **incrementa**
adjacent: **conterminus**
adolescence **juventus**
adult: **adultus**
adversary: **adversarius**
advised: **hortatus**
advocate: **homo forensis**
after: **post**

DOI: 10.4324/9781003255369-6

after birth: **post partum** or **postpartum**
after death: **post mortem** or **postmortem** or **post obitum**
after noon: **post meridiem**
after the event: **ex eventu**
after the fact: **ex post facto** or **post facto** or **post factum** or **postfactum**
after the fashion of: **ad instar**
after this manner: **in hunc modum**
against good morals: **adversus bonos mores**
against my will: **me invito**
against nature: **contra naturam**
against the law: **contra legem**
against the letter of the law: **contra formam statuti**
against the man: **ad hominem**
against the peace: **contra pacem**
against the person: **ad hominem** or **in personam**
against written testimony: **contra scriptum testimonium**
age: **aetas**
aggrieved party: **pars gravata**
agreement: **consensus** or **pactum** or **concordia**
agricultural: **georgicus**

aid: **auxilium**
alias: **alias dictus**
alimony: **rationabile estoverium**
alternate: **alternus**
alternately: **alternis vicibus**
always: **semper**
ambitious: **ambitiosus**
ambush: **insidiae**
amendment: **emendatio**
among equals: **inter pares**
among friends: **inter amicos**
among other persons: **inter alios**
among other things: **inter alia**
among the acts: **apud acta**
among the goods: **in bonis**
among the living: **inter vivos**
an existing condition: **status quo** or **status in quo**
anarchy: **leges nullae**
ancestors: **majores**
ancestral custom: **mos majorum** or **consuetudo majorum**
ancient: **vetustus**
ancient customs: **antiqua custuma**
ancient statutes: **antiqua statuta** or **vetera statua**
and elsewhere: **et alibi**
and husband: **et vir**
and other things: **et alia**
and others: **et aliae** or **et alii**
and so on: **et cetera**
and spouse: **et conjunx**

and the following: **et sequens**
and the like: **et similia**
and the rest: **et cetera**
and what follows: **et sequentes** or **et sequentia**
and wife: **et uxor**
anew: **de integro** or **de novo**
annually: **annuus** or **per annum** or **quotannis**
annuity: **annua pecunia** or **annuus reditus**
another: **alius**
antiquity: **vetustas**
appropriate: **accommodatus**
approved: **probatus**
appurtenances: **appenditia**
arbitrator: **compromisarius**
archived: **ad acta**
argument: **argumentum**
argument in court: **disputatio fori**
armed: **armatus** or **cum telo**
armed force: **armata vis** or **vis armata**
arson: **crimen incendii**
art: **ars**
artificial: **artificialis** or **factitius**
as a favor: **a gratia**
as a gift: **ex dono**
as a matter of form: **pro forma**
as a penalty: **in poenam**
as a precaution: **ad cautelam**
as above: **ut supra**
as confessed: **pro confesso**

as convicted: **pro convicto**
as directed: **more dicto** or **ut dictum**
as far as I know: **quantum scio** or **quod sciam**
as for the rest: **quod superest**
as if said: **quasi dictum**
as is customary: **ut assolet**
as matters stand: **e re nata**
as requested: **uti rogas**
as to the rest: **quod ultra**
assassin: **sicarius**
assembly: **consessus**
assessor: **consessor**
assistance: **adjumentum**
associate justice: **conjudex**
association: **consociatio**
at a certain day: **ad certum diem**
at a future time: **de futuro** or **in futuro**
at a moment's notice: **in promptu**
at common law: **ad communem legem**
at court: **ad curiam**
at full length: **in extenso**
at hand: **ad manum**
at home: **domi**
at issue: **ad exitum**
at large: **ad largum**
at last: **denique**
at length: **ad longum** or **demum**
at my own risk: **meo periculo**

at one's own risk: **suo periculo**
at our own risk: **nostro periculo**
at pleasure: **ad libitum**
at present: **de praesenti** or **de presenti**
at the agreed hour: **ad horam compositam**
at the appointed day: **ad diem**
at the beginning: **ad initium**
at the cost: **ad custum**
at the costs: **ad custagia**
at the discretion of the judge: **ex arbitrio judicis**
at the instance: **ad instantiam**
at the instance of a party: **ad instantiam partis**
at the last moment: **ad ultimum**
at the moment: **ex tempore**
at the moment of death: **in articulo mortis**
at the person: **ad hominem**
at the place: **ad locum**
at the point in time: **ad punctum temporis**
at the point of death: **in extremis**
at the present time: **in praesenti**
at the source: **ad fontes**
at the suit of: **ad sectam**
at this day: **ad hunc diem**
at this place: **ad hunc locum**
at this time: **hoc tempore**
at this word: **ad hanc vocem**
at times: **aliquando**
at will: **ad arbitrium** or **ad libitum** or **libitum**
author: **auctor**
autograph copy: **chirographum** or **chyrographum**
avenger of wrong: **vindex injuriae**
averting peril: **aversio periculi**

B

bad: **malum** or **malus**
bad conscience: **conscientia mala**
bad credit: **mala creditus**
bad faith: **mala fide** or **mala fides**
bad intention: **malus animus**
bad road: **via iniqua**
bad weather: **tempestas mala**
bail: **ballium** or **balium** or **salvus plegius**
balance of account: **reliqua**
banished: **bannitus** or **forbannitus** or **forisbanitus**
banishment: **exilium** or **exsilium**
banker: **mensularius**
banquet: **convivium**
bastard child: **nullius filius** or **filius populi**

before a judge: **coram judice**
before all things: **ante omnia**
before birth: **ante partum** or **antepartum**
before daybreak: **ante lucem**
before death: **ante mortem**
before midday: **ante meridianus**
before noon: **ante meridiem**
before one's peers: **coram paribus**
before the judge: **sub judice** or **pro tribunali**
before the war: **ante bellum**
beforehand: **ab ante** or **ab antecedente**
beheading: **decollatio**
behold the man: **ecce homo**
behold the sign: **ecce signum**
beneath one's dignity: **infra dignitatem**
beside the point: **nihil ad rem**
between husband and wife: **inter virum et uxorem**
between ourselves: **inter nos**
between the living: **inter vivos**
beware of cat: **cave felem**
beware of danger: **in cauda venenum**
beware of dog: **cave canem**
beyond one's power: **ultra vires** or **extra vires** or **supra vires**

beyond the law: **extra jus** or **praeter jus** or **praeter legem**
beyond the legal limit: **ultra licitum**
beyond the powers of: **extra vires** or **ultra vires**
beyond the value: **ultra valorem**
beyond the walls: **extra muros**
bill: **billa**
bill of complaint: **querela** or **querella**
bill of exchange: **billa excambii**
birth: **partus**
birthday: **dies natalis**
black and white: **atra et alba**
blind: **caecus**
blood: **sanguis**
bloodthirsty: **sanguinarius**
bodily ills: **dolores corporis**
bodily strength: **vires corporis**
body: **corpus**
body of law: **corpus juris**
body of the crime: **corpus delicti**
bond (pledge): **cautio**
bond (tie): **vinculum**
bond of matrimony: **vinculum matrimonii**
book: **liber**
booty: **praeda** or **praeda bellica**

born: **natus**
both: **ambo**
both of them: **uterque**
bound together: **consolidus**
boundary: **terminus**
boy: **puer**
brief: **brevis**
briefly: **breviter**
broken: **fractus**
brothel: **fornix**
brother: **frater**
brothers and sisters: **fratres**
burden of proof: **onus probandi**
buried: **sepultus**
burning of heretics: **auto da fe** or **combustio**
buyer: **emptor**
buying and selling: **emptio et venditio**
by a leap: **per saltum**
by accident: **per accidens** or **per infortunium**
by another hand: **alia manu**
by birth: **natu**
by command: **jussu**
by default: **per defaltam**
by divine right: **jure divino**
by evasion: **per ambages**
by far the stronger: **a multo fortiori**
by favor: **de gratia**
by fiction of law: **ex fictione juris**
by force: **manu forti** or **per vim**
by force of law: **per vim legis**
by force or fear: **vi aut metu**
by fraud: **per fraudem**
by grace: **ex gratia**
by heart: **ex memoria** or **memoriter**
by its associates: **a sociis**
by my own witness: **teste me ipso** or **teste meipso**
by necessity of law: **necessitate juris**
by neglect: **per incuriam**
by oath: **juramento**
by order: **jussu**
by permission: **permissu**
by profession: **ex professo**
by proxy: **per procurationem**
by reason of death: **causa mortis**
by right: **jure** or **de jure** or **in jure**
by right of office: **jus officii**
by statute: **ex statuto**
by stealth: **furtim**
by the book: **per librum**
by the day: **per diem** or **in diem**
by the fact itself: **ipso facto**
by the full court: **per totam curiam**
by the head: **capitatim**
by the hour: **per horam**
by the law itself: **ipso jure**
by the law of nations: **jure gentium**

English-Latin Index 239

by the month: **per mensem**
by the thousand: **per mille**
by the way: **obiter**
by turns: **in vicem** or **invicem** or **alternis vicibus**
by virtue of: **in virtute**
by virtue of law: **ex lege**
by virtue of office: **ex officio** or **virtute officii**
by way of argument: **arguendo**
by way of example: **in rei exemplum**
by way of mercy: **in misericordia**
by way of penalty: **in modum poene**
by way of proof: **in modum probationis**
by way of threat: **inter terrorem**
by ways and means: **viis et modis**
by what right?: **quo jure?**
by witnesses: **per testes**
by word of mouth: **ore tenus**

C

calendar: **calendarium**
called to the bar: **ad barram evocatus**
canon law: **jus canonicum** or **lex canonica**
capable of committing crime: **capax doli**
capital punishment: **judicium capitale**
care: **cura**
cared for: **curatus**
case: **casus** or **causa**
case of conscience: **casus conscientiae**
casting lots: **sortitio**
casual remark: **obiter dictum**
catalog: **repertorium**
cause of an action: **causa causans**
cause of mischief: **causa mali**
caution: **cautum** or **caveat**
censor of morals: **censor morum**
censure: **convicium**
certainly: **certo**
children: **liberi**
chosen: **electus**
chronicles: **annales**
circular reasoning: **circulus vitiosus**
circumlocution: **circuitus verborum**
citizen: **civis**
city: **civitas**
civil law: **jus civile**
civilly: **civiliter**
clause: **clausus** or **incisio**
clean slate: **tabula rasa**
clemency: **clementia**
clerical error: **vitium clerici**
clerk: **clericus**
close by: **prope** or **juxta**

closed: **clausum** or **clausus**
closeness: **propinquitas**
codicil: **elogium**
cohabitation: **consortium vitae**
collaterally: **de latere**
collection of laws: **codex**
college: **collegium**
college graduate: (m.) **alumnus** or (f.) **alumna** or (pl.) **alumni**
color of office: **colore officii**
comity among nations: **comitas inter gentes**
command: **dictum**
common: **communis** or **vulgaris**
common bond: **commune vinculum**
common good: **commune bonum** or **bonum publicum**
common law: **jus commune** or **lex communis**
common opinion: **communis opinio**
common plea: **commune placitum**
common pleas: **communia placita** or **placita communia**
common wall: **paries communis**
company: **consortium**
compare: **confer**
compassion: **misericordia**
complaint: **querimonia**
compound interest: **anatocismus**
compulsory: **in invitum**
concerning fraud: **de dolo malo**
condemned: **damnatus**
conditions of peace: **legis pacis**
conduct: **gestio**
confidentially: **sub rosa**
confiscated goods: **bona confiscata**
confusion of goods: **confusio bonorum**
conjugal affection: **affectio conjugalis**
connection: **nexus**
conscience: **conscientia**
consent: **consensus**
consent of the nations: **consensus gentium**
consequence: **consequentia**
conspiracy: **consensus audacium**
constable: **comes stabuli** or **constabularius**
contemplation of flight: **meditatio fugae**
continuance: **continentia** or **dies datus partibus**
contract: **contractus**
contrary to good morals: **contra bonos mores** or **adversus bonos mores**
convenient: **conveniens**
conveniently: **ex commodo**

conversely: **e converso** or **vice versa**
coroner: **coronator**
corporal punishment: **poena corporalis**
corporate body: **collegium**
corporation: **corpus corporatum**
corpse: **cadaver**
correction: **litura**
correspondence: **ab epistolis** or **ab epistulis**
corrupted: **corruptus**
cost: **custagium** or **custum**
costs: **custa** or **custagia** or **custantia**
council: **concilium**
counselor: **consiliarius**
counterclaim: **mutua petitio**
counterplea: **contra placitum**
country estate: **praedium rusticum**
county: **comitatus**
county court: **curia comitatus**
course: **cursus**
course of study: **curriculum**
court hours: **horae judiciae**
court of conscience: **forum conscientiae**
court of justice: **curia** or **forum**
court transcript: **ligula**
courtship: **consuetudo amatoria**

covertly: **clam**
credits: **accepta**
crime: **crimen** or **delictum**
crime of falsification: **falsi crimen**
criminal: **criminosus**
criminal act: **actus reus**
crocodile tears: **lacrimae simulatae**
culpable: **culpabilis**
curator: **curator** or **curatrix**
cure-all: **panacea**
curfew (bell): **ignitegium** or **pyritegium**
custodian of morals: **custos morum**
custody: **cura** or **custodia**
custody of the law: **custodia legis**
custom: **consuetudo**
customs: **mores**

D

daily: **in dies** or **indies** or **quotidie** or **quotidianus** or **cotidie** or **cotidianus**
daily food: **diarium**
daily records: **acta diurna**
damage: **damnum**
damned: **damnatus**
daughter: **filia**
daughter-in-law: **nurus**
day: **dies**
day of grace: **dies gratiae**
dead: **mortuus**

deaf: **surdus**
death: **mors**
death penalty: **ultimum supplicium**
debt(s): **debitum** or **aes alienum**
debtor: **debitor** or **obaeratus**
deceased: **defunctus** or **demortuus**
deceitful: **dolosus**
decided: **adjudicata**
declaration of war: **belli denuntiatio**
decree: **decretum**
deductive reasoning: **a priori**
deed: **carta** or **charta**
deed (act): **factum** or **res gesta** or **res gestae**
default: **defalta**
defect: **defectus**
defendant being absent: **reo absente**
defense of the public: **publica vindicta**
deformity: **deformitas**
delay: **mora**
delaying: **dilatio**
delegate: **legatus**
deliberating: **deliberabundus**
deliberation: **deliberatio**
delirium tremens: **mania a potu**
den of iniquity: **colluvies vitiorum**
denied: **negatum**
deposit: **sequestrum**

depraved: **pravus**
depravity: **improbitas**
deputy: **legatus** or **locum tenens**
devil's advocate: **advocatus diaboli**
diary: **adversaria**
did not submit: **non submissit**
died without issue: **obiit sine prole** or **decessit sine prole** or **defunctus sine prole**
digression: **excursus**
directly: **in recto** or **ex directo**
disinherited: **exheres**
dispatch: **expeditio**
disputed: **controversus**
divided: **partitus**
divine law: **jus divinum**
divorce: **a vinculo matrimonii**
do not admit: **ne admittas**
does not follow: **non sequitur**
domestic: **domesticus**
domestic court: **forum domesticum**
donation: **donatio**
done and transacted: **actum et tractatum**
double jeopardy: **non bis in idem**
doubtful: **dubius**
dowery: **dos**

English-Latin Index 243

dregs of society: **faex populi**
drunk: **ebrius**
duel: **duellum** or **bellum inter duos**
dull-minded: **brutus**
duress: **duritia**
during absence: **durante absentia**
during life: **durante vita**
during minority: **durante minore aetate**
during virginity: **durante virginitate**
during widowhood: **durante viduitate**
duty: **officium**
duty (tax): **vectigal**
dwelling place: **domicilium**

E

earnest money: **argentum Dei**
easily: **ex facili** or **facile**
easy: **facilis**
ecclesiastical court: **curia christianitatis** or **forum ecclesiasticum**
edict: **edictum**
elected: **electus**
elsewhere: **alibi**
emancipation: **manumissio**
empty: **vacat**
empty house: **vacuum domicilium**
empty space: **vacuum**
empty threat: **brutum fulmen** or **fulmen brutum**
enclosure: **clausura**
ending point: **terminus ad quem**
enemy: **hostis**
engaged: **occupatus**
English Parliament: **Curia Magna**
enough: **satis**
epitaph: **elogium**
equal guilt: **par delictum**
equal parts: **partes aequales**
equal to the burden: **par oneri**
equality: **aequalitas**
equality of condition: **paragium**
equally: **ex aequo** or **a pari**
equally at fault: **in pari delicto** or **pari delicto**
equipment: **apparatus**
equitable: **justus**
equitable law: **jus aequum**
equitably: **ex equitate**
equity: **aequitas** or **justitia**
error: **erratum** or **lapsus**
escheat: **res caduca**
established: **inveteratus**
established principle: **maxim**
estimate of damages: **litis aestimatio**
event: **eventum** or **eventus**
everything knowable: **omne scibile**

evident: **evidens**
evil: **malum** or **malus** or **pravus**
evil deed: **scelus**
evil in itself: **malum in se**
evil intent: **animus malus**
evildoer: **maleficus** or **homo maleficus** or **malefactor**
exact copy: **fac simile** or **facsimile**
examination: **probatio**
examining the womb: **ventre inspiciendo** or **de ventre inspiciendo**
example: **exemplum**
excerpts: **excerpta**
exchange: **excambium** or **cambium**
excuse: **excusatio**
excused: **excusatus**
execution by hanging: **suspensio per collum** or **suspendatur per collum**
executioner: **carnifex**
exempt: **immunis**
exile: **exilium** or **exsilium**
exotic: **exoticus**
expectation of gain: **odor lucri**
expense: **custus**
expert: **expertus**
explicitly: **expressis verbis**
external: **externus**
extortion: **res repetundae**
extracts: **excerpta**
eyewitness: **oculatus testis**

F

fact: **factum**
failure of issue: **defectus sanguinis**
faith: **fides**
fallacious: **fallax**
false allegation: **allegatio falsi**
false statement: **expressio falsi**
fame: **fama**
family estate: **res familiaris**
family tree: **gradus parentelae**
farmer: **agricola**
fate: **fatum**
father: **pater**
father of the nation: **pater patriae**
father-in-law: **socer**
fault: **culpa**
favor: **beneficium**
fear: **metus**
fear of perjury: **metus perjurii**
fearful: **timidus**
felony: **felonia**
female sex: **sexus muliebris**
female: **femina**
feminine: **femininum**
fertility: **fertilitas**
final proposal: **ultimatum**
finally: **ad finem** or **ad ultimum**
finding of the jury: **sententiae judicum**

fine: **mulcta**
first among equals: **primus inter pares**
first glance: **prima facie** or **primo intuiti**
first name: **praenomen**
first of all: **imprimis**
firstborn: **primogenitus** or **anecius** or **einetius**
fishing rights: **libera batella**
fit and capable person: **idoneus homo**
flourished: **floruit**
food: **cibus** or **cibatus**
food stuffs: **alimenta**
foolish judgment: **fatuum judicium**
foothold: **pedis possessio**
for a short time: **ad exiguum tempus**
for all contingencies: **ad omnes casus**
for all time: **ad vitam aeternam**
for another reason: **alia de causa**
for better or for worse: **de bono et malo**
for breach of faith: **pro laesione fidei**
for certain knowledge: **ex certa scientia**
for collecting: **ad colligendum**
for counsel given: **pro consilio impenso**

for each day: **in diem**
for example: **exempli gratia** or **exempli causa** or **verbi gratia** or **verbi causa**
for good and bad: **bono et malo**
for good behavior: **de bono gestu**
for greater caution: **ad majorem cautelam** or **in majorem cautelam**
for inquiry: **ad inquirendum**
for instance: **exempli gratia** or **exempli causa** or **verbi gratia** or **verbi causa**
for life: **ad vitam**
for life or until fault: **ad vitam aut culpam**
for many reasons: **multis de causis**
for many years: **ad multus annos**
for more abundant caution: **ad abundatiorem cautelam**
for now: **pro nunc**
for offense: **propter delictum**
for open display: **ad exhibendum**
for political reasons: **rei publicae causa**
for reference: **ad referendum**
for religious purposes: **ad pios usus** or **in pios usus**
for sale: **venalis**

for the benefit: **ad opus**
for the defendant: **pro defendente**
for the future: **in posterum**
for the last time: **ad postremum**
for the perpetual memory of the thing: **in perpetuam rei memoriam**
for the plaintiff: **pro querente**
for the public good: **pro bono publico**
for the sake of brevity: **brevitatis causa**
for the sake of gain: **lucri causa**
for the sake of honor: **honoris causa**
for the whole: **in solidum**
for this occasion: **pro hac vice**
for this purpose: **ad hoc**
for want of justice: **pro defectu justitiae**
for whatever reason: **ex quocunque capite**
for whose benefit?: **cui bono?** or **cui bono fuisset?** or **cui prodest?**
forbidden: **nefas**
force and fear: **vis et metis**
force or fear: **vis vel metus**
forcibly: **efforcialiter**
forever: **ad infinitum** or **ad perpetuitatem** or **in perpetuum** or **imperpetuum** or **in infinitum**
forfeited: **abandum** or **forisfactum**
forfeited goods: **bona forisfacta**
forger: **falsonarius**
form: **forma**
formal: **formalis**
formally: **formaliter**
formerly: **ab olim** or **quondam**
foster child: (m.) **alumnus** or (f.) **alumna**
fragile: **fragilis**
fraud: **fraus** or **dolus**
fraudulently: **ex dolo malo**
free: **liber**
free of cost: **gratis**
free person: **homo francus** or **homo liber** or **liber homo**
free service: **liberum servitium**
free will: **liberum arbitrium**
freedom: **libertas**
frenzy: **phrenesis**
friend of the court: **amicus curiae**
from a distance: **ex longinquo**
from antiquity: **ab antiquo**
from before: **ex ante**
from behind: **a retro** or **a tergo**
from birth: **a nativitate**

from boyhood: **a pueris** or **a puero**
from childhood: **a teneris annis** or **ab parvulis** or **de tenero ungui** or **ex pueris**
from day to day: **diem ex die** or **in dies** or **indies**
from delay: **ex mora**
from elsewhere: **aliunde**
from every side: **ab omni parte**
from hearsay: **ex auditu** or **de auditu**
from malfeasance: **ex maleficio**
from memory: **ex memoria** or **memoriter**
from offense: **ex delicto**
from one to all: **ab uno ad omnes**
from that day: **a die**
from the absurd: **ab absurdo** or **ad absurdum**
from the beginning: **ab initio** or **a principio** or **ab origine** or **ab ovo**
from the bond: **a vinculo**
from the bond of matrimony: **a vinculo matrimonii**
from the cradle: **ab incunabulis**
from the date: **a dato** or **a datu**
from the first: **a primo**
from the greatest to the least: **a maximis ad minima**
from the heart: **ex animo**
from the inside: **ab intra**
from the lesser to the greater: **a minori ad majus**
from the library of: **ex libris**
from the necessity of law: **ex necessitate legis**
from the outside: **ab extra**
from title to text: **a rubro ad nigrum**
from words to blows: **a verbis ad verbera**
fugitive from the law: **caput lupinum**
full: **plenus**
full faith: **plena fides**
full justice: **complementum justi**
full legal capacity: **sui juris**
full proof: **plena probatio** or **probatio plena**
fully: **ad plenum**
fungible things: **res fungibiles** or **fungibiles res**
furlough: **commeatus**
further consideration: **ulterius concilium**

G

gallows: **arbor infelix** or **furca**
game warden: **custos ferarum**
gap: **lacuna**

genealogy: **gradus parentelae**
generally speaking: **in genere**
genuine: **verus**
genuine credentials: **bona fides**
gift: **donatio** or **donum**
girl: **puella**
given as a gift: **dono dedit**
godfather: **patrinus**
good: **bene** or **bonus**
good and lawful men: **probi et legales homines**
good behavior: **bona gestura**
good conscience: **conscientia recta**
good deeds: **benefacta**
good faith: **bona fides**
good pleasure: **bene placitum** or **beneplacitum**
goods: **bona**
goods and chattels: **bona et catalla**
goodwill: **bona gratia**
governor: **gubernator**
gradually: **gradatim**
granddaughter: **neptis**
grandfather: **avus**
grandmother: **avia**
grandson: **nepos**
grant: **concessio**
gratuity: **honorarium**
greater: **major**
gross ignorance: **crassa ignorantia**
gross negligence: **crassa neglegentia** or **crassa negligentia**
guard: **custos**
guardian: **gardianus**
guardians of the peace: **custodes pacis**
guardianship: **custodia** or **tutela**
guest: **hospes** or **hospita**
guild: **gilda** or **collegium**
guilty: **nocent** or **culpabilis**
guilty mind: **mens rea**
guilty person: **homo reus**

H

habit: **habitus**
habitation: **habitatio**
habitually: **de more**
handcuffs: **manica**
handwritten: **chirographum** or **chyrographum** or **manuscriptum** or **manuscriptus**
hangman: **carnifex**
harmful: **nocivus**
harmony: **concordia**
he himself said it: **ipse dixit**
he or she died: **obiit** or **obit**
head: **caput**
hearing: **auditus**
hearsay: **testimonium de auditu** or **de auditu** or **oratio obliqua** or **dictum de dicto**

heir: **heres**
heirloom: **res hereditaria**
heirs: **heredes**
here and now: **hic et nunc**
here and there: **passim**
here lies buried: **hic iacet sepultus** or **hic jacet sepultus**
hereditary: **hereditarius**
hidden places: **abscondita**
high and low: **alto et basso**
high priced: **magno pretio**
high seas: **altum mare**
high treason: **laesa majestas** or **alta proditio**
highway: **via alta** or **alta via**
highway robbery: **insidiatio viarum**
hindrance: **impedimentum**
hodgepodge: **mixtum compositum**
holidays: **feriae**
home: **domicilium**
homeless: **domo carens**
homicide: **homicidium**
honorary: **honoris gratia**
hope: **spes**
horsetrack: **hippodromos**
hour: **hora**
hourly: **in horas**
house: **domus**
house arrest: **custodia libera**
how much damage?: **quantum damnificatus**
huckster: **pede pulverosus**

hue and cry: **vociferatio**
human: **humanus**
human body: **corpus humanum**
human species: **homo sapiens**
humankind: **genus humanum** or **humanum genus**
husband: **vir** or **maritus**
husband and wife: **vir et uxor**
hybrid: **hybridus** or **hibridus**

I

I: **ego**
I am absent: **absum**
I am present: **adsum**
I am sorry: **me paenitet**
I have granted: **concessi**
I have spoken: **dixi**
I myself: **ego ipse**
I say no: **nego**
I say yes and I say no: **aio et nego**
I withdraw the statement: **hoc indictum volo**
idiocy: **amentia**
if necessary: **si opus sit**
ignorance of fact: **ignorantia facti**
ill fortune: **adversa fortuna**
ill will: **malevolentia**
illegal: **illicitus** or **inlicitus**

illegible: **illegibilis**
illicit: **illicitus** or **inlicitus** or **impermissus**
immediately: **statim**
immoral: **turpis**
immovable goods: **bona immobilia**
impartial judge: **judex incorruptus**
impassable: **impervius**
impeached: **impescatus**
impose a fine: **finem facere**
impunity: **impunitas**
in a bad sense: **sensu malo**
in a body: **in corpore**
in a broad sense: **lato sensu** or **sensu lato**
in a circuit: **in circuitu**
in a fit of anger: **ab irato**
in a friendly way: **amiciter**
in a good sense: **sensu bono**
in a judicial proceeding: **in judicio**
in a milder sense: **mitiori sensu**
in a nutshell: **in nuce**
in a quarrel: **in rixa**
in a similar case: **in consimili casu**
in a strict sense: **sensu stricto** or **stricto sensu**
in a vacuum: **in vacuo**
in a word: **uno verbo**
in absence: **in absentia**
in advance: **ab ante**
in aid: **in subsidium**
in all directions: **in omnes partes**
in all things: **in omnibus**
in allegiance: **ad fidem**
in an analogous case: **in pari materia**
in another place: **in alio loco**
in arrears: **a retro**
in bad faith: **in mala fide**
in both cases: **in utraque re**
in chains: **in vinculis**
in chambers: **in camera**
in common: **in communi**
in contemplation of flight: **in meditatione fugae**
in contempt of: **in contumaciam**
in court: **in foro**
in custody: **in custodiam**
in default: **in mora**
in delay: **in mora**
in different ways: **alius aliter**
in doubt: **in dubio** or **in ambiguo**
in due time: **ad tempus** or **debito tempore** or **justo tempore**
in equal right: **in aequali jure** or **in pari jure**
in equilibrium: **in equilibrio**
in error: **ex errore**
in every respect: **omnibus rebus**
in exchange: **in excambio**
in exile: **in exilium** or **in exsilium**

in expectation: **in spe**
in express terms: **expressis verbis**
in fact: **de facto** or **in facto**
in fault: **in delicto**
in favor of liberty: **in favorem libertatis**
in favor of life: **in favorem vitae**
in fee: **in feodo**
in full: **in pleno**
in full court: **in banco**
in full life: **in plena vita**
in good faith: **bona fide** or **ex bona fide**
in hand: **in manu**
in hatred: **in odium**
in its place: **in situ**
in jest: **per jocum**
in kind: **in specie**
in lieu of: **in loco**
in life: **in vita**
in like manner: **a pari** or **similiter**
in manner and form: **modo et forma**
in memory of: **in memoriam**
in my judgment: **me judice**
in name only: **in nomine solum**
in one's own name: **suo nomine**
in one's own right: **suo jure**
in open court: **in curia**
in payment: **in solutum**
in perpetuity: **ad perpetuitatem**
in person: **in persona**
in place of: **in loco** or **ad vicem**
in place of a guardian: **loco tutoris**
in place of a parent: **in loco parentis** or **loco parentis**
in place of the heir: **in loco haeredis**
in plain words: **nudis verbis**
in pledge: **in vadio**
in prison: **in carcerem** or **in vinculis** or **in custodiam**
in private: **in privato**
in public: **in publico**
in public view: **in oculis civium**
in safety: **in tuto**
in secret: **in pectore** or **in subterduco** or **januis clausis**
in self-defense: **se defendendo**
in so many words: **totidem verbis**
in some respect: **aliqua ex parte**
in strict right: **in stricto jure**
in strictness of law: **in rigore juris**
in sum: **ad summam**
in suspense: **in suspenso** or **in pendente** or **in pendenti**

in terror: **in terrorem**
in that place: **ad illic**
in the beginning: **in initio** or **in principio**
in the bosom of the law: **in gremio legis**
in the cause: **in causa**
in the custody of the law: **in custodia legis**
in the event: **in eventu**
in the first place: **in primis**
in the future: **in autea**
in the heart of the judge: **in pectore judicis**
in the king's bench: **in banco regis**
in the matter of: **in re** or **in materia**
in the meantime: **ad interim** or **interim** or **interea**
in the middle: **in medio**
in the midst of things: **in medias res**
in the name of: **in nomine**
in the name of God: **in nomine Dei**
in the name of the Lord: **in nomine Domini**
in the nature of things: **in rerum natura**
in the notes: **in notis**
in the nude: **in naturalibus**
in the place cited: **in loco citato** or **loco citato**
in the place of a parent: **in loco parentis**
in the power of a parent: **in potestate parentis**
in the presence of the court: **in facie curiae**
in the same place: **ibidem**
in the very act of the crime: **in flagrante delicto** or **flagrante delicto**
in the very words: **ipsissimis verbis**
in the womb: **in utero**
in the work cited: **opere citato**
in the year of our Lord: **anno Domini**
in the year of the reign: **anno regni**
in these words: **in haec verba**
in this month: **hoc mense**
in this name: **hoc nomine**
in this order: **hoc ordine**
in this place: **hoc loco**
in this sense: **hoc sensu**
in this year: **hoc anno**
in time of war: **in bello** or **inter arma**
in times past: **ab olim**
in total: **in toto**
in transit: **in transitu**
in trust: **in commendam**
in whatever manner: **quovis modo**
in witness: **in testimonium**
indebted: **indebitatus**

indirectly: **in obliquo** or **per obliqua** or **per obliquum**
indispensable condition: **sine qua non** or **causa sine qua non**
individual right: **jus individuum**
inductive reasoning: **a posteriori**
industrial: **industrialis**
infant: **infans**
informer: **delator**
inheritance: **hereditas**
inherited property: **patrimonium**
injurious: **nocivus**
injury: **injuria** or **vulnus**
innkeeper: **hospitator communis**
innocence: **innocentia**
innocent: **innocens**
inquest: **questa**
insane: **insanus** or **amens** or **demens**
insanity: **vesania** or **amentia** or **dementia**
inscription: **inscriptio** or **epigramma**
inspection of the body: **inspectio corporis**
instead of: **ad vicem**
insurance premium: **pretium periculi**
intent: **animus** or **mens**
interest: **usura**
intermediate: **intermedius**
internal: **internus**
international law: **jus gentium**
intestate: **ab intestato**
intoxicated: **ebrius**
irresistible force: **vis major**
issued: **editus**
it does not follow: **non sequitur**
it follows: **sequitur**
it has been proven: **probatum est**
it is adjourned: **adjournatur**
it is agreed: **convenit** or **placet**
it is apparent: **liquet**
it is done: **factum est**
it is evident: **constat**
it is just: **aequum est**
it is legal: **licet**
it is permitted: **licet** or **fas est**
it is remitted: **remittitur**

J

jack-of-all-trades: **factotum**
jailbird: **furcifer**
jeweler: **gemmarius**
joined to the land: **adscripti glebae**
joined together: **continens**
joint heir: **coheres**
jointly: **in simul** or **insimul**
jointly and severally: **conjunctim et divisim**
journal: **adversaria**

judge (n.): **judex**
judge (v.): **judicare**
judge's chambers: **camera**
judgment of God: **Dei judicium**
judicial authority: **jurisdictio**
judicial decision: **res adjudicata** or **res judicata**
judicial ordeal: **lex judicialis**
judicial reason: **ratio juris**
judicial right: **jus judicium**
judicial writs: **brevia judicialia**
juridical: **juridicus**
jurisprudence: **jurisprudentia**
juror: **jurator**
jury: **jurata** or **duodena** or **duodecima manus**
just: **justus**
just and good: **aequum et bonum**
just cause: **justa causa**
justice: **justitia**
juvenile: **juvenilis**

K

keeper of the land: **custos terrae**
keeper of the seal: **custos sigilli**
kind: **benignus**
king: **rex**
King's Bench: **Bancus Regis**
King's Court: **Curia Regis**

knowingly: **scienter**
known cause: **causa cognita**

L

labor: **labor** or **laboris**
language: **lingua**
lapse: **lapsus**
larceny: **latrocinium**
lastly: **ad postremum**
lately deceased: **nuper obiit**
law: **lex** or **jus**
law and statute: **jus et lex**
law of nature: **jus naturae**
law of retaliation: **lex talionis**
law of the court: **lex fori**
law of the land: **lex terrae**
law of the place: **lex loci**
law of war: **jus belli**
lawful: **licitus**
lawful detention: **habeas corpu**
lawful power: **legitima potestas**
lawless: **inlex**
laws: **jura** or **leges**
laws of England: **leges Anglia**
lawsuit: **lis**
lawyer: **juris consultus** or **jurisconsultus**
leap year: **annus bisextus**
lease: **concessio** or **locatio**
leave of absence: **commeatus**
ledger book: **graffium** or **grafium**

left: **laevus** or **sinister**
left hand: **sinistra**
left-hand page: **verso folio** or **verso**
legal: **legitimus** or **legibus**
legal act: **actus legitimus**
legal case: **casus** or **causa**
legal complaint: **postulatus** or **postulatio actiones**
legal decision: **judicium**
legal dispute: **controversia**
legal expert: **juris peritus** or **jurisperitus** or **legis peritus** or **legisperitus**
legal marriage: **justae nuptiae**
legal name: **nomen juris**
legal opinion: **judicatio**
legal precedent: **stare decisis**
legal presumption: **presumptio juris**
legal reason: **ratio legis**
legal right: **jus** or **jus legitimum**
legal standing: **locus standi**
legitimate: **legitimus**
let it stand: **stet**
let the buyer beware: **caveat emptor**
let the seller beware: **caveat venditor**
let the traveler beware: **caveat viator**
letter: **epistola** or **epistula**
letter carrier: **tabellarius**
libel: **libellus famosus**

liberty: **libertas**
liberty under the laws: **libertas in legibus**
library: **bibliotheca**
license: **licentia**
lie (n.): **mendacium**
life: **vita**
life principle: **aura vitalis**
life-force: **vis vitae** or **vis vitalis**
lifelike: **ad vivum**
lifespan: **summa vitae** or **vitae summa**
limitless: **ad infinitum**
line of descent: **linea**
literally: **ad literam** or **ad litteram** or **ad verbum** or **de verbo** or **e verbo**
litigant: **causator**
litigious: **legiosus**
loan: **pecunia mutua** or **creditum** or **commodatum**
loophole: **fenestra**
loss: **damnum**
loss and injury: **damnum et injuria**
lost: **adiratus**
love: **amor**
loyal tenant: **affidatus**
lunatic: **furiosus**

M

madness: **furor** or **mania** or **phrenesis**

magistrate: **magistratus**
majesty: **majestus**
make it known: **scire facias**
male: **mas** or **masculus**
male sex: **sexus virilis**
malice aforethought: **malitia praecogitata**
malicious: **malevolus** or **malignus**
malicious prosecution: **calumnia**
malpractice: **mala praxis** or **malapraxis**
man: **homo** or **vir**
manager of an estate: **actor dominae**
manager of church property: **actor ecclesiae**
mandate: **edictum**
manacles: **manica**
manner: **modus**
manual labor: **opus manificum**
manuscript: **manu scriptum** or **manuscriptum** or **manuscriptus**
marginal: **marginalis**
marginal notes: **marginalia**
marine: **maritimus**
marital affection: **affectio maritalis**
market: **emporium**
marriage: **conjugium** or **connubium** or **nuptiae**
marriage record: **nuptiales tabulae**

married: **nupta**
masculine: **masculinus**
master: **magister**
masterpiece: **magnum opus** or **opus magnum**
matrimony: **matrimonialiter**
matters of public concern: **acta publica**
measure: **mensura**
medical excuse: **aegrotat**
meeting of the minds: **aggregatio mentium**
memorandum (memo): **memorandum** or **hypomnema**
memory: **memoria**
merchandise: **merx**
merchant: **mercator**
mercy: **misericordia**
message: **nuntium**
messenger: **nuntius** or **nuntia**
midwife: **obstetrix**
mind: **mens**
mindful: **memor**
miscarriage of justice: **judicium perversum**
misrepresentation: **suggestio falsi**
mob: **mobile vulgus**
mockery: **derisus**
moderation: **mediocritas**
moment of death: **articulo mortis**
money: **nummus**
money lenders: **argentarius**

month: **mensis**
monthly: **menstruus**
more or less: **magis minusve**
mortgage: **vadium mortuum** or **mortuum vadium**
mother: **mater** or **matrix**
movable goods: **bona mobilia**
movable things: **res mobiles**
murder: **homicidium**
murderous: **internecivus**
mutual consent: **mutuus consensus** or **assensio mentium**
my fault: **mea culpa**

N

name: **nomen**
name change: **mutato nomine**
namely: **scilicet** or **videlicet**
narrative: **narratio**
nation: **natio**
native land: **patria**
native soil: **natale solum**
native-born inhabitant: **indigena**
natural: **naturalis**
natural instinct: **instinctu naturae**
natural law: **lex naturale** or **jus naturale**
natural reason: **ratio naturalis** or **naturalis ratio**
natural right: **jus naturae** or **jus naturale**
necessary changes being made: **mutatis mutandis**
negligent: **negligiens**
neighbor: **vicinus**
nephew: **nepos**
network: **plexus**
neutral: **neutralis**
new: **novus**
new law: **jus novum**
news: **nuntium**
nickname: **agnomen**
night: **nox**
no: **non**
no objection: **nihil obstat**
no offense intended: **absit invidia**
no one: **nemo**
no one contradicting: **nemine contradicente**
no one dissenting: **nemine dissentiente**
no third choice: **non datur tertium**
no trespassing: **transitus vetitus**
nobility: **nobilitas**
non-citizen: **advena**
nonsense: **nugae**
not allowed: **inconcessus**
not guilty: **non culpabilis**
not injured: **non damnificatus**
not of sound mind: **non compos mentis** or **non sanae mentis**

not permitted: **non licet**
not pleasing: **non libet**
not proven: **non liquet**
not published: **nondum editus** or **ineditus**
not said: **indictus**
not without cause: **non sine causa**
notary: **graffarius** or **tabularius**
notary public: **registrarius**
note well: **nota bene**
nothing: **nihil** or **nil**
notwithstanding: **non obstante**
novelty: **novitas**
now: **nunc** or **jam**
now and then: **interdum**
number: **numerus**

O

oath: **jusjurandum** or **juramentum**
objection: **praejudicium**
obligation: **obligatio**
occupant: **occupans**
of a wild nature: **ferae naturae**
of all goods or effects: **omnium bonorum**
of another kind: **alieni generis**
of both parties: **ab utraque parte**
of counsel: **de consilio** or **a consiliis**
of course: **de cursu**
of divine right: **juris divini**
of doubtful law or right: **juris dubii** or **dubii juris**
of his or her age or lifetime: **aetatis suae** or **aetatis**
of its own accord: **ex proprio motu**
of law: **juris**
of necessity: **ex necessitate**
of no legal force: **nullus juris**
of one's own accord: **sponte sua** or **sua sponte** or **ex mero motu**
of private right: **juris privati** or **privati juris**
of public right: **juris publici** or **publici juris**
of sound mind: **compos mentis** or **sanae mentis**
of the bench: **de banco**
of the body: **de corpore**
of the same kind: **ejus generis** or **ejusdem generis**
offspring: **fetus** or **foetus**
old: **vetus**
old age: **senectus** or **geraticus** or **fessa aetas**
old fashioned: **vetustus**
old law: **jus antiquum** or **jus vetus**
on another's land: **alieno solo**
on deposit: **in deposito**
on either side: **ex utraque parte**

on equal terms: **in aequo**
on good security: **certis nominibus**
on hand: **in manibus**
on my word of honor: **fide mea**
on the contrary: **e contra** or **e converso** or **ex contrario** or **per contra**
on the death bed: **in lecto mortali**
on the father's side: **ex parte paterna**
on the left: **a sinistra** or **laevo**
on the morrow: **crastinus**
on the mother's side: **ex parte materna**
on the other hand: **a contrario sensu**
on the right: **a dextra**
on the whole: **ex toto** or **in toto** or **ad summam** or **in summa**
one of a kind: **sui generis**
opinion: **sententia**
opposed to: **anti** or **adversus** or **adversum** or **versus**
opposite party: **pars adversa**
other enormities: **alia enormia**
other things being equal: **ceteris paribus**
otherwise called: **alias dictus**
out of abundant caution: **ex abundanti cautela** or **ex abundante cautem**
out of court: **ex curia** or **extra judicium**
out of courtesy: **ex comitate**
outcry: **vociferatio**
outlaw (as a class): **exlegalitas**
outlaw: **exlegatus** or **exlex** or **diligiatus** or **contumax** or **civiliter mortuus**
outside: **extra**
overt act: **apertum factum**
owner: **dominus**

P

pact: **pactio** or **concordatus**
page: **folium**
pages: **folia**
panel of jurors: **judicis**
pardon my words: **sit venia verbis**
parent: **parens**
parental: **parentalis**
part: **pars**
part for the whole: **pars pro toto**
partner in crime: **socius criminis**
partnership: **consortium**
party to the crime: **particeps criminis**
path of crime: **iter criminis**
patriot: **civis bonus**
pay a fine: **finem facere**
pay the penalty: **solvere poenas**

payment: **solutio** or **merces**
peddler (pedlar): **institor**
penal: **poenalis**
penal actions: **actiones penales**
penalty: **poena**
pending the suit: **lis pendens** or **pendente lite** or **lite pendente**
perishable goods: **bona peritura**
perjury: **perjurium**
personal secretary: **amanuensis**
petition: **libellus**
petty treason: **parva proditio**
physician: **medicus**
pickpockets: **saccularii**
pirate: **pirata** or **malandrinus**
pirates (as a class): **hostes humani generis**
place: **locus**
place of the seal: **locus sigilli**
plaintiff: **actor** or **quaerens** or **querens** or **petitor**
plea of no contest: **nolo contendere**
pledge: **pignus**
plunder: **praeda**
point for point: **punctatim**
point of time: **punctum temporis**
political power: **potentatus**
posture: **gestus**
power: **potentia** or **potestas**

precepts: **praecepta**
premature: **praecox**
presence of mind: **praesentia animi**
present in court: **praesens in curia**
preservation: **conservatio**
previous act: **ante factum** or **ante gestum**
prison: **carcer**
private property: **res privitae**
private right: **jus privatum**
privately: **privatim**
privilege: **beneficium**
procedural law: **ordinandi lex**
procurable: **parabilis**
profit: **lucrum**
prohibition: **interdictum**
proof: **probatio**
proper name: **nomen proprium**
property: **bona** or **averum**
proportion: **quota**
proportionally: **in pari passu**
proprietor: **dominus**
protection: **aegis**
provisions (food): **alimenta**
public: **publicus**
public actions: **actiones populares**
public affairs: **negotia publica**
public archives: **tabulae publicae**
public enemy: **inimicus**

public interest: **e republica** or **e re publica**
public land: **ager publicus**
public office: **munus publicum**
public opinion: **vulgi opinio**
public place: **locus communis**
public property: **res publicae** or **bona fiscalia**
public right: **jus publicum**
publication of a law: **divulgatio legis**
punishment: **poena**

Q

queen: **regina**
Queen's Bench: **Bancus Reginae**
question: **quaestio** or **questio**
question of fact: **quaestio facti**
question of intention: **quaestio voluntatis**
question of law: **quaestio juris**
quickly: **cito**

R

ransom: **redemptiones**
rape: **raptus**
read between the lines: **sub audi** or **subaudi**
ready for use: **ad manum**
reason: **ratio**
reasonable part: **pars rationabilis**
reasoning: **ratiocinatio**
receipts: **accepta**
recent crime: **flagrans crimen**
recently: **de recenti**
record: **album** or **littera** or **litera**
records: **annales**
red ink: **rubramentum**
refugee: **domo profugus**
regarding: **in re** or **re**
register: **tabula** or **graffium** or **grafium**
related by birth: **cognatus**
related by blood: **consanguineus**
remembrance: **memoria**
rent: **redditus** or **reditus**
rental period: **ad die datus**
repeatedly: **identidem**
reputation: **fama**
request: **rogatio**
required: **requisitus**
résumé: **curriculum vitae** or **vitae curriculum** or **vita**
retroactive: **nunc pro tunc**
revocable will: **ambulatoria voluntas**
reward: **praemium** or **premium**
rich: **dives**
right: **dexter**

right hand: **dextra** or **dextera**
right of citizenship: **jus civitatis**
right of inheritance: **jus hereditatis**
right of navigation: **jus navigandi**
right of possession: **jus possessionis**
right of the first night: **jus primae noctis**
right of the firstborn: **jus primogeniturae** or **jus aesneciae**
right of the widow: **jus relictae** or **jus relicti**
right to vote: **jus suffragii**
right-hand page: **recto folio** or **recto**
rights: **jura**
rights and obligations: **jura et munera**
rigor of the law: **strictum juris**
robber: **praedo**
robbery: **rapina** or **furtum** or **crimen roberiae**
room for doubt: **ambigendi locus**
royal: **regalis** or **regius**
royal court: **forum regium**
rule: **norma** or **regula**
rumor: **fama**
rural and urban: **rustica et urbana**

S

said and done: **dictum factum**
sanction: **sanctio**
sanctuary: **asylum**
sane: **sanus**
scene of the crime: **locus criminis** or **locus delicti**
seal: **sigillum**
sealed letters: **litterae sigillatae**
sealed records: **litterae clausae**
seat of honor: **sedes honoris**
second marriage: **nuptiae secundae**
second self: **alter ego** or **alter idem**
second to none: **nulli secundus**
secondhand story (hearsay): **dictum de dicto** or **oratio obliqua**
secret: **arcanus**
secretarial matters: **ab epistolis** or **ab epistulis**
secular law: **jus non sacrum**
security: **cautio**
see above: **vide supra**
see below: **vide infra**
seized: **captus**
send such: **mitte tales**
seriousness: **gravitas**
settled: **adjudicata**
settled out of court: **intra parietes**

English-Latin Index 263

settlement: **solutio**
sexual union: **coitus** or **coetus**
shameless: **procax**
sheriff: **comes stabuli** or **vicecomes** or **vice comes**
sheriff's posse: **posse comitatus**
shipwreck: **naufragium**
shopkeeper: **tabernarius**
shrewd person: **emunctus**
sideways: **per obliqua**
signature: **signatura** or **subscriptio** or **subscriptum**
sister: **soror**
slander: **maledicus**
slip of the memory: **lapsus memoriae**
slip of the pen: **lapsus calami** or **lapsus plumae**
slip of the tongue: **lapsus linguae**
smaller: **minor**
smoke: **fumus**
snake in the grass: **anguis in herba**
so help me God: **sicut me Deus adjuvet** or **ita te Deus adjuvet** or **medius fidius**
so it is: **ita est**:
so ordered: **ordinatum est**
sociable: **gregarius**
sojourner: **advena**
solid land: **terra firma**
son: **filius**

son-in-law: **gener**
speedy remedy: **festinum remedium**
spirit of the law: **voluntas legis**
spoken: **locutus**
sponsorship: **aegis**
spouse: **sponsus** or **sponsa** or **conjunx** or **conjux**
spurious: **bogus**
standard: **norma** or **regula** or **mensura**
starting point: **terminus a quo**
state secrets: **arcana imperii**
statistical account: **rationarium**
statute law: **lex** or **lex scripta**
stepfather: **vitricus**
stepmother: **noverca**
stipulation: **proviso**
storehouse: **thesaurus** or **thesaurium**
stranger: **hospes**
strayed: **adiratus**
stronger: **fortior**
students of the law: **jurisprudentes**
such is the law: **ita lex scripta est**
sufficient security: **idonea cautio**
suicide: **felo-de-se**
suitable: **aptus** or **accommodatus** or **commodus** or **habilis** or **idoneus**

summarily: **acervatim** or **brevi manu** or **manu brevi**
summary proceedings: **judicia summaria**
summit: **apex**
summons: **summoneas** or **accitus**
sundial: **solarium**
supplement: **addendum**
suppression of the truth: **suppressio veri**
supreme power: **suprema potestas**
surname: **cognomen**
surveyor: **mensor** or **metator**
sworn document: **jurat**
sworn statement of fact: **affidavit**

T

tacitly: **ex tacito**
tape recording: **magnetophonicus**
taste: **gustus**
tax: **tallagium** or **talagium** or **tributum** or **vectigal**
teacher: **magister**
temporarily: **ad interim** or **ex tempore** or **pro tempore** or **in tempus**
that and that alone: **id demum**
that is: **id est**
that is to say: **videlicet** or **scilicet**
the accused: **reus**
the best: **optimus**
the city: **urbs**
the country: **rus**
the defendant being absent: **reo absente** or **absente reo**
the defendant being present: **reo praesente**
the end: **finis**
the greatest: **maximus**
the least of evils: **minima de malis**
the left hand: **manus sinistra**
the majority: **major pars**
the question arises: **quaeritur**
the rest is wanting: **cetera desunt** or **desunt cetera**
the right hand: **manus dextra**
the right to vote: **suffragium**
the same as above: **idem** or **idem quod**
The Twelve Tables: **Lex Duodecim Tabularum**
the very words: **ipsissima verba**
theft: **furtum**
then and there: **ad tunc**
there and then: **ibi**
therefore: **ergo**
these being witnesses: **his testibus** or **hiis testibus**
thief: **fur**
things done: **res gestae**

this for that: **quid pro quo**
thus: **sic**
time for deliberation: **tempus deliberandi**
title: **titulus**
to abide by legal precedent: **stare decisis**
to all the pleas: **ad omnia placita**
to answer: **ad respondendum**
to be corrected: **corrigendum**
to consider further: **ad avizandum**
to deliver to jail: **ad goalam deliberandam**
to have and to hold: **habendum et tenendum**
to infinity: **ad infinitum**
to injure no one: **alterum non laedere**
to join in aid: **ad jungendum auxilium**
to meet an accusation: **ad rectum**
to or for the suit: **ad litem** or **in litem**
to render an account: **ad computum reddendum**
to satisfy: **ad satisfaciendum**
to similar cases: **ad consimiles casus** or **ad pares casus** or **ad similes casus**
to summon to court: **ad curiam vocare** or **in jus vocare**
to swear an oath: **facere sacramentum**
to the common nuisance: **ad commune nocumentum**
to the detriment: **ad nocumentum**
to the extreme: **ad extremum**
to the former condition: **ad pristinum statum**
to the grievance: **ad gravamen**
to the highest authority: **ad limina**
to the injury: **ad nocumentum**
to the letter: **ad literam** or **ad litteram**
to the loss (damage): **ad damnum** or **ad quod damnum**
to the matter: **ad rem**
to the people: **ad populum**
to the point of disgust: **ad nauseam**
to the point of extermination: **ad internecionem**
to the same degree: **ad eundem gradum**
today: **hodie**
toll: **tallagium** or **talagium**
tomorrow: **cras** or **crastino**
toward insolvency **ad inopiam**
townsfolk: **urbani**
tracked down: **evestigatus**

treasury: **thesaurus** or **thesaurium**
trial: **judicium** or **probatio**
trial by combat: **duellum**
trial by fire: **ignis judicium**
trial by hot iron: **canfara**
trial by jury: **judicium parium**
trial by ordeal: **Dei judicium** or **judicium Dei** or **lex manifesta**
trial by water ordeal: **judicium aquae**
trifle: **minutia**
trifles: **apinae** or **nugae**
trifling: **de minimis** or **ineptiae**
true: **verus**
trust: **fiducia**
trust the expert: **experto credite**
truth: **veritas**
twice as much: **alterum tantum**
twice demanded: **bis petitum**
twilight: **crepusculum**
typewritten: **typographum**

U

unabridged: **in extenso**
unacceptable person: **persona non grata**
unaided: **sine auxilio**
unanimous: **omnes ad unum** or **nemine dissentiente**
unanimously: **una voce** or **uno animo** or **uno consensu** or **uno ore** or **ad unum omnes**
unavenged: **inultus**
unborn: **nondum natus** or **nasciturus**
unburied: **inhumatus**
uncertain: **incertus**
unclaimed goods: **bona vacantia**
uncle (maternal): **avunculus**
uncle (paternal): **patruus**
under arms: **in armis**
under oath: **juratus**
under penalty: **sub poena** or **subpoena**
under seal: **sub sigillo** or **sub pede sigilli**
under the name of: **sub nomine**
under this title: **hoc titulo**
undivided: **indivisum** or **indivisus**
unfaithful: **infidelis**
ungrateful: **male gratus**
unintended harm: **aberratio ictus**
unisexual: **dioicus**
universal consent: **consensus omnium**
universal custom: **consuetudo universa**
universally: **in universum**
unjust: **injustus**

unknown: **ignotus** or **incognito**
unlawful: **nefas** or **impermissus**
unlettered: **illiterati**
unprepared: **imparatus** or **impromptus**
unprovoked: **non laccessitus**
unpublished: **nondum editus** or **ineditus**
unsafe: **intutus**
unsealed records: **litterae patentes**
unsealed writ: **apertum breve**
unskilled: **indoctus**
until misconduct: **ad culpam**
untrained: **indoctus**
unwilling: **invitus**
unwilling to prosecute: **nolle prosequi**
unwillingly: **ab invito**
unwritten law: **lex non scripta** or **jus ex non scripto** or **jus non scriptum**
unwritten laws: **leges non scriptae**
upright in court: **rectus in curia**
urban tenement: **praedium urbanum**
usury: **usura**
utterly destructive: **internecinus**

V

verbal obligation: **verborum obligatio** or **obligatio verborum**
verdict: **veredictum**
veteran: **emerita** or **emeritus**
vexing question: **quaestio vexata** or **vexata quaestio**
vicious circle: **circulus vitiosus**
victim: **hostia**
voice of the people: **vox populi**
voluntary statement: **gratis dictum**

W

wages: **merces**
war: **bellum**
war of atrocities: **bellum atrocissimum**
warden: **custos**
warlike: **bellicus** or **bellicosus**
warning: **caveat**
water: **aqua**
wax seal: **cera impressa**
way: **via**
weakness: **debilitas**
weapons: **arma**
week: **hebdomada**
well: **bene**
well-heeled person: **habentes homines**

which see: **quod vide** or **quae vide**
which the court granted: **quod curia concessit**
which was to be demonstrated: **quod erat demonstrandum**
which was to be done: **quod erat faciendum**
white and black: **alba et atra**
whom will it harm?: **cui malo?**
widow: **vidua**
widowed: **relicta** or **relictus**
wife: **uxor** or **conjunx** or **conjux**
wild: **ferus**
wild beasts: **ferae bestiae**
will: **testamentum**
willy-nilly: **nolens volens**
with a calm mind: **aequo animo**
with a grain of salt: **cum grano salis**
with additional rights: **cum pertinentiis**
with aid and counsel: **ope et consilio**
with authority: **ex cathedra**
with cause: **cum causa**
with effect: **cum effectu**
with every advantage: **cum omni causa**
with force and arms: **vi et armis**
with full right: **optimo jure**
with good memory: **bona memoria**
with great care: **magna cum cura**
with greater force: **a fortiori**
with its burden: **cum suo onere**
with malice aforethought: **ex praecogitata malicia**
with many others: **cum multis aliis**
with reservation: **cum nota**
with the consent of the court: **ex assensu curiae**
with this law: **hac lege**
with what intent?: **quo animo?**
within: **infra** or **intra** or **intus**
within a year: **infra annum**
within earshot: **in auditu**
within the jurisdiction: **infra jurisdictionem**
within the law: **intra legem**
within the limit(s): **infra metas**
within the powers (of): **intra vires**
within the realm: **infra regnum**
within the state: **infra civitatem**
without: **sine** or **absque**
without a hearing: **indicta causa**
without any complaint: **sine ulla querela** or **sine ulla querella**

without any condition: **absque ulla conditione**
without any mark: **absque ulla nota**
without care: **sine cura** or **sinecura**
without counsel: **inops consilii**
without date: **sine anno**
without deceit: **sine fraude**
without delay: **sine mora** or **sine dilatione** or **ex incontinenti**
without dispute: **sine controversia**
without doubt: **sine dubio**
without end: **ad infinitum**
without exception: **ad unum**
without injury: **absque injuria**
without issue (offspring): **sine prole**
without judgment: **sine judico**
without limit: **in infinitum**
without means: **inops**
without mercy: **absque misericordia**
without probable cause: **absque probabili causa**
without waste: **absque vasti**
without witnesses: **sine testibus**
witness: **testis**
witness to a will: **obsignator**
woman: **femina** or **mulier**
womb: **venter** or **matrix**
word: **verbum**
word for word: **ad verbum** or **de verbo in verbum** or **verbatim**
word to the wise: **verbum sapienti**
work: **labor** or **laboris**
world: **orbis terrarum**
wound: **vulnus**
writ: **breve**
writ of inquiry: **scire fieri**
written contract: **obligatio litterarum** or **obligatio litteris** or **obligatio literis**
written documents: **tabulae**
written law(s): **lex scripta** or **jus scriptum** or **leges scriptae**

Y

year: **annus**
yearly: **annuus**
yearly rent: **annuus reditus**
yes: **certo**
yesterday: **heri**
you may approach the court: **accedas ad curiam**
youth: **adolescens** or **juventus**

Printed in the United States
by Baker & Taylor Publisher Services